Wiltshire Record Society

(formerly the Records Branch of the Wiltshire
Archaeological and Natural History Society)

VOLUME 55

FOR THE YEAR 1999

Impression of 500 copies

*Cornbury Mill, West Lavington, c. 1855. George Butcher was the miller here until 1854/55, when his tax assessment was £100 (**315**, p. 66). His successor, Joseph Webb, appealed against his £100 assessment in 1856/ 57, and it was reduced to £90. It was further reduced, to £70, the following year (**343**, p. 73)*

DEVIZES DIVISION INCOME TAX ASSESSMENTS, 1842 – 1860

EDITED BY

ROBERT COLLEY
University of Wales, Aberystwyth

TROWBRIDGE

2002

ISBN 0 901333 32 8

Typeset by John Chandler
Produced for the Society by
Salisbury Printing Company Ltd, Salisbury
Printed in Great Britain

CONTENTS

PREFACE

The idea for this study by Dr. Colley was born out of research for a doctoral thesis on the mid-Victorian income tax at the Department of Law, University of Wales, Aberystwyth in the mid-1990s. During research undertaken in over twenty-five County Record Offices in England and Wales, he came upon what appeared to be a unique collection of assessments of the self-employed in mid-Victorian England, in a deposit at the Wiltshire and Swindon Record Office (WSRO 1090/81). What he found threw into sharp contrast the theoretical and actual workings of the income tax and significantly changed his preconceptions of its administration. Although essentially a legal historian, he began to see the possibility that the material offered a hitherto uncharted source of research material for other historians. His interest lies essentially in the relationship between the state and civil society, and he therefore approached the local history of Devizes with some apprehension because there are others who have devoted many years to this particular study. He decided, therefore, to concentrate purely on the material which he found without moving into this specialization, and to edit it in a way which those well versed in the story of the Devizes area can use for their own purposes.

Dr. Colley warmly acknowledges the many people who have assisted his research, through conversation and correspondence, and by providing facilities: Steven Hobbs and the staff of the Wiltshire & Swindon Record Office; Dr Lorna Haycock, Sandell Librarian, Wiltshire Archaeological & Natural History Society; the staff of the Computer Department of the University of Wales, Aberystwyth; the staff of the National Library of Wales for providing a microfilm reader and a room in which to work in peace and tranquillity for over two years; the Library of Pembroke College, Oxford, for generously supplying material from *Country Banks*; Richard Ireland of the University of Wales, Aberystwyth, and Basil Sabine, OBE, for reading the introduction to this volume. He wishes to thank Professor Jeremy Black, editor of *Archives*, for permission to use in the introduction to this volume material relating to the disposal of tax papers previously published in that journal (vol. 25, 2000, no. 102, pp. 74-87). He also wishes to pay tribute to the imagination and enthusiasm shown to him by the Committee of the Wiltshire Record Society, and to the regular advice and support, especially in the final typesetting and layout of the work, given him by me in my capacity as the Society's General Editor. Finally, Dr. Colley and the Wiltshire Record Society express our gratitude to Mr G. A. Awdry of the firm of solicitors, Messrs Awdry, Bailey and Douglas, Devizes, for permission to publish this material.

JOHN CHANDLER

INTRODUCTION

The income tax was initially a temporary phenomenon. First enacted between 1799 and 1816 as the tax that beat Napoleon, it was perceived essentially as a war tax or meant to be re-enacted only for some unique national purpose. Resuscitated by Peel in 1842,[1] the emergency was a financial one and the tax was a postulate for the extensive tariff reform that was part of his Free Trade programme. Gladstone extended its life in 1853 but with a terminable existence expressly defined, the rates of tax gradually reducing until its proposed (but unrealized) extinction in 1860.

It was expedient, both politically and methodologically, to repose the day to day administration of what was meant to be a temporary visitant in the existing centuries' old framework of tax assessment and collection which relied almost entirely on the amateur service of members of the traditional local hegemony. These personalities already had jurisdiction over the land tax and the assessed taxes (the taxes on windows, servants, carriages, sporting dogs and armorial bearings). They were, *mutatis mutandis*, Justices of the Peace, Members of Parliament, Poor Law Guardians, Street or Improvement Commissioners and Land Tax Commissioners – the wealthy, and invariably landed, representatives of politics, law, banking and church.

Peel dignified the continuance of a system of such great antiquity in his appeal to the constitutional principle that the assessment of the income tax should not depend upon the will of Government but should be undertaken by local personalities.[2] It is arguable, however, that the acceptance of the tax by Parliament was largely dependent on the continuing supremacy of these local oligarchs in its execution and their capacity to exercise patronage and influence in the control of assessment. On the one hand, it must be acknowledged that one of the distinguishing marks of landed society in the mid-nineteenth century was the acceptance and discharge of authority and responsibility which the absence of any cohesive apparatus of centralized administration left to it.[3] But on the other hand, it must equally be recognized that these local élites were strongly opposed to the extending tendrils of state intervention in the life of the individual as well as fearful of the accompanying growing erosion of their powers, any encroachment on which would have generated sufficient opposition to defeat the re-introduction of the income tax.

---

1   5 & 6 Vict., c.35
2   Hansard, *HCDebs.*, 3rd. ser., 61, col. 911, 18 Mar. 1842
3   F.M.L. Thompson, *English Landed Society in the Nineteenth Century*, 1963, p.8

THE DIVISION OF DEVIZES AND THE GENERAL COMMISSIONERS

Peel's constitutional ideal of the separation of central and local powers was translated into an intensely localized administration. The geographic jurisdiction of this local administration was the division, an area which had first been defined in 1688 when the Commissioners appointed to execute the first land tax were empowered to divide themselves into administrative units 'in such Manner and Forme as to them shall seeme expedient'.[4] They resembled more or less closely the hundred divisions of each county which were either consolidated or sub-divided into larger or smaller units respectively. These same limitations were adopted for the purposes of the income tax in 1842 resulting in 693 divisions in England and Wales.[5] These units were sometimes termed 'districts', though the correct statutory term 'division' has been preferred in this study. The division of Devizes was formed by the amalgamation of the two hundreds of Potterne & Cannings and Swanborough. The former included the town of Devizes (recorded in separate units as the parishes of St.John and St.Mary the Virgin, and the tithings of Bedborough and Week) and its environs, Bromham, Rowde, West Lavington and several smaller parishes; the latter comprised Market Lavington, Urchfont, Upavon and the several parishes along the Vale of Pewsey. These are shown in more detail on the map opposite.

At the pinnacle of the local administration were the 'commissioners for the general purposes of the (Income Tax) Act' – called almost immediately by their shortened title General Commissioners.[6] They had both an executive and appellate jurisdiction. They comprised seven men of substance and station who were to be appointed by the Land Tax Commissioners from amongst their own numbers in each division.[7] They were invariably magistrates. The first of these office holders were Thomas Henry Sutton Sotheron Estcourt, Member of Parliament for Devizes, great nephew of the former Prime Minister Henry Addington, and later President of the Poor Law Board and

---

4   1 W & M, c.20, s.5; 1 W & M, Sess. 2, c.1, s.5, (1688). The divisions were to be fixed at meetings held on or before 5 Feb. 1689. The Act 4 W & M, c.1 (1692) is generally regarded as introducing the first Land Tax proper but for the purposes of identifying the date of creation of the divisions it is necessary to refer to look to the earlier Act. W.Phillips in his article 'A New Light on Addington's Income Tax', *British Tax Review*, 1967, 271-81, at pp.275-6 firmly expounds the 'end of the 1692 myth'.

5   5 & 6 Vict., c.35, s.4. Although by 4 & 5 Will.IV, c.60, s.1, (1834), the Land Tax Commissioners were given power to transfer parishes from one jurisdiction to another or to create new divisions, there does not appear to have been any major alteration in the divisions which have been encountered by the writer during his research. The number of divisions is confirmed in House of Commons, (hereafter HC) Parliamentary Papers (hereafter PP), (1871) xxxvii 242

6   The first use of the shortened title is noted by Dr.A.Farnsworth in a side-note to an amending Act, 39 Geo.III, c.22, s.14, (1799) in his article 'The Income Tax Commissioners', *Law Quarterly Review* 64 (1948) 372-88 at p.373

7   5 & 6 Vict., c.35, s.4

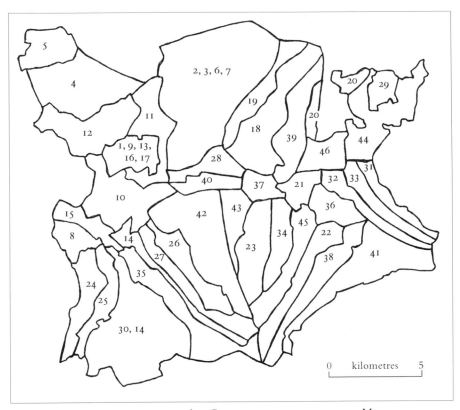

1	BEDBOROUGH	18	ALL CANNINGS	35	MARKET LAVINGTON
2	BISHOP'S CANNINGS	19	ALLINGTON		
3	BOURTON & EASTON	20	ALTON BARNES	36	NORTH NEWNTON & HILLCOTT
4	BROMHAM	21	BEECHING STOKE		
5	CHITTOE	22	CHARLTON	37	PATNEY
6	COATE	23	CHIRTON	38	RUSHALL
7	HORTON	24	CHEVERELL MAGNA	39	STANTON ST. BERNARD
8	MARSTON	25	CHEVERELL PARVA		
9	NURSTEED	26	EASTCOTT	40	STERT
10	POTTERNE	27	EASTERTON	41	UPAVON
11	ROUNDWAY	28	ETCHILHAMPTON	42	URCHFONT
12	ROWDE	29	HUISH	43	WEDHAMPTON
13	WEEK	30	LITTLETON PANNELL	44	WILCOT, OARE & DRAYCOTT
14	WEST LAVINGTON	31	MANNINGFORD ABBOTTS		
15	WORTON	32	MANNINGFORD BOHUNE	45	WILSFORD
16	DEVIZES ST. JOHN	33	MANNINGFORD BRUCE	46	WOODBOROUGH
17	DEVIZES ST. MARY	34	MARDEN		

[NOTE: WEST LAVINGTON (14) INCLUDES FIDDINGTON (DETACHED); ALTON BARNES (20) INCLUDES SHAW (DETACHED). PATNEY (37) IS INCLUDED IN THE INCOME TAX DIVISION THOUGH NOT IN SWANBOROUGH HUNDRED.]

Map of parishes and townships in the Division of Devizes

Secretary of State for the Home Office; his kinsman, Wadham Locke, son of the banker Wadham Locke who was a former Member of Parliament for Devizes; William Hughes, banker of St. John Street; Col. Henry Stephen Olivier of Potterne Manor; Thomas Hunt Grubbe of Potterne and Eastwell; Ven. Archdeacon William MacDonald, Vicar of Bishop's Cannings and Archdeacon of Wiltshire; and John Edward Andrew Starkey of Spye Park.[8] The last named died within a year of appointment and was replaced by Revd. Alfred Smith of Old Park, Perpetual Curate of Southbroom.

Clergy representation in the administration of the income tax was common, some divisions having as many as four out of the seven General Commissioners drawn from the Anglican clergy.[9] Usually every division also had among its Commissioners the incumbent Member of Parliament, in this instance Sotheron Estcourt, and one of its leading bankers. William Hughes and Wadham Locke's brother F.A.S. Locke were partners in the banking firm of Hughes, Locke & Co. This later became Locke, Olivier & Tugwell when Colonel Olivier became a partner and William Edmund Tugwell of the law firm of Tugwell & Meek, also a later Commissioner, joined the bank.[10] Alexander Meek, his partner in the firm of solicitors and a later partner in the banking firm of Locke, Tugwell & Meek, was Clerk to the General Commissioners, the officer appointed by them to deal with the day to day executive process. This was a closely-knit group with a finger on the pulse of the life of the community and a typical selection from the world of politics, law, banking and church.

THE SCHEDULAR NATURE OF THE INCOME TAX

The income tax was a duty imposed on the subject in the form of an assessment at a pound rate, of so many pence, on his income. For administrative purposes income assessable to the income tax was divided into five discrete categories, termed Schedules. These were broadly described in the taxing statute as follows: income from property was assessable under Schedule A, income from farming and market gardening under Schedule B, profits from trades, professions and vocations and wages from private sector entities under Schedule D, and income from public offices and employments under Schedule E. The receipt of interest on certain investments was also assessable under Schedule D. These were the main categories of income which were subject to many sub-divisions and as many rules but they are sufficient to give a broad outline.[11]

---

8   *Devizes Gazette*, 15 July 1842, supplemented by reference to contemporary genealogical and biographical directories

9   These were largely, but not exclusively, in rural districts. Caernarfon, in North Wales, for example, comprised 4 out of 7. In the Chester division of Wirral there were 3 out of 7.

10   M. Dawes & C.N. Ward-Perkins, *Country Banks in England & Wales, 1688-1953*, CIB, 2000, at p.198

11   5 & 6 Vict., c.35, ss. 60, 63, 100, and 146; Schedule C (s.88) related to annuities and dividends paid out of the public revenue, limited companies and other bodies corporate, and lies outside the scope of this study

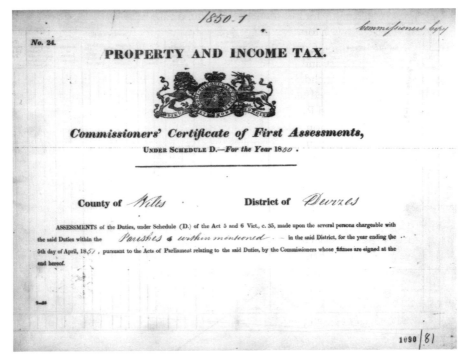

Title page of Schedule D Certificate (WSRO 1090/81)

The deciding factor as to which employees should be assessed under Schedule D and which under Schedule E, was the status of the employer. Those working for a private firm or partnership would be assessable under Schedule D while those working for a limited company or public concern, under Schedule E. So, for example, Richard Falkner (**454**), most likely manager at the unincorporated bank of Locke, Olivier & Tugwell (**537**), was assessable on his salary under Schedule D, while Richard Maysmore (**556, 797**), manager of the incorporated Wilts & Dorset Bank and Edward King (**517**), manager of the incorporated North Wilts Bank, were assessable under Schedule E.

These strict rules were not always observed (or perhaps sometimes not fully understood) and so, at times, the assessment lists include bank managers (irrespective of which bank they worked for); some curates were assessed on their stipends, like Revd. Joseph MacCormick (**543**) or Revd. William Dewdney Walke (**641**); the Relieving Officers, John Butcher (**226**) and J.P. Akerman (**1091**) were assessed; and employees such as Revd. Alexander Manning, chaplain of the New Prison (**192**) or John Thurnham [*sic,* but generally spelled Thurnam], superintendent of the County Asylum (**289**), were brought into the lists before being transferred to the Schedule E certificates. Income under each Schedule was assessed in a slightly different way and since it is with income arising from trades, professions and vocations and certain wages assessable under Schedule D with which this volume is principally concerned, a brief description of this procedure will be given.

Under Schedule D each party was required to make a return of his profits from any trade, manufacture, adventure or concern upon a fair and just average of three years ending either on the fifth day of April or on a date to which accounts had been usually made up immediately preceding the year of assessment.[12] Profits from professions, employments and vocations were computed on the basis of the income for the one year ended on the previous **5** April.[13] The term 'profits' was nowhere defined in the taxing Acts, its concept being largely parallel to that understood by the trading and professional community as being the gross income less the expenses incurred in realizing that income. The main differences were that the statute prohibited the deduction from profits of certain items which were recognized by the commercial community as proper, (the most important of which were loan interest and depreciation of plant and equipment)[14] and the profits from the trade of a married woman living with her husband were deemed to be those of the husband and charged in his name.[15] Thus, Samuel Adlam, painter and glazier of Devizes St.Mary (**667**) was also assessed in respect of his wife's profits as a straw bonnet maker.

THE ASSESSMENT

Each year the General Commissioners appointed an assessor for each parish within the division to undertake certain preliminary duties: to post a general notice on the church door or in the market place requiring returns of income to be made, to serve notices on each individual to make a return of income, to draw up the lists of those on whom assessments should be made, to insert in the list the amounts returned by the parties and to make an estimate of income where a person failed to make a return.[16] The assessor was named in vestry. He was usually a small tradesman and his office was compulsory, failure to act resulting in a fine of £20.[17] He received remuneration by way of poundage of one and a half pence for every pound of tax collected.

It was an unpopular task. His own business interests often clashed with those of the Crown, favoured customers being omitted from the assessment lists. Assessors were, at times, criticized for making assessments carelessly and inaccurately, in rural areas for being illiterate, and in towns for using their official papers for the purpose of advertising their own trades, especially those connected with debt collection.[18]

---

12 Ibid., s.100, r.1 of Case I
13 Ibid., r.2 of Case II confirmed by evidence given before the Hume Committee, (1852) ix qq. 949, 959-61
14 Ibid., s.100, r.3 of Case I
15 Ibid., s.45
16 Ibid., ss.46-8, 57-8
17 43 Geo.III, c.99, s.16, (1803) Examples of prosecution are given at HC, PP, (1856) 1 25
18 *6th Report of the Commissioners of Inland Revenue* (hereafter CIR), PP (1862) xxvii 327, 345; *Report of the Select Committee on Inland Revenue and Customs Establishments*, (hereafter IR & CE) PP (1863) vi 303 at p.32; W.Astle, *The History of Stockport*, 1822, repr. 1971 at p.55

In order not to leave the delicate matter of the assessment of the trading community to such officers, the General Commissioners were required to appoint Additional Commissioners for the purpose of making assessments under Schedule D.[19] The assessors still dealt with the preliminary detail but the Additional Commissioners reviewed the returns, made any necessary estimates and signed the assessments. Invariably the General Commissioners selected two of their own number to act in this capacity, or two of the supply Commissioners appointed to fill vacancies in their divisional complement. Since each Commissioner had to satisfy a property qualification, this practice was encouraged because it gave a greater degree of security.[20] In Devizes the Commissioners who acted most frequently in this capacity were Revd. Alfred Smith, John Locke, a brother of Wadham Locke, Colonel H.S. Olivier and later, W.E. Tugwell, both partners in the banking firm of Locke, Olivier & Tugwell. Later in the period, W.B. Seagram, physician and John Hayward, most likely the land agent, occasionally acted in this capacity. The returns of the trading and professional community, therefore, came under scrutiny by the Commissioners themselves.

Of course, the interests of the state needed to be protected against omission and delay and to ensure the timely assessment and collection of the tax. There were some 140 centrally remunerated officials in England and Wales termed Surveyors of Taxes who represented Government at a local level for this purpose.[21] In the early years of the re-introduced income tax, their role was essentially managerial: ensuring that the assessors made assessments within the time limits stipulated by law, that tax collected was paid over to the Board of Inland Revenue and that all those who ought to be assessed were assessed. They also played a pivotal role in examining taxpayers' claims for exemption. They were each responsible for a large area of the county. Wiltshire was divided into three tax districts, of which Chippenham included the division of Devizes. Here the Surveyors were William Tennant, from Sheffield, who moved on to Chester in about 1852 and was succeeded by James Cottell, a Swindon man.

Although the Surveyor also possessed certain statutory powers in the assessment process, these were very much subordinate to the functions of the General Commissioners. Peel was careful to inculcate forbearance in trespassing on the Commissioners' jurisdiction in order to sustain deference to the parameters of local assessment and so maintain the constitutional separation of powers on which the income tax relied for its survival. But as both the assessor and Surveyor were present at the meeting at which the Additional Commissioners made the assessments, they (and the Surveyor in particular) were able to comment on the sufficiency of the returns made and offer their observations on any estimates considered necessary.[22] This was an occasion on which the Surveyor might, and often did, influence the amounts in which assessments were made.

19 5 & 6 Vict., c.35, s.16
20 Ibid., ss. 16, 21, 59, 111; 45 *Justice of the Peace* (1842) 706
21 Number compiled from a return by each Surveyor of Taxes to the Select Committee on the Income & Property Tax of 1851/52 (hereafter Hume Committee), HC, PP, (1852) ix pp.905-9
22 Minutes of evidence taken before the Hume Committee (hereafter Hume Committee evidence), (1852) ix qq.1517-19

Not every person made a return of income every year. Large businesses such as Paul & Edward Anstie (**375**), tobacco and snuff manufacturers, the bankers Locke, Olivier & Tugwell (**537**), Hitchcock and Ives (**1014**), the surgeons of Market Lavington, and clergymen-tutors such as Revd. George Parker Cleather, curate of Chirton (**917**), returned an exact sum each year. Many smaller businesses, too, returned exact amounts annually, *inter alia*, R & W Edmonds, French teachers (**446**), and William Blackwell Jones, law stationer (**514**), of Devizes St.John.

But more often, the taxpayer would make a return in a round sum perhaps only every three years. Although provisions existed for the imposition of penalties for default in making an annual return, alongside these sanctions was the provision to deal with the matter in another way: the propulsive force behind the income tax legislation and the machinery of its enforcement was not that those who failed to make a return of income should be punished, but that an estimated assessment should be made so that the collection of the tax should move forward as smoothly and as quickly as possible.[23] The thrust of the income tax was to get at the money in the pockets of the people, not to make criminals. The penalty provisions were meant to be experienced as a threat *in terrorem* to encourage production of a return of income.

As an, albeit primitive, check against possible omission and procrastination, the Additional Commissioners were granted the power to make an estimated assessment where the taxpayer had failed to make any return. They were also empowered to disregard the amount of income declared by the taxpayer in cases where they doubted the sufficiency of the sum returned and to make an estimate according to the best of their judgement.[24] The power of arbitrary assessment was 'necessarily entrusted to the (C)ommissioners as the last defence against the taxpayer's power of concealment'.[25] Unless an appeal were made to the General Commissioners, estimated assessments were final and conclusive.[26] These were the elementary ways in which under- or non-assessment might be minimized.

Making a best judgement assessment was a function central to checking evasion, since neither the Additional Commissioners nor the Surveyor had any powers to compel the production of information, such as trading accounts or other corroborative evidence, to support a return of income. Only the General Commissioners had the power to enquire beyond the return, but this was originated only on the taxpayer's appeal against an estimated assessment.[27] The rationale on which this was based saw the estimate as final unless the appellant could satisfy the General Commissioners that it ought properly to be reduced. This entailed producing whatever information the General Commissioners required before they altered the estimate, which often meant production of the books of account of the taxpayer.

23 5 & 6 Vict., c.35, ss.52, 55
24 Ibid., s.113
25 H.H.Monroe, *Intolerable Inquisition? Reflections on the Law of Income Tax*, 1981, p.71
26 *Allen v Sharp*, (1848), 2 Ex. 352, 361, and see Baron Parke at 363
27 5 & 6 Vict., c.35, s.120

The reluctance to reveal the true state of a man's business to Commissioners who might be his own bankers, competitors, creditors or creditors' bankers, tended to deflect the taxpayer from appeal.[28] Because of the social and commercial constraints which thus worked against making an appeal, or simply because of the desire to escape a sufficient assessment, appeals were few. The exercise of the powers of estimation using local knowledge was, therefore, an essential feature of the assessment process. The figures compiled for the purposes of the Select Committee on the Income and Property Tax of 1851/52, (hereafter called the Hume Committee), show that at least 40 per cent of Schedule D assessments in England and Wales made for 1848/49 were estimated. On average, 27 per cent of these were appealed against.[29] For Devizes itself for the same year, 38 per cent of assessments on which tax was ultimately payable were estimated either in the absence of a return or in sums increased over and above the sum returned. 25 per cent of estimated assessments either greater than £150 or increased on the return were appealed against. This compares with 21 per cent for the entire tax district of Chippenham and 21 per cent for the county of Wiltshire.

In order to overcome the apparent problem of appealing to the local Commissioners, an alternative route was permitted whereby the appellant under Schedule D could make an application to be assessed by the Special Commissioners.[30] These were three Government officials, based at Somerset House, who travelled on circuit to hear appeals. This was a provision of which few availed themselves because of the perception that remunerated officers of the Crown might be more likely to make increased assessments. In Devizes, only the solicitor John Raikes Bayley (**384**) and the law firm of MacDonald & Olivier (**544**) elected to be assessed by the Special Commissioners.

As a further measure to maintain confidentiality, (which extended only to assessments made under Schedule D), the taxpayer could elect to be assessed under letter instead of name,[31] though the degree to which strict confidentiality was thus attained is questionable. In any event, few opted for this treatment – notably George Washington Anstie, solicitor of St. Mary (**669**); Thomas Blackwell, civil engineer of Rowde (**165**); John Hayward, land agent of Rowde (**182**); Thomas Chandler, maltster of Week (**230**); John Raikes Bayley, solicitor of St. John (**384**); and innkeepers James Chandler of the Old Crown (**693**), William Grace of the Castle (**746**), James Macklin of the White Bear (**787**) and William Joyce of the Pelican (**515**).

EXEMPTION

Between 1842 and 1852 the tax threshold was £150. Those with a total annual income of £150 and above paid tax on the whole of their income, while those below were

28 Hansard, *HCDebs.*, 3rd. ser., 161, col.642, 8 Apr.1856; *The Times*, 21 Jan.1856
29 Hume Committee evidence, p.909 and PP (1851) xxxi 397 re Schedule D
30 5 & 6 Vict., c.35, s.130 (appeal), s.131 (assessment)
31 Ibid., ss.137-9

excepted, provided that they made a formal claim for exemption.[32] This entailed making a declaration of total income under all Schedules. Without such a claim, tax remained payable even though the taxpayer might be eligible for exemption. Few people with incomes well below the threshold (generally those earning between £50 and £100 annually in country parishes and in the parish of Devizes St.Mary) made returns. The Additional Commissioners exercised their powers of estimation widely in these areas. In 1848/49 (to continue the comparison with figures from the Hume Committee Report) 93 per cent of assessments made in sums below £150 in Devizes were estimated. Of the total assessments made in whatever sum, 67 per cent were discharged on a claim for exemption. Of course, proof of income is implicit in the fact that a formal claim was a precondition of relief.

Initially, an assessment had to be made on every taxpayer irrespective of the potential for exemption and the claimant had to prove the level of his income either before the Surveyor or the General Commissioners. It was a kind of means test on what might cautiously and loosely be termed the lower or lower middle classes before the assessment might be discharged. Claimants either produced calculations of their total income and were tested by oral enquiry, or acquiesced in the estimate made by the Additional Commissioners.

The formal ritual of assessment and claim for exemption was observed in the division of Devizes until 1850 when, probably in order to reduce the workload of the administrative personnel, parties who were continually being relieved from tax were eliminated altogether from the assessment process. However, after 1853 when the exemption limit was lowered to £100, a closer scrutiny of lower income taxpayers was again introduced. In the text, therefore, an assessment for the years 1850/51 to 1852/53 will sometimes be absent in respect of those whose incomes were obviously well below the exemption limit. This fact is recorded in the footnotes by stating '1850/51-1852/53 no assessments made'.

It is at the margins of tax liability that an early form of legal tax avoidance is witnessed. The exclusivity of the exemption limit where an annual income of £150 was wholly taxable while an annual income of £149 19s.11d. was wholly exempt created a fiscal precipice which tested the ingenuity of the taxpayer.[33] Employees were in a better position than most to prove the level of their incomes because they could produce corroborative evidence from their employers. Thomas Glossop Thorp, surveyor's clerk (**29**), of Bedborough, returned and was assessed on a salary of £150 up to 1847/48. For 1848/49 and 1849/50 he was assessed at £150 but proved that he had arranged with his employer a salary of £149, so making an overall saving (with a tax rate of seven pence in the pound) of £3 7s. 6d. Similar arrangements can be seen in the records of Thomas Watson Anderson, solicitor's clerk (**373**), and William Palmer Coxhead, schoolmaster (**427**), both of Devizes St.John.

---

32 Ibid., s.163
33 Hume Committee evidence, qq. 3019,3020,3235

APPEALS

Once the Additional Commissioners had made the assessment at or above £150 (or £100 after 1853) it could be displaced only by appeal to the General Commissioners. Even where made at a figure below the exemption limit, without an appeal, the figure remained the sum which had to be included in the proof of income. On appeal, the taxpayer was required to adduce such evidence as the General Commissioners considered necessary before the assessment would be reduced. This often entailed a *viva voce* examination.

The General Commissioners had wide powers of enquiry on appeal and could issue a precept for particulars in writing, for example, for a statement of debtors and creditors, or computation of profits, which might also be sworn on oath. In the main, appeals were successful but this was not universal. Often the result was a compromise after ascertaining the facts. In 1856/57 John & Thomas Chandler, corn dealers and maltsters of Week (**229**), having returned £160 were increased by the Additional Commissioners to £720; on appeal the assessment was confirmed at £550. In 1849/50 Robert Coates, innkeeper of the Odd Fellows' Arms in Sidmouth Street, Devizes (**703**), returned £100, was increased to £150 to incite an appeal and the assessment settled at £117 on which exemption was successfully claimed. Occasionally the evidence was not enough to displace the estimate: in 1842/43 John & James Sainsbury, timber dealers and wheelwrights of West Lavington (**339**), were assessed at £50 each by the Additional Commissioners and on appeal the assessments were sustained at this sum.

Statutorily no estimated assessment could be displaced except on appeal, although where exemption was clearly due and a formal claim was made, in practice, the assessment often seems to have been discharged without a formal appeal. Thus, in 1850/51, Richard Berry, miller & corndealer of Horton (**109**), who returned £100, was assessed at £150 and his assessment was reduced to £134 19s. 6d. on his proof of income alone. It may be that the figure included in the 'Amount of Income Proved' column is the total income rather then the specific Schedule D income. It is impossible to ascertain this with certainty, though isolated examples suggest this as a possibility. For example, in 1848/49 Benjamin Webb, lime burner of Bromham (**99**), was assessed at £100 but proved his income at £120. The following year he was assessed in the absence of a return at £50 which seems incongruous until it is proposed that his total income may have comprised £50 Schedule D profits and £70 other (unspecified) income. Similar examples, among many others, can be seen at entries **105, 115, 193, 214** and **311**.

In the main, up to the late 1850s, the returns of certain taxpayers were accepted as a matter of course while others were doubted. The criteria which activated the preferences and prejudices of the Additional Commissioners were inevitably many and varied and often subjective. But there is a prevailing and imperceptible undercurrent, certainly in the work of the Hume Committee, which suggests that although there would have been exceptions, returns of income above a certain figure were generally accepted by the Commissioners without question. What this figure was is difficult to ascertain. The terms 'small trader' or 'small manufacturer' were used as phrases of convenience to describe those who were scrutinized more closely. But these terms, too, present a difficulty in terminology in defining such a group for the purposes of the income tax and leave ambiguities and inconsistencies, chiefly about where to draw the high cut-off lines, although the low cut-off point was somewhere just below the exemption limit.

Throughout the evidence given before the Hume Committee, the examples of evasion put forward by the witnesses relate almost exclusively to small traders and manufacturers and instances relating to the larger industrialists and merchants are conspicuous by their absence. The presumption which pervaded the work of the Committee and was explicit in the evidence it received was that while the small trader would go to any lengths to reduce the amount returned as his profits, the larger taxpayers returned more than they needed. Contemporaries who discussed evasion in the 1840s and 1850s perceived it largely as the province of those whose incomes lay at the margins of the exemption limit. In 1848/49, nationally, 43 per cent of assessments increased over and above the return related to persons who had returned incomes below £150 but had been assessed at £150 or upwards to make them appeal or pay the tax.[34] Perhaps this mentality, which identified small traders as those who were most tempted to evade the tax, and so should be scrutinized more closely, is one of the most striking features of the mid-Victorian income tax. It can be seen particularly in the case of Isaiah Dangerfield, fishmonger of St. John (**433**).

This notion was to be shattered in the mid-1850s[35] but it can be seen in cases such as George Simpson, newspaper proprietor (**612**), Revd. Richard Elliott, dissenting minister and schoolmaster (**447**), Thomas Browne Anstie, surgeon (**670**), or William Cunnington & Sons, wine merchants of the Bottle and the Old Town Hall (**234**), among many others whose returns were largely accepted and whose assessments remained relatively constant. But instances such as the brewers James Oram of Northgate Street, Devizes (**810**) and James Banks of Bromham (**61**), the rising fortunes of George Taylor Sainsbury, brickmaker of Rowde (**201**) or of John & Thomas Chandler, retail maltsters of Week (**229**), and, to a lesser extent, of the ironfounders of Bedborough, Messrs Brown & May (**4**), reveal a policy of aggressive increases by the Additional Commissioners, perhaps stimulated, too, by attempts by the Surveyor of Taxes to raise assessment levels. It signals a move away from the general attitude that the word of a gentleman was accepted without question and perhaps indicates either a more discerning approach by the Commissioners of this division or a readiness to accede to the suggestions of the Surveyor of Taxes for an increase in the estimate.

Their reaction to local conditions and events, which reflected falling profits as well as expanding businesses, is clearly seen in the assessments of the lunatic asylums of

34 Hume Committee evidence, qq. 360-3 and p. 909
35 This arose primarily from the compensation claims following the Cannon Street Improvements (*Report of the Select Committee on Income Tax*, PP (1861) vi q.2174), and from the abolition of offices under the Court of Probate Act and the Matrimonial Causes Act of 1857 (Hansard, *HCDebs.*, 3rd. ser., 157, col.1203). See also 8th CIR PP (1864) xxx 423 re compensation claims upon public companies

Thomas Phillips at Bellevue, Week (**276**) and of Charles Hitchcock (successor to Robert Willett) at Fiddington House, West Lavington (**327**). These show a downturn after 1852 with the beginning of the transfer of pauper patients to the newly opened County Asylum, as recorded in a manuscript note against the name of Phillips. The assessments at Bellevue, which housed a larger proportion of paupers than Fiddington House, fell from £850 in 1852/53 to £75 by 1856/57 reflecting the fact that between 1851 and 1855 the number of pauper patients fell from 144 to 4. The assessment on Fiddington House fell from £1,000 to £380 over the same period as the number of pauper patients fell from 146 to 3, though the Commissioners in this instance were more resistant to a greater reduction, even on appeal by Hitchcock, perhaps aware of his accommodation of private patients, which continued at much the same level as before.[36]

THE CERTIFICATE OF ASSESSMENTS

The process of the assessment to income tax began when a notice of return was delivered to each inhabitant in the division by the assessors. These officers and the Schedular nature of the income tax have been described earlier, but the following will help to reinforce the essential effect of this scheme.

There was no composite return of income as there is today. Each person was required to complete a declaration of his income separately under each Schedule, so that where he owned or occupied property or used it for the purposes of farming or market gardening, he would make a return under Schedules A & B; where his income was derived from a trade, profession or vocation, from certain wages or salaries, or certain interest on investments, under Schedule D; and where he received income from a public office or employment, under Schedule E. When the declarations of income were returned, the Clerk to the Commissioners, with assistance from the assessors, drew up a list of all persons on whom a notice of return had been served, termed a Certificate of Assessments, under each separate Schedule for each township or parish within the division. These were central to the record of returns and assessments for each fiscal year and of the final charge to duty.

The Certificate of Assessments is the key administrative record. It comprised an alphabetical list of the 'Christian and Surnames of persons charged' and a 'Description of the Trade, Profession, Vocation or other Profits chargeable under Schedule D'. Against each name is written a columnar history of the stages of assessment which shows the amounts of income returned by the parties and indicates those who made no return. The next column shows the 'Amount assessed by the Additional Commissioners', from which can be deduced the estimates made both in the absence of a return and where the Commissioners were dissatisfied with the sufficiency of the sum returned. An example

---

36 *6th Report of the Commissioners in Lunacy*, PP (1851) xxiii 353 and *9th Report of the Commissioners in Lunacy*, PP (1854/55) xvii 533

of the Certificate of Assessments showing part of the entries relating to the township of Bedborough is reproduced below.

There was also a column which recorded any assessment which the Surveyor of Taxes considered insufficient so that the General Commissioners could take this into account in deciding the quantum to be assessed; but this was used infrequently and usually reserved for instances where the Surveyor laid a formal Information before the Commissioners in cases of evasion or under-assessment. In the division of Devizes this power does not seem to have been invoked. Instead, the Surveyor's observations were put forward when he attended the meeting at which the Additional Commissioners made the assessments. The forms accommodate a manuscript note for the result of appeals made to the General Commissioners against estimated assessments, from which it is possible to ascertain the proportion of taxpayers who appealed against estimated assessments and the number of appeals that were successful. Later in the period a system of abatement was introduced whereby those having an assessable income between the exemption limit and £150 were charged at a lower rate of tax. A separate column, headed 'Amount of Income Proved' records those persons relieved from the payment of duty on a claim for exemption where their total incomes lay below the tax threshold. The final columns show the amount of duty discharged, (in appropriate years) abated, and finally payable by each person.

Traders who had businesses both in Devizes and elsewhere were assessed in the division in which they resided but their presence in the division where they carried on

Sample page of a Certificate of Assessments, relating to Bedborough (WSRO 1090/81)

a trade was nevertheless noted: William Lawes & Co., carriers, who traded at the Wagon Office in Devizes St.Mary (**779**), made returns and were assessed at Chippenham, their principal place of business and residence until 1849/50 when part of the business was taken over by Horatio Nelson Perry (**24**), who resided in and was assessed at Bedborough; Jonah Reeve, upholsterer of Devizes St.John (**596**) from 1842 to 1860 also carried on the business of auctioneer, appraiser and cabinet maker at Marlborough where he made his returns; John North, coach builder at Week (**268**), made returns at Melksham between 1846 and 1855 but was assessed at Devizes St.John from 1856/57-1859/60. Thus, every businessman who traded in the division at any time between 1842 and 1860, was noted, whether or not an assessment was made.

The Certificates are signed by the Additional Commissioners at the time they made the assessments and by the General Commissioners after all appeals had been heard. By signing and, in statutory terms, 'allowing the assessments', the General Commissioners created the legal charge to tax. The Certificates for each township or parish in the division were bound together with ribbon under each Schedule, for the convenience of the Commissioners. Thus, there is a set of documents which records the number of manufacturers, tradesmen, professional men and certain classes of employees respectively and the amounts on which they paid duty. The record includes both men and women.

But however useful the statistics compiled from this source might be to the historian generally, some reorganization of the basic components included in each Certificate has been considered desirable – and indeed, necessary – if the information was to be made accessible to a wider group, for example, to the social or local historian, to the population or family historian, as well as to the casual genealogist, all of whom have a legitimate claim to be interested in this historical record. In order to achieve this, the information comprised in each Certificate has been dissected and the details for each taxpayer analysed and reallocated to form a personal history of each individual or business within the division, covering the period from 1842 to 1860. The mechanism of this process is described in more detail in the section on Editorial Method.

The question must of course be posed – how accurate a reflection of the incomes of the trading and professional people of Devizes are the assessments incorporated in the Certificates? Perhaps we shall never know for certain. The cynic may argue that their accuracy is commensurate with the honesty and integrity of each taxpayer and, in the main, he would probably be right. But the exercise by the Additional Commissioners of their judgement on the sufficiency of the sum returned and on the estimates made, under Schedule D, and the resolve of the Surveyor to ensure as high an assessment as possible, helps to lessen this concern, at least in respect of the smaller tradesmen.

Their preferences and prejudices, however, (to which reference has already been made) are still factors which must be borne in mind when considering a number of assessments made. It may well be that the incomes of the more well-to-do are understated rather than overstated. Certainly, the assessments on Tugwell & Meek, solicitors (**638**) display a remarkable uniformity, and those of Alexander Meek, solicitor (**557**) and Clerk to the Commissioners, are evidently largely repetitive amounts. On the other hand, as already noted, firms like Locke, Olivier & Tugwell, bankers (**537**) and Paul &

Edward Anstie, tobacco and snuff manufacturers (**375**) returned precise amounts. And instances such as the brewers James Oram (**810**) and James Banks (**61**) among many others, where high estimated assessments displaced the sums returned, also help to dispel fears of complacency in the assessing process.

But one answer to all such self-inflicted criticism is that this is probably the closest we will come to a construct of the incomes and profits of such a wide cross-section of people in this stratified mid-Victorian commercial community for so long a period. And in spite of nagging doubts, it is possible to discern a marked sensitivity in estimating the assessments of the various types of business. Indeed, not all tradesmen in the same category were treated the same. Each entry seems to have been considered subjectively, so that, for example, in the parish of St.Mary, the range of figures for assessments on innkeepers is significantly varied from business to business – the assessments on Henry Blencowe of the Castle (**683**) range from £118–£200; on Richard Trueman of the White Lion (**862**), £65–£100; on Isaiah Dangerfield of the White Hart (**712**), £40–£60; on James Chandler of the Three Crowns (**694**), £75–£130. And although Decimus Wild of the White Bear (**883**) made seemingly precise returns every year, these were disregarded and estimates made, rising sharply from £150 to £300 in one year. This suggests that taxpayers came under some scrutiny and that the assessments represent the exercise of local knowledge and were based on local conditions.

INCOME TAX RECORDS – THE STATUTORY REQUIREMENTS

The temporary characteristic of the income tax is reflected nowhere more clearly than in the legislative attitude to the records that were created by the system, the documents which formed the day to day administration of the income tax. This is witnessed in the legislation which envisaged a local administration, under which the custody of records was entrusted to the General Commissioners. Although the tax was a temporary measure, in order to make the system workable, custody of the records had to be subject, to an extent at least, to some continuity and the reason behind this can be seen in a consolidating Act of 1803, which related to the management of direct taxes, when it was stated (in a rather more unwieldy form than the abridged version which follows):

> . . . many Difficulties and Inconveniencies have arisen to the Commissioners . . . upon the Death or Removal of their respective Clerks, into whose Custody all the . . . Books and Papers . . . have been delivered; such Clerks so removed, or the Executors Administrators or Legal Representatives of such Clerk so dying, frequently refusing to deliver up the . . . Books and Papers . . . under a Pretence that the said Commissioners have no property in the same, and are without remedy for the Recovery thereof.[37]

---

37 43 Geo.III, c.99, s.67 (1803)

This Act, as a consequence, declared the books of assessment and all other books and papers to be the property of the local Commissioners 'for the Time being, and in succession'. The Certificates of First Assessments for the division of Devizes were prepared under the supervision of, and kept by, the Clerk to the Commissioners, Alexander Meek (**557**). He was a solicitor of 33, St.John Street, Devizes and was a partner with William Edmund Tugwell in the firm of Tugwell & Meek (**638**). The firm traced its history at least back to William Salmon in the late 18th century. After 1852, Meek practiced alone. He was also County Treasurer, Town Clerk, Clerk to the Magistrates, and a Justice of the Peace. Later he became a partner in the banking firm of Locke, Tugwell & Meek (see Locke, Olivier & Tugwell, bankers, **537**).[38]

The statutory control of local papers which was introduced by the Act of 1803 was focused on current material as opposed to past papers and concentrated on facilitating the transfer of the impedimenta of assessment and collection to newly appointed clerks on the death or retirement of their predecessors, so that the process could continue uninterrupted. The documentation created by the process was directed at a specific managerial function, that of collection of the tax for a definite period, after which such records became obsolete and, as a result, disposable. The legislation was not directed at a long-term retention of material and the Act of 1842, by which the Victorian income tax was re-introduced, still regulated by the Act of 1803, provided for the returns to be

> filed in the Office of the said Commissioners and carefully kept so long as the Accounts of the said Duties for such District, or any Part thereof, shall remain unpaid to Her Majesty.[39]

So, once the tax for the year had been paid, the purpose of the returns and assessments, or any documentation which emanated from them, became superfluous. Even papers or abstracts which the Surveyor of Taxes was permitted to take, do not appear to have been retained. For example, having been requested by the Secretary of the Board of Inland Revenue to furnish a return of assessments and appeals for the information of the Hume Committee, one Surveyor replied that he could not 'give 1842-47 because the whole of the assessments, etc., have been destroyed, agreeable to the directions given by the Board to the Clerk to the Commissioners for this district'.[40] By 1853 a general instruction to all Surveyors urged that old papers should be burned,

38 He remained a partner until 1883 when the bank was merged with Capital & Counties Bank. He lived at Hillworth House and at his death in 1888 left a remarkable fortune of £83,843. By his marriage to the daughter of John Grant of Manningford, he had a son Alexander Grant Meek who continued the law practice and is recorded in Trade Directories of 1875 and 1885. He married the niece of Revd. Benjamin Charles Dowding, Perpetual Curate of Southbroom (**7**) and his descendants were still living in the area in the 1950s, after which the estate passed to a kinsman and member of the Dowding family.
39 5 & 6 Vict., c.35, s.59
40 Hume Committee evidence, correspondence 29 Mar.1852 John Nicholson to Thomas Keogh

usually on a bonfire, though some seem to have been consigned to furnaces to ensure complete combustion.[41]

Although a central involvement suggests central records, these did not extend systematically, at least in relation to any other than the current or preceding two years, beyond a summary compiled from the aggregate numbers of assessments made and total incomes assessable for each division. The Surveyor of Taxes was permitted to abstract details from the Commissioners' lists of assessments but in practice appears to have used the original documents for whatever purposes he needed them. There would inevitably have been a flow of instructions and correspondence between the Surveyor and Somerset House but for perhaps the whole of the period with which this volume is concerned, the records of the Board at the Public Record Office are piecemeal, comprising, essentially, no more than random examples of correspondence and instructions, covering, in the main, only the years 1843 and 1860.[42] The record of the day to day assessment of the income tax was firmly rooted in the division. Indeed, the source of the figures from which the official income tax statistics that were compiled on a national basis for each year from 1842 onward of the total numbers of assessments made and the total amounts of income assessed under each Schedule was the divisional record of assessment.

That the documentation created by the procedure of taxation were records in the sense that they were contemporary officially authenticated statements of acts and proceedings in public affairs, is self-evident. But tax papers were not yet records in the sense that they had a secondary purpose over and above their limited function as the means of arriving at a public contribution for some specific purpose. Perhaps the word 'data', albeit the right word in the wrong century, is a better way to describe the facts which were collated as a consequence of the procedure. It might be said that such data were not processed in any way other than that for which they were brought into existence. The usefulness of the returns and assessments was essentially finite: they possessed no connotative quality beyond the immediate purpose for which they were created. For example, their application in providing a personal history of assessment for a taxpayer and hence their subsidiary utility as a means of creating an information base that could be used to detect instances of under or non-assessment over a period of time, does not seem to have been considered. There was not yet the desire, nor the manpower, to collect and organize local information for the purpose of better control; that is, there was no use of data as records of assessment which might have another dimension within a wider philosophy of taxation. This may now seem naive, but this was not yet the system of permanent taxation in which the Government Department most interested in its assessment could influence the process, nor yet the system in which the Commissioners intervened beyond the making of an assessment for one year and beyond acting as its stamp of authority. This was still the world of the autocrat not the bureaucrat. The survival of the Certificates of Assessments for Devizes, in this light, is fortuitous.

41 Chester Record Office D6148/80, The Henzell Collection, 14 June 1853. I am grateful to Mr Stephen Matthews for drawing my attention to this collection, which until recently was in private hands.

42 IR40 class file

DISPOSAL OF INCOME TAX PAPERS AND THEIR RARITY VALUE

Used paper, printed or written on, was a marketable commodity, much in demand for a great variety of uses in the wrapping of fish and groceries or many other commercial or domestic uses. Once the primary function of the income tax papers had ceased, if they no longer possessed value as a record of assessment, they did possess value as waste paper. Anecdotal evidence about the disposal of income tax papers, at first blush, seems apocryphal or at least replicated, since it normally comprises accounts of grocers delivering butter or cheese wrapped up in the customer's own return form. But the disposal of income tax returns and papers to tradesmen is recorded in several parts of the country over a substantial period, among which, the butcher at King's Cross who purchased nearly the whole of the income tax returns for the parishes of St.Mary, Islington and St.Luke in 1848;[43] the grocer near Brixton in 1851/2 who obtained for waste paper several large bales of returns, schedules and claims for exemption;[44] the shopkeeper who purchased 3cwt of returns of the inhabitants of Westbury, Devizes and Trowbridge in 1856;[45] as well as in Leeds, where the shopkeeper acquired not only returns and schedules but also 'the pieces of paper attached, with the remarks and calculations of the Commissioners'. They included the papers of two clergymen (one of whom was a distinguished leader in the Oxford movement and a chaplain to Queen Victoria) five surgeons and doctors, seven solicitors and barristers, five booksellers, six druggists, six corn-factors, eleven merchants, two curriers, five wine merchants and four tea dealers (including an alderman of the City of London).[46]

The position reached crisis point in 1858 when several hundredweight of income tax papers relating to the City of London, comprising 1000 to 1200 returns, found their way into Billingsgate fish market and the Surveyor, Edward Welsh, visited shops in several different wards and bought back as many papers as possible in order to get possession of them. A charwoman at the Commissioners' offices had sold them as waste paper and although she selected only a few at a time from various batches, the quantity discovered by Welsh was considerable: Walter Blanchard, a waste paper dealer of Bell Alley, Moorgate Street had purchased half a hundredweight from her over a three month period; Henry Barber, a fish salesman of Lower Thames Street had purchased one hundredweight and another half hundredweight was sold to Dearsley the fishmonger of Billingsgate.[47]

While revelations of laxity led to investigations by both the local personnel and the Board of Inland Revenue, the importance is, perhaps, not only that after being

---

43 *Liverpool Mercury*, 12 May 1848

44 *The Times*, 26 Jan.1852; *Chester Chronicle*, 7 Feb.1852

45 Article in *Wiltshire County Mirror* reproduced in *The Times*, 4 Dec.1856

46 *The Times*, 24,28 & 29 Aug.1857

47 IR & CE evidence, PP (1862) xii q.2414; PP (1857/58) xxxiv 97 *et seq.*, correspondence Edward Welsh to Thomas Keogh, 11 Feb.1858; *The Times*, 12 Feb.1858; B.E.V.Sabine, 'Victorian Paper Chase', *British Tax Review*, 1969, 10-15

retained for a number of years, such records were ordered to be disposed of, but because such material found its way, whether accidentally or otherwise, into the public gaze, a more stringent policy of supervised destruction was adopted. In the City of London, for example, in the mid-fifties, it was the practice to take records 'by rail some distance from the town, and having had a good dinner, to make a good bonfire of them somewhere down the river'.[48] Gradually, probably as a result of adverse publicity, it became the practice for income tax returns and papers, once they were done with, to be sold to the highest bidder of about five persons who were in the habit of purchasing mill waste, generally Messrs Waterlow and Sons,[49] and it is apparent that, for most of the mid-Victorian period, income tax records were themselves temporary and when finished with were consigned to disposal. Sensational newspaper reports relating to such breaches of confidentiality only resulted in a stricter policy of the disposal of income tax records and even inevitably accelerated their destruction. Though it has to be said that instances existed where this, too, became lax: in Warrington in Lancashire in 1880, an inspection of the attic of the office of the Surveyor revealed the floor strewn with old letters, papers and assessments in a state of great disarray, and orders were given for their destruction.[50]

That the papers were brought into existence for only a limited purpose reflects the temporary nature of the mid-Victorian income tax: that they were sometimes disposed of in a seemingly incredible manner may account for their present-day scarcity. The survival of the Certificates of Assessments for the division of Devizes for so long a period, therefore, is remarkable, and signals the unique quality of this source of material. But it also introduces the historian to a different mentality, far removed from even the kind of bureaucracy that would later become more recognizable to the modern world. Custody of the records, while they still retained their primary utility, was entrusted to the General Commissioners and kept in the offices of a local solicitor or attorney who acted as their Clerk. The paperwork and organization of the assessments was carried out by an administrative framework which was statutorily distanced from the Government Department. This was still the world of personalities in which the executive function in relation to the income tax was carried out by members of the local oligarchy, not yet the world of officialdom. Any social disciplines which controlled the safe-keeping of the Certificates of Assessments and other books and papers were as yet largely unorchestrated by a uniform bureaucracy.

THE CERTIFICATES IN THEIR HISTORIOGRAPHICAL CONTEXT

Each of the episodes to which reference has been made suggests that the disposal of tax papers was more the rule than the exception. More than anything they stress the unique

48 *Chester Chronicle*, 12 Aug.1854
49 *Report from the Select Committee on Public Departments (Purchases and Sale of Materials and Stores)*, PP (1873) xvii 1, 364, q.8120
50 PRO IR 40/1507, Report by George Phillips on George Hemment, Surveyor at Warrington, 30 Oct.1880. Similar report by William Smiles, 9 Oct.1880

quality of any surviving material. Their existence today is largely the result of the care taken by the firm(s) of solicitors which succeeded to Meek's practice and deposited the Certificates with the Wiltshire & Swindon Record Office (WSRO 1090/81). This firm is now represented by Messrs Awdry, Bailey & Douglas. The preservation of this record is important for the interpretation of official income tax statistics, as well as of the more general data obtained from these sources that might be used in population and socio-economic studies. The usefulness of income tax statistics has ever been marred to some extent by the uncertainties which surrounded them. The possibility of placing them in the context of the actual practice of taxation opens up a new awareness of these figures and may perhaps lead to a re-evaluation of accepted thinking about mid-Victorian incomes. The Certificate of Assessments provides the golden key which unlocks what was really being done at a local level, and allows us to approach more intimately the workings of the income tax which neither the statute, the Reports of the Board of Inland Revenue, central statistics or other more formalized reports, alone, permit.

Economic histories, particularly those which concern the size and distribution of middle or lower-middle class wealth have relied to some extent on official income tax statistics. These works have invariably acknowledged the limitations of these figures and that far more work needed to be done on the practices of the local administrative personnel before they could be accepted as a reasonable reflection of the social and geographic distribution of income. Social histories which have addressed the income tax have also been concerned almost exclusively with its political progress as opposed to its social impact and have been based largely on central records.

Although there have been some invaluable tax histories written during the last century or more by only a handful of writers, an understanding of the income tax in legal, social and economic terms has, in the main, been understandably doctrinal in the absence of substantive local records and the relation between the statute law and actual practice has lacked substantial empirical analysis. With some few exceptions they have had little to say about local administrative practices, which is understandable given the scarcity of surviving local material.

Almost every Record Office will boast some ephemera relating to the income tax: a batch of returns for a particular parish, the tax Commissioners' minute books recording the swearing in of the assessors and collectors, a few random notices of assessment, some minutes of appeal meetings or discrete correspondence between the taxpayer and the Clerk to the Commissioners. The density of preservation is an issue which has to be considered. The ephemera such as individual returns or assessments discovered sporadically in archival deposits may often act as tiny lanterns in a dark world in the absence of anything more substantial. But these are no more than isolated fragments which, although useful, contribute in only a minor way to a scientific understanding of the wider scheme of taxation. The value of income tax records in historical research often remains unrealized. The Certificates of Assessments for Devizes open up a new awareness of income tax records as source material for the historian.

Income statistics compiled and publicised by the Board of Inland Revenue during the third quarter of the nineteenth century were drawn directly from summaries of the Certificates of Assessments prepared by the Clerks to the Commissioners for each division. Perhaps one of the most widely held assumptions about these statistics is that they are based on information of a similar quality to the data which are created by the present day system – that is, that there is a close relation between the actual income of, the return made by, and the assessment made on the taxpayer. That the accuracy of such statistics is questionable because of the unknown quantity of evasion is generally the main concern of the historian, but the possibility that the figures may, in certain instances, be little more than estimates in the first place, is not usually considered. The usefulness of such statistics has ever been marred to some extent by the uncertainties which surrounded them. The possibility of placing them in the context of the actual practices of taxation may invite a re-evaluation of accepted thinking about how they were compiled. This is still relatively uncharted territory and more work still needs to be done to ascertain whether more examples of this primary source survive in other parts of the country. It is hoped that this study will generate a greater interest in income tax records as source material and help those who come to such material to understand its context and meaning.

EDITORIAL METHOD
EXPLANATIONS TO THE TEXT

THE MATERIAL

This volume comprises a complete analysis of the Certificates of Assessments for the year 1842/43 and the period 1846/47 to 1859/60. The first year coincides with the re-introduction of the income tax in 1842. There is a gap between 1843 and 1846 after which there is a continuous record. This record extends beyond 1860 but after this date there were subtle changes in, and outward influences on, the making of assessments which would make year on year comparisons unreliable. And as a consequence, a variety of methodological constraints make the recorded data after this date difficult to handle in a format consistent with earlier years. For this reason, this particular study ends at 1860. In order to make the material useful to historians generally, as opposed to the tax historian specifically, the data are presented in the form of a personal history of assessment for each individual or business within the division for this period.

ORGANIZATION OF MATERIAL

The division of Devizes was formed by the amalgamation of the two hundreds of Potterne & Cannings, and Swanborough. Each hundred comprised many parishes and tithings, which became the administration units within the division. A separate Certificate of Assessments was prepared for each one. The Certificates for each unit were bound together in a largely alphabetical order with two exceptions: firstly, the separation of the hundreds was observed in the ordering of the units, so that those comprised in Potterne

& Cannings are listed together, followed by those in Swanborough; and secondly, the parishes of St. John and St.Mary the Virgin, Devizes, invariably follow Worton within the hundred of Potterne and Cannings. The text, therefore, begins with Bedborough, continues to Worton, followed by St.John and St.Mary. These are followed immediately by Allcannings and continue to Woodborough. This reflects the original ordering of the Certificates of Assessments which was observed almost throughout the period.

ENTRY HEADINGS

Each entry is ordered by surname. The forename(s) are recorded where they appear at some time in the Certificates of Assessments. The heading includes the occupation(s), business name and other familial names by which the business was carried on. These are explained in more detail below:

Surnames
The first entry in each heading is the surname. Spelling variants are more frequent at the earlier dates, perhaps as a result of the lists being compiled from largely oral or hearsay evidence. Towards the middle of the period spellings were refined, perhaps when written evidence, such as returns of income and claims for exemption bearing the signatures of the taxpayers, had been obtained. On the basis that later entries reflect the accepted spelling, this form is recorded in the entry heading. Variants and the years for which they existed are recorded by way of footnote. For example, for five out of fifteen years George Randell, baker of St.Mary (**829**) is entered as George Randle; the entry heading is under Randell and the spelling variant noted by footnote.

Forename(s)
Full names are given in the entry heading where they are recorded at some time in the series. For example, J.R.Bayley, solicitor of St.John (**384**) and St.Mary (**676**) is often entered in the Certificates by initials but at other times by his full name of John Raikes Bayley. The entry heading records the full name. Where forenames (other than initials) have been ascertainable only from contemporary directories (for example the Clergy List) these are shown as follows: Cleather, Revd G(eorge) P(arker) (**917**). Variants other than initials are recorded by footnote. Original abbreviations, such as Jno. for John, Jas. for James, are replaced by the full form where this has been recorded at some time in the Certificates. Omissions have been rectified on a few occasions where this was plainly possible, for example Revd. Peter Almerick Leh(eup) Wood (**659**), or the T(urn) P(ike) Trust (**291**).

Occupations
In the entry heading all occupations recorded at any time in the period are included. For example, the heading for William Harding who was described as a farrier from 1842/43 to 1849/50 and as a veterinary surgeon between 1853/54 and 1859/60, is HARDING, William, farrier, veterinary surgeon (**15**); where dual or multiple occupations subsisted throughout the whole period for which a record exists, these are shown

conjoined – PERRETT,William, baker & shopkeeper (**93**).The years for which different occupations are recorded are shown by way of footnote.

Business names
Where noted at some time in the period, the business name is given in the heading and the years noted recorded by footnote.The business name has also been included in the entry heading.This applies mostly to inns, taverns and public houses, but brewers and maltsters are also included. For example, SLOPER, Edwin, innkeeper, Elm Tree (**617**); HUMBY, Frederick Peter, Southbroom Brewery (**254**).Where the business name has been recorded for a successor only or obtained from Pigot & Co's Directory of 1842, the name is shown as follows: CROOK,William, innkeeper [by comparison Hare & Hounds] (**430**). Here, the note was recorded in the assessment record for his successor Nathaniel Millwaters.

Familial successions
Two types of succession are included in the entry heading – succession by a family member and succession by a wife or husband.An example of the first is Robert Blake, grocer, builder and assistant overseer of West Lavington between 1852/53 and 1854/55 succeeded by Christopher Blake, grocer & carpenter from 1855/56 to 1859/60.The heading reads BLAKE, Christopher, grocer, builder, carpenter, assistant overseer [also BLAKE, Robert] (**311**) on the basis that Christopher Blake was recorded in five out of eight years.An example of the second is Edward Davies, innkeeper of the Bear from 1842/43 to 1850/51 followed by Elizabeth Davies between 1851/52 and 1859/60. Here, the entry heading is DAVIES, Elizabeth, innkeeper, Bear [also DAVIES, Edward] (**434**).The entry is made under Elizabeth Davies because this is the name in which the trade was carried on for the greatest number of years recorded.The exception is where the successor has a separate entry, for example, Charles Hook, confectioner (**496**) was succeeded by Eliza & Emma Hook(**497**), who were already recorded separately as schoolmistresses but changed their occupation to confectioners after the date of succession.All successions are noted by way of footnote, recording the exact wording of the entry.

Partnerships
Partnerships are entered in headings under the name of the first named partner. For example, the partnership of tailors Spencer & Plummer is entered under SPENCER, Thomas C. and Plummer, John Alderson (**624**). Exceptionally, the changing partnership of surgeons in Market Lavington, where Charles Hitchcock appears to have been the principal partner throughout the period, is recorded under HITCHCOCK, Charles in order to maintain the integrity of this particular business entity and the heading extended to the other partners as they changed by square brackets: HITCHCOCK, Charles, surgeon [also IVES, John; HAYWARD, John; WHITE, Frederick George; PEPLER, William Brown] (**1014**) and separate headings recording individual partners occur in appropriate alphabetical places in the text and cross-referenced to HITCHCOCK.

FOOTNOTE COMMENTARY

Footnotes to each entry record all original textual commentary. This is dealt with under the following categories.

Spelling
Variants and surnames have been explained above. In all footnote entries the original spelling has been retained – for example, Cottle for Cottell; Poulshot for Poulshott.

Original comments
Comments inserted in the Certificates of Assessments have been reproduced *verbatim* and included by way of footnote with a note of the appropriate year. These are mainly comments such as 'dead', 'gone to -', 'left', 'now -', 'removed to -', 'late -', 'insolvent', 'business ceased', 'return at -', 'at Devizes', 'charged in -'.

Occupation variations
As stated above, entry headings include all occupations recorded at any given time in the period. The years for which they were recorded are given by footnote. For example, the entry heading GILLMAN, Charles, reporter, bookseller, profits on printing, dissenting preacher (**469**), would show in the footnotes 1854/55 reporter & profits on printing, dissenting preacher, 1855/56 reporter, 1856/57 reporter & bookseller, 1857/58–1859/60 bookseller.

Successions
Successions to businesses are recorded by footnote commentary showing the year in which noted. For example, JONES, William Blackwell (**514**) for 1857/58 marked 'dead, innkeeper Crown, now Charles Rhodes Plank' or LYNE, Thomas William (**542**) marked in 1850/51 'Lyne late Lavington, Samuel, grocer' and in 1856/57 'Long, John late Lyne, grocer'. This practice is extended in many instances to bank employees, as in KING, Edward, bank manager, North Wilts Bank (**517**), 1848/49 marked 'King late Copeman' in a reference to his predecessor W.W.Copeman. In 1857/58 his agency commission is marked 'transferred to Mr.Calf and Mr.Humby' in a reference to James Humby's succession as manager and Henry Calf's position as bank clerk (**57**). Occasionally the succession is implicit, for example, Eliza Allen, innkeeper of Bromham was entered and assessed in 1846/47 but in 1847/48 the entry is struck out and replaced by Richard Stone, innkeeper, in the same alphabetical position as Allen in the assessment list.

Life assurance relief
In later years relief was granted in respect of premiums paid under life assurance contracts. The relief was given in the form of a discharge of tax rather than a reduction in assessment. The amount of the premium is recorded in a footnote together with the year of note.

Schedule E
Certain employees deriving income from public offices or limited companies – for example, certain bank managers, the chaplain to the New Prison, Relieving Officers,

Prison Governors – are recorded but not assessed, since they were more correctly assessable under Schedule E. However, in the early years, the statutory requirements were at times honoured more in the breach than the observance. For example, James Humby, bank clerk at the North Wilts Bank (**256**, **507**) was assessed under Schedule D between 1852/53 and 1854/55 and having been appointed manager, his name and salary were entered under Schedule D between 1856/57 and 1858/59 but marked 'Schedule E' to denote the fact that an assessment was made under another Schedule. Similarly, John Thurnham, Superintendent of the new County Asylum (**289**) was entered in 1852/43 and marked Schedule E.

CROSS REFERENCES AND NOTES

Textual cross references relate in the main to successions, where all proprietors who carried on the business at any time during the period are included. For example, under the entry JONES, William Blackwell, law stationer, innkeeper, Crown (**514**), cross references are extended not only to the immediate predecessor Benjamin Palmer and the immediate successor Charles Rhodes Plank, but to George King (including Elizabeth Gale King) who had earlier carried on the same business. Similarly the entry JOHNSTONE, Bayntun, chemist (**511**), is cross referenced to Fitzherbert Bridges, Henry Cripps and Robert Hayward. In this way a consecutive history of each business can be seen at a glance.

All appropriate entries are cross referenced to Pigot & Co's Trade Directory of 1842 which is included in Volume 47 of the Wiltshire Record Society series. For example, the footnote to the entry BIGGS, Richard William, schoolmaster, interest on securities, possessions in Ireland (**388**), records Richard W. Biggs, (boarding) school, Long Street.

Certain explanations arising from textual material accompany the entry in note form. For example, a commentary on early forms of lawful tax avoidance is included in the entry THORP, Thomas Glossop, surveyor's clerk (**29**); a comment on bank manager's salaries is included in the entry KING, Edward, bank manager (**517**); or a note concerning the brief history of the wine merchant's business in the entry relating to Edwin Giddings and George Ellis (**464**, **465**).

Extra-textual cross references have been kept to a minimum and have been made only where corroboration was necessary to verify facts.

Assessment by letter
As a measure to ensure confidentiality, (which extended only to assessments made under Schedule D), the taxpayer could elect to be assessed under letter instead of name, though the degree to which strict confidentiality was thus attained is questionable. The fact that such an election was made is recorded by a capital letter placed against the sum assessed in each year. Few opted for this treatment – notably George Washington Anstie, solicitor (**669**); Thomas Blackwell, civil engineer (**165**); John Hayward, land agent (**182**); Thomas Chandler, maltster (**230**); and innkeepers such as James Chandler of the Old

Crown (**693**), William Grace of the Castle (**746**), James Macklin of the White Bear (**787**) and William Joyce of the Pelican (**515**).

Assessment by Special Commissioners
The Schedule D taxpayer could make an application to be assessed by the Special Commissioners, three Government officials based at Somerset House, who travelled on circuit to hear appeals. This was a provision of which few availed themselves because of the perception that remunerated officers of the Crown might be more likely to make increased assessments. In Devizes, only the solicitors John Raikes Bayley (**384**) and the firm of MacDonald & Olivier (**544**) elected to be assessed by the Special Commissioners. The years for which such an election was made is included in the notes to each entry.

ABBREVIATIONS

The most frequently used abbreviations in the text are 'a' against an assessment to denote that an appeal was made against an estimate; and 'i' against a sum to denote that it was interest on a loan or investment. Abbreviations specific to a particular entry are recorded separately. For example, under the entry KNEE, Nathaniel, schoolmaster, clerk, commercial traveller, baby linen warehouse (**525**), the abbreviations 's', 'c'. 'ct' and 'b' respectively are noted in the assessment record.

TERMINOLOGY USED IN THE TEXT

Much of the terminology used must be gleaned from the introduction in order to appreciate fully the meaning, but the following broadly represent a brief outline of the most common terms.

Returned – the word signifies that the taxpayer made a return of income of the amount shown.

Assessed – the word records the fact that an assessment was made by the Additional Commissioners either in the sum returned by the taxpayer or estimated by them (which one is evident from each entry).

Appeal – a formal appeal was made to the General Commissioners against an estimated assessment made by the Additional Commissioners.

Income proved – the term shows that a claim for exemption was made by the taxpayer, the exact results of which were entered in the income proved column, proving that his total income lay below the tax threshold.

Exempt – this term is used where the sum assessed is extended to the income proved column so signifying a formal claim for exemption. In later years, particularly 1856/57 to 1859/60 the names of persons continually and obviously below the tax threshold were entered but no assessments were made. In such circumstances the textual entry reads 'recorded; no assessment made; exempt.' In other cases, where the claimant was evidently below the exemption limit, the assessment was wholly discharged although no sum was recorded. The entry for the year is marked 'exempt' in the text and the fact recorded by footnote. It is important to appreciate that where any assessment is not marked 'exempt', even where the amount lay below the tax threshold, tax was payable.

First – the word "First" in the title "Certificates of First Assessments" implies that there was another, and later, assessment. The bulk of assessments were meant to be, and were, included in the Certificates of First Assessments. Any taxpayers who were omitted from the main assessment were, statutorily, included in a supplementary assessment. In the division of Devizes, these additional or supplementary assessments were very few, and were recorded by way of addition to the Certificates of First Assessments, rather than a separate list. All such entries have been included in this volume.

Assessed in absence of return – in almost every case this means that, in the absence of a return, an estimated assessment was made by the Additional Commissioners. In one or two instances the figures assessed appear to be actual rather than estimated figures, and it is possible that a late return was delivered to the Additional Commissioners before the meeting at which they made the assessments. These instances are few but needed clarification.

THE COMMISSIONERS' CERTIFICATES OF FIRST ASSESSMENTS UNDER SCHEDULE D FOR THE DIVISION OF DEVIZES 1842–1860

BEDBOROUGH

1 ABRAHAMS, Joseph, grocer, coal merchant.

Year	Amount returned £	Commissioners' estimate £	Final assessment £
1842/43	150	–	150
1846/47	110	160	160
1847/48	–	200	200
1848/49	160	200	200
1849/50	–	200	200
1850/51	200	–	200
1851/52	175	200	200
1852/53	170	200	200
1853/54	–	200	200
1854/55	–	200	200
1855/56	170	200	200
1856/57	200	–	200
1857/58	200	–	200
1858/59	170	200	200
1859/60	–	200	200

1842/43, 1846/47-1851/52 Abraham; 1852/53-1859/60 Abrahams.
1842/43, 1846/47 coal merchant & grocer; 1847/48-1859/60 grocer, etc.
Pigot & Co"s Directory, 1842: Joseph Abraham, coal merchant & dealer, grocer & tea dealer, Back Lane.

2 ASHLEY, James, mealman.

1846/47-1849/50 assessed in absence of return £50; exempt.
1853/54 assessed in absence of return £50 and £26 pension; exempt.
1854/55 assessed in absence of return £100, income proved at £70; exempt.
1855/56 assessed in absence of return £70; exempt.
1856/57-1859/60 recorded; no assessment made; exempt.

1846/47-1849/50 no occupation noted; 1853/54-1859/60 mealman.
1853/54 pension assessed.
1850/51-1852/53 no assessments made.

3 BOWERING, Benjamin, beerhouse keeper.

1842/43 returned and assessed £50; exempt.
1846/47-1849/50 assessed in absence of return £40; exempt.

Pigot & Co"s Directory, 1842: Benjamin Bowering, retailer of beer, baker, Green.

4 BROWN, William & MAY, Charles, ironfounders.

Year	Amount returned £	Commissioners' estimate £	Final assessment £
1854/55	–	–	–
1855/56	200	300	300
1856/57	300	400	400
1857/58	400	500	500
1858/59	–	500	500
1859/60	500	600	600

1854/55-1855/56 Brown & May; 1856/57-1859/60 forenames inserted.
1858/59 marked "see return".

5 CHANDLER, John, maltster & gate keeper.

1842/43 entry deleted; no assessment made.

Cross reference: Chandler, John, toll keeper & mealman, St.Mary.

6 COLE, Robert, innkeeper, brewer, Bell.

Year	Amount returned £	Commissioners' estimate £	Final assessment £
1842/43	150	200	200
1846/47	176	220a	179.16.3
1847/48	161.12.4	–	161.12.4
1848/49	203.10.8	–	203.10.8
1849/50	240	–	240
1850/51	250	–	250
1851/52	250	–	250
1852/53	250	–	250
1853/54	250	300	300
1854/55	166.13.4	300	200
1855/56	–	200	200
1856/57	150	200	200

1857/58	150	200	200
1858/59	150	200	200

1842/43, 1846/47-1853/54, 1855/56-1859/60 innkeeper; 1854/55 innkeeper & brewer.
1854/55 assessment reduced but no appeal noted.
1858/59 Bell noted.
1859/60 marked "now Decimus Wild".
Pigot & Co"s Directory, 1842: Robert Cole, innkeeper, Bell, Green.
Cross reference: Wild, Decimus, innkeeper, Bedborough; innkeeper, St.Mary.

7 DOWDING, Revd.Benjamin Charles, pew rents.

1847/48 returned and assessed £74.12.2.
1848/49-1849/50 assessed in absence of return £74.12.2.
1850/51-1851/52 returned and assessed £74.12.2.
1852/53 assessed in absence of return £74.12.2.
1853/54 returned and assessed £74.5.8.
1854/55 assessed in absence of return £74.5.8.
1855/56 returned and assessed £101.
1856/57 returned and assessed £104.2.9.
1857/58 returned £42.6.0; assessed £57.10.0.
1858/59 returned £22.10.0; assessed £55.
1859/60 returned £20; assessed £51.10.0.

1842/43 marked "clerk see Schedule A & B".
1847/48 recorded as clergyman.
1856/57 pew rents recorded.
1857/58 noted "£57.10.0 Mr.Gundry's for Mr.Dowding".
Pigot & Co"s Directory, 1842: Revd.Benjamin Dowding, Potterne Road, clergyman.

8 DURNFORD, Thomas, blacksmith.

1842/43 returned and assessed at £40; exempt.
1846/47 returned £50; increased £80 on appeal; exempt.
1847/48-1849/50 assessed in absence of return £80; exempt.

1848/49 recorded at £30 which seems a mis-numbering.
Pigot & Co"s Directory, 1842: Thomas Durnford, blacksmith, Green.

9 DYKE, Richard, plasterer & tiler.

1842/43 returned and assessed £20; exempt.
1846/47-1849/50 assessed in absence of return £20; exempt.

10 EDMONDS, Richard, teacher of French.

1848/49-1849/50 assessed in absence of return £50; exempt.

1848/49 teacher of French; 1849/50 French teacher.
Pigot & Co"s Directory, 1842: E.Edmonds, schoolmistress, Infants' School, Sheep Street.
Cross references: Edmonds, R, French teacher, St.Mary & St.John; Edmonds, R & W, school-
    masters, St.John.

11 ELLEN, Henry, lime burner. [also ELLEN, William]

1842/43 returned £60, assessed £100; exempt.
1846/47-1849/50 assessed in absence of return £50; exempt.
1853/54 assessed in absence of return £75; exempt.
1854/55 assessed in absence of return £80.
1855/56 assessed in absence of return £80; exempt.
1856/57-1859/60 recorded; no assessments made; exempt.

1842/43 William Ellen; 1846/47-1859/60 Henry Ellen.
1850/51-1852/53 no assessments made.
Pigot & Co"s Directory, 1842: William Ellen, lime burner, Green.

12 FILLIS, John, whitesmith.

1846/47-1849/50 assessed in absence of return £100; exempt.

Pigot & Co"s Directory, 1842: John Fillis, brightsmith, Green.

13 GEORGE, Frank, clerk.

1853/54-1854/55 entries made in absence of return £105 but deleted.

Cross reference: George, Francis(sic), law clerk, Week.

14 GUNDRY, George, tea dealer, grocer. [also GUNDRY, Samuel; GUNDRY & SMITH]

Year	Amount returned	Commissioners' estimate	Final assessment
	£	£	£
1842/43	208	–	208
1846/47	190	–	190
1847/48	–	190	190
1848/49	–	190	190

1849/50	–	190	190
1850/51	190	–	190
1851/52	200	–	200
1852/53	–	200	200
1853/54	150	200	200
1854/55	–	200	200
1855/56	–	200	200
1856/57	170	200	200
1857/58	150	200	200
1858/59	170	200	200
1859/60	150	200	200

1842/43, 1846/47-1850/51 Samuel Gundry; 1851/52-1853/54, 1857/58-1859/60 George Gundry; 1854/55-1856/57 Gundry & Smith.
1842/43, 1846/47 tea dealer & grocer; 1847/48-1859/60 tea dealer(s), etc.
Pigot & Co"s Directory, 1842: Peter Gundry & Son, grocer & tea dealer, agent to Imperial Fire Office, Green.

15 HARDING, William, farrier, veterinary surgeon.

1842/43 returned and assessed £40; exempt.
1846/47-1849/50 assessed in absence of return £60; exempt.
1853/54-1855/56 assessed in absence of return £70; exempt.
1856/57-1859/60 recorded; no assessments made; exempt.

1842/43, 1846/47-1849/50 farrier, 1853/54-1859/60 veterinary surgeon.
1850/51-1852/53 no assessments made.
Pigot & Co"s Directory, 1842: William Harding, blacksmith & farrier, Monday Market Street.

16 HARRISON, John, stonemason.

1842/43 assessed in absence of return £150.
1846/47 returned and assessed £76; exempt.
1847/48-1849/50 assessed in absence of return £76; exempt.
1853/54-1855/56 assessed in absence of return £75; exempt.
1856/57-1859/60 recorded; no assessments made; exempt.

1850/51-1852/53 no assessments made.
Pigot & Co"s Directory, 1842: Harrison, stone & marble mason, Green.

17 LONG, James, innkeeper, British Lion.

1858/59 entry only but deleted.
Cross references: Long, James, innkeeper, Week; West, Henry, innkeeper, Bedborough.

18 MASLEN, John, pig killer.

1842/43 returned and assessed £10.5.0; exempt.
1846-47-1849-50 assessed in absence of return £20; exempt.

19 MATTHEWS, Richard D, clerk.

1853/54-1855/56 assessed in absence of return £115.

1856/57 marked "removed to St.John's".
1858/59 marked "dead".
Cross reference: Matthews, R.D, St.John.

20 MULLINGS, Benoni, builder, etc.

Year	Amount returned £	Commissioners' estimate £	Income proved £	Final assessment £
1852/53	100	120	100	
1853/54	–	200	116	
1854/55	100	150	–	150
1855/56	120	150	–	150
1856/57	130	150	–	150
1857/58	–	200	–	200
1858/59	160	200	–	200
1859/60	150	200	–	200

1852/53 marked "late White".
Cross references: White, Benoni Thomas, builder, Bedborough; White, T.B, St.John; Young & White, St.John.

21 NEATE, Charles & John, blacksmiths. [also NEATE, Mrs.]

1846/47-1849/50 assessed in absence of return £50; exempt.
1853/54 returned and assessed £80; exempt.
1854/55-1855/56 assessed in absence of return £80; exempt.
1856/57-1859/60 recorded; no assessments made; exempt.

1846/47-1849/50 Mrs Neate, blacksmith; 1853/54-1859/60 Charles & John Neate, black-smiths.
1850/51-1852/53 no assessments made.
Pigot & Co"s Directory, 1842: Sophia Neate, blacksmith, Green.

22 NEATE, John, carpenter, timber dealer.

1846/47-1849/50 assessed in absence of return £50; exempt.
1853/54 assessed in absence of return £50; exempt.
1854/55 assessed in absence of return £60; income proved at £25; exempt.
1855/56 assessed in absence of return £25; exempt.
1856/57-1859/60 recorded; no assessments made; exempt.

1842/43, 1846/47-1853/54 carpenter; 1854/55-1859/60 timber dealer.
1850/51-1852/53 no assessments made.

23 ORIEL, William, shopkeeper.

1842/43 returned and assessed £50; exempt.

Pigot & Co"s Directory, 1842: William Oriel, grocer & tea dealer, Green.

24 PERRY, Horatio Nelson, agent to Lawes & Co. Van, carrier.

1842/43, 1846/47-1847/48 returned and assessed £40.
1848/49 assessed in absence of return £40.
1849/50 returned and assessed £40.
1850/51 assessed in absence of return £70.
1851/52-1852/53 returned £50; assessed £70.

1842/43, 1846/47-1848/49 agent to Lawes & Co.; 1849/50-1852/53 carrier.
1849/50 [St Mary] marked "William Lawes & Co now Perry".
1852/53 marked "deceased".
Cross reference: Lawes, William & Co., carriers, wagon office, St Mary.

25 PLANK, Charles Rhodes, builder.

1842/43 returned £200; assessed £250.
1846/47-1847/48 assessed in absence of return £250.
1848/49-1849/50 returned £150; assessed £200.
1850/51 assessed in absence of return £200.
1851/52 returned and assessed £200.
1852/53 assessed in absence of return £200.
1853/54 returned and assessed £200.
1854/55-1856/57 returned £150; assessed £200.
1857/58 returned £150; assessed £225.
1858/59-1859/60 returned £150; assessed £200.

1842/43, 1846/47-1854/55, 1859/60 Charles Rhodes Plank; 1855/56-1858/59 Charles Plank.

Pigot & Co"s Directory, 1842: Charles Plank, carpenter, builder & wheelwright, Green.
Cross references: Plank, Charles Rhodes, innkeeper, St.John; Plank, Charles, builder, Week.

26 RANSOM, William, woolstapler.

1853/54 returned £32 and £30 interest; assessed £82.
1854/55 assessed in absence of return £50; increased by General Commissioners to £25 and £30 interest.
1855/56 assessed in absence of return £55.
1856/57 assessed in absence of return £25.
1857/58 returned £25; assessed £30.
1858/59 returned and assessed £30.
1859/60 assessed in absence of return £30.

1854/55 assessment increased by General Commissioners; no appeal noted.
1856/57 confirmed on appeal.
Cross reference: Ransom, William, woolstapler & publican, St. John.

27 SALMON, Charles, stonemason.

1858/59-1859/60 recorded; no assessments made; exempt.

28 TARRANT, Nathaniel, schoolmaster.

1858/59-1859/60 recorded; no assessments made; exempt.

29 THORP, Thomas Glossop, surveyor's clerk.

1842/43, 1846/47-1847/48 returned and assessed £150.
1848/49 assessed in absence of return £150; reduced to £149 on appeal; exempt.
1849/50 assessed in absence of return £150; income proved at £149; exempt.
1850/51 returned and assessed £149; exempt.
1851/52-1852/53 assessed in absence of return £149; exempt.

1848/49 is an example of an early form of tax avoidance. On incomes of £150, tax was payable on the whole amount. Incomes below this sum were eligible to be wholly relieved on a claim for exemption. By agreeing with the employer to fix the salary at £149, the taxpayer would be better off by £3.7.6. (Evidence taken before the Select Committee on the Income and Property Tax, House of Commons. Parliamentary Papers. (1852) ix qq.3019, 3235).
1849/50 no appeal noted.
1852/53 marked "removed to Southampton".
Cross references: (similar instance of early legal tax avoidance) Anderson, T.W., solicitor's clerk, St.John; Coxhead, W.P., schoolmaster, St. John.

30 WALKER, Frederick, silk throwster, silk manufacturer. [also WALKER, Peter]

Year	Amount returned £	Commissioners' estimate £	Income proved £	Final assessment £
1842/43	–	200	100	–
1846/47	125	169	–	169
1847/48	152	200	–	200
1848/49	–	200a	–	157
1849/50	97	–	97	–
1850/51	–	200	–	200
1851/52	135	200	–	200
1852/53	156	200	–	200
1853/54	200	–	–	200
1854/55	187	250	–	250
1855/56	163	400	–	400
1856/57	200	400	–	400
1857/58	130	300	–	300
1858/59	–	200	–	200
1859/60	100	300	–	300

1842/43 Walker, Peter, silk manufacturer, entered and deleted.
1842/43 silk manufacturer; 1846/47-1859/60 silk throwster.
1842/43 no appeal noted.
Pigot & Co"s Directory, 1842: Frederick Walker, silk throwster, Belvedere Mill.

31 WATSON, Charles, tea dealer.

1842/43 No assessment made.

Pigot & Co"s Directory, 1842: Charles Watson, tea dealer & linen & woollen draper, Green.
Cross reference: Watson, John, (Charles deleted), draper & tea dealer, St.John.

32 WEST, Henry, beerhouse keeper, British Lion.

1857/58 no assessment made.
1858/59 recorded; no assessment made; exempt.
1859/60 assessed in absence of return £80; reduced £65.

1858/59 British Lion noted.
1859/60 no appeal noted.
Cross references: Long, James, innkeeper, Bedborough; West, Henry, innkeeper, Week.

33 WHEELER, Robert, beerhouse keeper.

1842/43 assessed in absence of return £20; exempt.
1846/47-1849/50 assessed in absence of return £50; exempt.

1842/43 pig killer deleted.
Pigot & Co"s Directory, 1842: R. Wheeler, retailer of beer, Green.

34 WHITE, Benoni Thomas, builder.

1842/43 marked "return made in St. John's".
1852/53 marked "Mullings, Benoni, builder late White".
1852/53 [St.John] marked "White now Mullings, Benoni, builder".
Cross references: Mullings, Benoni, builder, Bedborough; White, T.B, St.John; Young & White, St.John.

35 WILD, Decimus, innkeeper, Bell.

1859/60 returned and assessed £200.

1859/60 marked "late Cole, innkeeper, Bell".
Cross references: Cole, Robert, innkeeper, Bedborough; Wild, Decimus, innkeeper, St.Mary.

36 WILSON, Sandar, master of workhouse.

1842/43 entered but deleted; marked "See Schedule E".

Note: Incomes from public offices and employments were assessable under Schedule E.
Pigot & Co"s Directory, 1842: Union Workhouse, Back Lane, Sandar Wilson, governor.

BISHOP'S CANNINGS

37 BERRY, Isaac, beerhouse keeper.

1846/47-1847/48 assessed in absence of return £50; exempt.
1848/49-1849/50 assessed in absence of return £90; exempt.

38 COCKLE, William, innkeeper.

1847/48 assessed in absence of return £50; exempt.

1848/49 marked "Cockle, William, late now Rumming".
Cross references: Cockle, William, innkeeper, Bourton & Easton; Rumming, Thomas, inn-
    keeper, Bishop's Cannings.

39 DAVIS, William, provision & cheese dealer.

1858/59 returned and assessed £100.

1858/59 marked "to be charged next year in Bourton where he resides".
1859/60 marked "in Bourton".
Cross reference: Davis, William, provision & cheese dealer, Bourton & Easton.

40 KERTON, James, grocer & baker.

1853/54-1855/56 assessed in absence of return £75; exempt.

1856/57 marked "dead".

41 MACDONALD, Archdeacon [William].

1854/55 returned £393 but no assessment made.
1855/56 estimated in absence of return £268 but no assessment made.

1854/55 marked [partly illegible] "Tithe Charge".

42 RUMMING, Thomas, innkeeper.

1848/49 assessed in absence of return £50; exempt.
1849/50 assessed in absence of return £20; exempt.

1848/49 marked "Cockle, William, late now Rumming".
1849/50 marked "Rumming, Thomas late Cockle, innkeeper".
Cross reference: Cockle, William, innkeeper, Bishop's Cannings.

43 SAVAGE, William, curate.

1855/56 estimated in absence of return £268 but no assessment made. [blurred]

44 SCOTT, Revd. Thomas, curate.

1842/43 returned £70 but no assessment made.

45 SLOPER, James, miller, baker, shopkeeper, farmer.

Year	Amount returned £	Commissioners' estimate £	Final assessment £		
1842/43	50m	100	100	(70bs	30s)
1846/47	–	100	100		
1847/48	43	100	100		
1848/49	–	100	100		
1849/50	120	–	120		
1850/51	–	120a	80		
1851/52	20	80	80		
1852/53	70	80	80		
1853/54	60	80	80		
1854/55	–	110	110		
1855/56	–	110	110		
1856/57	–	110	110		
1857/58	–	125	125		
1858/59	–	130	130		
1859/60	–	130	130		

Abbreviations: m, miller at Rowde; bs, baker & shopkeeper at Bishop's Cannings; s, shopkeeper at Avebury.
1842/43 miller, baker & shopkeeper; 1847/48-1853/54, 1856/57-1859/60 baker;
1854/55-1855/56 baker & farmer; 1857/58 baker & miller.

46 SLOPER, Simon, harness maker, blacksmith.

1853/54 returned £20; assessed £75; exempt.
1854/55-1857/58 assessed in absence of return £75.
1858/59 assessed in absence of return £80.
1859/60 returned £60; assessed £80.

47 SLOPER, William, innkeeper, maltster. [by comparison, Crown]

1842/43 returned £60i, £15m; assessed £100.
1846/47 assessed in absence of return £100.
1847/48 returned £70; assessed £100.
1848/49 assessed in absence of return £100.
1849/50 returned and £115; exempt.
1850/51 assessed in absence of return £115; reduced to £103.10.0 on appeal.
1851/52 returned £50; assessed £100.
1852/53 assessed in absence of return £100.

Abbreviations: i, innkeeper; m, maltster.
1842/43, 1846/47 innkeeper & maltster; 1847/48-1852/53 innkeeper.

1842/43 possibly confirmed on appeal.
1852/53 marked "Spreadbury now".
Cross reference: Spreadbury, Charles, innkeeper, Bishops's Cannings.

48 SMITH, George, beerseller, grocer, baker.

1849/50 assessed in absence of return £20; exempt.
1853/54 returned £20; assessed £50; exempt.
1854/55-1855/56 assessed in absence of return £50; exempt.
1856/57 assessed in absence of return £100.
1857/58 assessed in absence of return £120; reduced to £100 but no appeal noted.
1858/59 assessed in absence of return £120.
1859/60 returned £100; assessed £120.

1849/50 beerseller; 1853/54-1855/56 grocer & beerseller; 1856/57-1859/60 grocer, baker & beerseller.
1850/51-1852/53 no assessments made.

49 SMITH, John, baker & beerhouse keeper.

1842/43 assessed in absence of return £75; exempt.

50 SPREADBURY, Charles, innkeeper, Crown.

1853/54 returned £60; assessed £100; income proved at £75; exempt.
1854/55-1855/56 assessed in absence of return £75; exempt.
1856/57 assessed in absence of return £100; reduced to £97 on appeal; exempt.
1857/58 returned £70; assessed £105; income proved at £70; exempt.
1858/59-1859/60 recorded; no assessments made; exempt.

1852/53 marked "Sloper, William, Spreadbury now".
Cross reference: Sloper, William, innkeeper, Bishop's Cannings.

BOURTON & EASTON

Note: Bourton & Easton was subsumed into Bishop's Cannings 1847/48; resumed separate identity 1859/60.

51 COCKLE, William, innkeeper.

1846/47 assessed in absence of return £50; exempt.

Cross references: Cockle, William, innkeeper, Bishop's Cannings; Lucas, John, innkeeper, Bourton & Easton (probable); Rumming, Thomas, innkeeper, Bishop's Cannings.

52 DAVIS, William, provision & cheese dealer.

1859/60 returned £100; assessed £120.

1858/59 [Bishop's Cannings] marked "to be charged next year in Bourton & Easton where he resides".
Cross reference: Davis, William, provision & cheese dealer, Bishop's Cannings.

53 LUCAS, John, innkeeper.

1842/43 returned and assessed £15; exempt.

Cross references: Cockle, William, innkeeper, Bourton & Easton, (probable).

BROMHAM

54 AKERMAN, James, beerseller, beerhouse keeper, innkeeper, grocer.

1842/43, 1846/47-1849/50 assessed in absence of return £20; exempt.
1853/54 returned £20; assessed £60; exempt.
1854/55 returned and assessed £20; exempt.
1855/56 assessed in absence of return £20; exempt.
1856/57-1859/60 recorded; no assessments made; exempt.

1842/43, 1846/47-1849/50 beerseller; 1853/54 innkeeper & grocer; 1854/55 beerhouse keeper & grocer; 1855/56-1859/60 beerhouse keeper.
1850/51-1852/53 no assessments made.
1857/58-1858/59 noted £80 in margin.

55 AKERMAN, John, beerhouse keeper, innkeeper, New Inn.
[also AKERMAN, Elizabeth]

1842/43, 1846/47-1847/48 assessed in absence of return £40; exempt.
1848/49 returned £25; assessed £40; exempt.
1849/50 assessed in absence of return £40; exempt.
1854/55-1855/56 assessed in absence of return £40; exempt.
1856/57-1859/60 recorded; no assessments made; exempt.

1842/43, 1846/47-1857/58 John Akerman; 1858/59-1859/60 Elizabeth Akerman.
1850/51-1853/54 no assessments made.
1854/55 New Inn noted.

56 AKERMAN, Robert, baker & shopkeeper.

1852/53 returned and assessed £70; exempt.
1853/54 returned £60; assessed £70; exempt.
1854/55-1855/56 assessed in absence of return £70; exempt.
1856/57-1859/60 recorded; no assessments made; exempt.

57 ALLEN, Eliza, innkeeper.

1846/47 assessed in absence of return £40; exempt.

1847/48 Allen is replaced by Richard Stone, innkeeper. The position of Stone in the alphabetical list suggests that he succeeded to Allen's business.
Cross reference: Stone, Richard, innkeeper, Bromham.

58 ATTWOOD, James, blacksmith.

1842/43, 1846/47-1847/48 assessed in absence of return £50; exempt.
1848/49 returned £20; assessed £50; income proved at £67.4.6; exempt.
1849/50 assessed in absence of return £50; income proved at £67.4.6; exempt.

1848/49 Atwood.

59 ATTWOOD, Thomas, smith.

1842/43, 1846/47-1849/50 assessed in absence of return £20; exempt.

1848/49 Atwood.

60 BAILEY, Thomas, innkeeper.

1842/43 assessed in absence of return £40; exempt.

61 BANKS, James, brewer, maltster.

Year	Amount returned £	Commissioners' estimate £	Final assessment £
1842/43	415	–	415
1846/47	355	415	415
1847/48	290	415	415
1848/49	240	415	415

1849/50	250	450	450
1850/51	395	450	450
1851/52	278	450	450
1852/53	310	450	450
1853/54	350	450	450
1854/55	250	450	450
1855/56	210	400	400
1856/57	320	500	500
1857/58	300	420	420
1858/59	250	500	500
1859/60	250	600	600

1842/43, 1846/47-1852/53 brewer & maltster; 1853/54-1859/60 brewer.

62 BARTON, Benjamin, miller.

1857/58 returned £150; assessed at £62; exempt.
1858/59 returned £40; assessed £100; income proved at £56; exempt.
1859/60 recorded; no assessment made; exempt.

1857/58 marked "Hitchens, John, miller, see Benjamin Barton".
1858/59 marked "no exemption claimed" but assessment discharged.
Cross reference: Hitchens, John, miller, Bromham.

63 BENGER, John, turner.

1842/43, 1846/47-1849/50 assessed in absence of return £70; exempt.
1853/54 returned and assessed £40; exempt.
1854/55-1855/56 assessed in absence of return £20; exempt.
1856/57-1859/60 recorded; no assessments made; exempt.

1850/51-1852/53 no assessments made.

64 BLACKMAN, James, baker & shopkeeper.

1842/43 returned £110; assessed £150.
1846/47 returned £68; assessed £150.
1847/48-1851/52 assessed in absence of return £150.
1852/53 returned and assessed £150.
1853/54 assessed in absence of return £150.

1854/55 marked "out of business 2 years".

65 BROWN, John, turner.

1853/54 returned and assessed £30; exempt.
1854/55 assessed in absence of return £20; exempt.
1855/56 assessed in absence of return £30; exempt.
1856/57–1859/60 recorded; no assessments made; exempt.

66 BROWN, Revd. M[eredith], clergyman.

1848/49 entry only.

67 BUTLER, Edward, miller.

1842/43 assessed in absence of return £50; exempt.

68 CHARLES, James, bailiff.

1853/54 returned and assessed £100; income proved at £90; exempt.
1854/55 returned and assessed £80; exempt.
1855/56 assessed in absence of return £90; exempt.
1856/57–1858/59 recorded; no assessments made; exempt.

1859/60 marked "now – bailiff'", (no name inserted).

69 COUZENS, Jane, beerhouse keeper.

1846/47–1849/50 assessed in absence of return £50; exempt.

1842/43 recorded but no assessment made.

70 DANGERFIELD, Henry, innkeeper, Greyhound.

1855/56 assessed in absence of return £60; exempt.
1856/57–1859/60 recorded; no assessments made; exempt.

1855/56 marked "Hunt, Jacob (deleted) Henry Dangerfield".
1857/58 returned £60 but no assessment made.
1858/59 Greyhound noted.
Cross reference: Hunt, Jacob, innkeeper, Bromham.

71 DAVIS, William, grocer.

1842/43 returned and assessed £10; exempt.
1846/47-1849/50 assessed in absence of return £20; exempt.

72 DRURY, Revd. Henry, fees from private tuition.

1842/43 returned and assessed £150.

1842/43 "fees as curate" deleted; returned £9.8.0 curate deleted, marked Schedule A.

73 DUCK, Hannah, smith.

1842/43 recorded but no assessment made.
1846/47-1848/49 assessed in absence of return £10; exempt.

74 EDGELL, Revd. -, clergyman, surplice fees.

1847/48 returned £150 (deleted); assessed £10.
1848/49 returned £150 curate, £10 surplice fees; no assessment made.

75 FENNELL, William, butcher.

1853/54-1854/55 returned £25; assessed £40; exempt.
1855/56 assessed in absence of return £40; exempt.
1856/57-1859/60 recorded; no assessments made; exempt.

76 GEE, James, butcher.

1842/43 assessed in absence of return £25; exempt.
1846/47 assessed in absence of return £40; exempt.
1847/48 returned £60; exempt.
1848/49 assessed in absence of return £60; income proved at £45.2.4; exempt.
1849/50 assessed in absence of return £60; income proved at £45.2.11; exempt.

77 GEE, John, shopkeeper, baker, farmer.

1842/43 returned £50; assessed £75; exempt.
1846/47 assessed in absence of return £75; exempt.
1847/48 returned and assessed £75; exempt.
1848/49-1849/50 assessed in absence of return £75; exempt.

1851/52-1852/53 returned £50; assessed £75; exempt 1851/52.
1853/54-1854/55 returned £70; assessed £75.
1855/56-1856/57 assessed in absence of return £75.
1857/58 returned and assessed £75.
1858/59-1859/60 assessed in absence of return £85.

1842/43, 1846/47-1849/50 shopkeeper; 1851/52-1853/54, baker, etc.; 1854/55-1855/56
    baker & farmer; 1856/57-1859/60 baker.
1850/51 no assessment made.

78 GIBBONS, Thomas, grocer.

1853/54 returned £20; assessed £40; exempt.
1854/55-1855/56 assessed in absence of return £40; exempt.
1856/57-1859/60 recorded; no assessments made; exempt.

79 HAND, John, innkeeper, Bell, St. Ediths Marsh.

1849/50 assessed in absence of return £70; exempt.
1853/54 assessed in absence of return £80; exempt.
1854/55-1855/56 assessed in absence of return £100.
1856/57 estimated in absence of return £60; no assessment made; exempt.
1857/58 recorded; no assessment made; exempt.
1858/59 returned and assessed £78.19.4; exempt.
1859/60 recorded; no assessment made; exempt.

1849/50 marked "Hand, John (late Smith) innkeeper".
1850/51-1852/53 no assessments made.
1858/59 Bell, St. Ediths Marsh noted.
Cross reference: Smith, John, innkeeper, Bromham.

80 HEALE, Ralph, bailiff.

1853/54-1856/57 assessed in absence of return £90.
1857/58 assessed in absence of return £90; exempt.
1858/59 returned and assessed £90; exempt.
1859/60 recorded; no assessment made; exempt.

1858/59 Hale.

81 HITCHENS, John, miller.

1842/43, 1846/47-1849/50 assessed in absence of return £50; exempt.
1853/54 assessed in absence of return £100; income proved at £95; exempt.

1854/55 assessed in absence of return £100; income proved at £80; exempt.
1855/56 assessed in absence of return £80; exempt.

1847/48-1849/50 Hitchins.
1850/51-1852/53 no assessments made.
1856/57 marked "now removed to Potterne".
1857/58 marked "see Benjamin Barton".
Cross references: Barton, Benjamin, miller, Bromham; Hitchens, John, miller, Potterne.

82 HORN, John, miller.

1853/54 returned and assessed £70; exempt.
1854/55 returned £70; assessed £75; income proved at £70; exempt.
1855/56 assessed in absence of return £70; exempt.
1856/57-1859/60 recorded; no assessments made; exempt.

1853/54 miller, etc.

83 HUGHES, -, miller.

1846/47 assessed in absence of return £75; exempt.
1847/48-1849/50 assessed in absence of return £80; exempt.

84 HUNT, Jacob, innkeeper. [by comparison, Greyhound]

1853/54 returned £30; assessed £60; exempt.
1854/55 returned £40; assessed £60; exempt.

1853/54 James entered but deleted.
1855/56 name deleted, Henry Dangerfield substituted.
Cross reference: Dangerfield, Henry, innkeeper, Bromham.

85 LEWIS, James, surgeon.

1851/52 returned and assessed £70; exempt.
1852/53 assessed in absence of return £70; income proved at £24; exempt.

1853/54-1854/55 marked "Schedule E".

86 LOTT, Thomas, innkeeper.

1842/43 returned and assessed £140; exempt.

87 MASON, Thomas, innkeeper, Shoulder of Mutton.

1858/59 returned and assessed £90; exempt.
1859/60 recorded; no assessment made; exempt.

1858/59 marked "Thomas Westaway now Thomas Mason, Shoulder of Mutton".
Cross references: Westaway, Thomas, innkeeper, Bromham; Wootten David, innkeeper, Bromham.

88 MEREDITH, Samuel, Chief Constable.

1846/47 entry only.

89 MILSOM, James, mop spinner.

1842/43 returned £10; exempt.
1846/47-1847/48 assessed in absence of return £15; exempt.

90 MOORE, Thomas, gentleman. [poet]

1842/43, 1846/47 recorded; no assessment made.
1847/48 assessed in absence of return £100.
1848/49 recorded; no assessment made.

1842/43 marked "Schedule B".
1846/47 marked "Return".

91 ORCHARD, Edward, beerhouse keeper, shopkeeper.

1842/43 returned and assessed £60; exempt.
1846/47-1847/48 assessed in absence of return £35; exempt.
1848/49 returned and assessed £64; exempt.
1849/50 assessed in absence of return £64; exempt.
1851/52 returned and assessed £70; exempt.
1852/53 assessed in absence of return £70; exempt.
1859/60 recorded but no assessment made.

1842/43, 1846/47-1849/50 beerhouse keeper; 1851/52-1852/53 shopkeeper; 1859/60 no
　　occupation noted.
1850/51 no assessment made.

92 PERRETT, James, baker & retail dealer.

1842/43 assessed in absence of return £30; exempt.
1846/47-1849/50 assessed in absence of return £32; exempt.

93 PERRETT, William, baker & shopkeeper.

1842/43 returned £35; assessed £100; exempt.
1846/47-1850/51 assessed in absence of return £100.

1851/52 marked "now William Webb, carpenter".
Cross reference: Webb, William, carpenter, Bromham.

94 POWNEY, Charles.

1842/43 returned and assessed £91; exempt.
1846/47-1849/50 assessed in absence of return £91; exempt.

No occupation noted.

95 RUDDLE, James, harness maker.

1842/43, 1846/47-1849/50 assessed in absence of return £40; exempt.

96 SANSOM, James, bricklayer.

1842/43 assessed in absence of return £75; exempt.
1846/47-1848/49 assessed in absence of return £61.10.0; exempt.
1849/50 assessed in absence of return £60; exempt.

97 SMITH, John, innkeeper. [by comparison, Bell, St. Ediths Marsh]

1846/47-1848/49 assessed in absence of return £70; exempt.

1849/50 marked "see Hand".
Cross reference: Hand, John, innkeeper, Bromham".

98 STONE, Richard, innkeeper, wheelwright.

1847/48 assessed in absence of return £40; exempt.
1848/49 returned and assessed £50 innkeeper, £40 wheelwright; exempt.
1849/50 assessed in absence of return £50; exempt.

1847/48 innkeeper; 1848/49-1849/50 innkeeper & wheelwright.
Cross reference: Allen, Elizabeth, innkeeper, Bromham.

99 WEBB, Benjamin, lime burner.

1842/43 assessed in absence of return £50; exempt.
1846/47 assessed in absence of return £75; exempt.
1847/48 assessed in absence of return £100; exempt.
1848/49 assessed in absence of return £100; income proved at £120; exempt.
1849/50 assessed in absence of return £50; exempt.

100 WEBB, William,baker, shopkeeper, carpenter.

1852/53 returned £70; assessed £100; assessment discharged on appeal.
1853/54 assessed in absence of return £100; income proved at £90; exempt.
1854/55 assessed in absence of return £100; reduced to £80.
1855/56-1856/57 assessed in absence of return £80; exempt.
1857/58 returned £60; no assessment made; exempt.
1858/59-1859/60 recorded; no assessments made; exempt.

1852/53 no sum recorded.
1856/57 assessment appealed against and assessment discharged but no sum recorded.
1852/53 baker & shopkeeper; 1853/54-1855/56 baker etc.; 1856/57 shopkeeper;
1857/58-1859/60 shopkeeper & carpenter.
1851/52 marked "Perrett, William now William Webb, carpenter".
Cross reference: Perrett, William, baker & shopkeeper, Bromham.

101 WESTAWAY, Thomas, innkeeper, Shoulder of Mutton.

1856/57-1857/58 recorded; no assessments made; exempt.

1855/56 marked "Wootten, David now Thomas Westaway, innkeeper".
1858/59 marked "Westaway, Thomas now Thomas Mason, Shoulder of Mutton".
Cross references: Mason, Thomas, innkeeper, Bromham; Wootten, David, innkeeper, Bromham.

102 WOOTTEN, David, farrier, innkeeper. [by comparison, Shoulder of Mutton]

1842/43, 1846/47 assessed in absence of return £50; exempt.
1847/48 assessed in absence of return £70; exempt.
1848/49 returned £54; assessed £70; exempt.
1849/50 returned £50; assessed £70; exempt.
1852/53 assessed in absence of return £75; exempt.
1853/54 returned £20; assessed £100; reduced to £52.
1854/55 returned £60; assessed £52.
1855/56 assessed in absence of return £50; exempt.

1842/43 Wootton, Junior.
1850/51-1851/52 no assessments made.

1852/53 innkeeper & farrier.
1853/54 income proved column entered but duty marked as payable.
1855/56 marked "now Thomas Westaway, innkeeper".
Cross references: Mason, Thomas, innkeeper, Bromham; Westaway, Thomas, innkeeper, Bromham.

103 WOOTTEN, David, carpenter.

1842/43 assessed in absence of return £80; exempt.
1846/47-1849/50 assessed in absence of return £50; exempt.

1842/43 Senior.

104 WOOTTEN, Joseph, grocer, etc.

1842/43, 1846/47-1849/50 assessed in absence of return £30; exempt.

105 WOOTTEN, Stephen, carpenter.

1851/52 returned £26; assessed £50; income proved at £112.3.4; exempt.
1852/53 assessed in absence of return £50; exempt.
1853/54 returned £20; assessed £50; exempt.
1854/55-1855/56 assessed in absence of return £50; exempt.
1856/57-1859/60 recorded; no assessments made; exempt.

CHITTOE

106 EARLE, John, wheelwright.

1842/43, 1846/47-1849/50 assessed in absence of return £40; exempt.

COATE

107 NEATE, William, carpenter, timber dealer.

Year	Amount returned £	Commissioners' estimate £	Income proved £	Final assessment £
1842/43	–	75	75	–
1846/47	–	120a	80	–

1847/48	–	120	80	–
1848/49	–	80	80	–
1849/50	–	80	80	–
1851/52	80	–	80	–
1852/53	–	80	80	–
1853/54	25	80	–	50
1854/55	50	–	–	50
1855/56	–	50	–	50
1856/57	–	50	–	50
1857/58	50	–	–	50
1858/59	–	50	–	50
1859/60	–	60	–	60

1842/43 no occupation noted; 1846/47–1849/50 timber dealer; 1851/52–1858/59 carpenter; 1859/60 carpenter & timber dealer.
1850/51 no assessment made.

HORTON

108 BERRY, Isaac, baker & miller.

1848/49 returned £90 but deleted.

109 BERRY, Richard, miller & corndealer.

1850/51 returned £100; assessed £150; reduced to £134.19.6; exempt.

No appeal noted.

110 DREW, John, miller, dealer, baker, innkeeper.

1842/43 returned £150; assessed £175.
1846/47–1847/48 assessed in absence of return £125.
1848/49 returned £60; assessed £125.
1849/50 returned £60; assessed £150.
1850/51 returned £50; assessed £150.
1851/52 returned £60; assessed £175.
1852/53 assessed in absence of return £175.
1853/54–1854/55 returned £60; assessed £175.
1855/56 returned £80; assessed £175.
1856/57 returned £80; assessed £120.
1857/58 returned £100; assessed £150.
1858/59 returned £150; assessed £180.
1859/60 returned £80; assessed £180.

1842/43, 1846/47–1848/49, 1856/57–1857/58 miller; 1849/50–1852/53 miller & innkeeper; 1853/54–1855/56 innkeeper & baker; 1858/59–1859/60 miller & dealer.
1856/57 marked "baking business ceased" "Sloper, Michael late Drew, innkeeper & baker".
Cross reference: Sloper, Michael, innkeeper & baker, Horton.

111 SLOPER, Michael, innkeeper, baker, beerhouse keeper.

1856/57 assessed in absence of return £75; confirmed on appeal; exempt.
1857/58 recorded; no assessment made; exempt.
1858/59–1859/60 assessed in absence of return £100.

1856/57–1858/59 innkeeper & baker; 1859/60 beerhouse keeper & baker.
1856/57 marked "late Drew, innkeeper & baker".
Cross reference: Drew, John, innkeeper & baker, Horton".

MARSTON

112 PERRETT, James, beerhouse keeper, innkeeper, baker.

1842/43, 1846/47 assessed in absence of return £40; exempt.
1847/48 assessed in absence of return £70; exempt.
1848/49 returned £20; assessed £70; exempt.
1849/50 assessed in absence of return £40; exempt.
1850/51 assessed in absence of return £50; exempt.
1851/52 returned £10; assessed £50; exempt.
1852/53–1854/55 assessed in absence of return £50; exempt.

1842/43, 1847/48–1850/51 beerhouse keeper; 1846/47 innkeeper; 1851/52–1854/55 beerhouse keeper & baker.

113 ROSE, Job, beerhouse keeper & maltster.

1855/56 assessed in absence of return £80; assessment deleted.

1855/56–1856/57 marked "transferred to Worton". (no entry traced in Worton)

NURSTEED

114 CALF, Henry, bank clerk.

1855/56 assessed in absence of return £100.

1855/56 marked "return in St.John" (deleted).
1856/57 marked "removed to St.John and assessed there".
1857/58 marked "charged in St.John".
Cross reference: Calf, Henry, bank clerk, St.John.

115 FARR, James, beerhouse keeper, etc.

1846/47 assessed in absence of return £50; exempt.
1847/48 assessed in absence of return £70; income proved at £108; exempt.
1848/49 assessed in absence of return £70; exempt.
1849/50 assessed in absence of return £60; exempt.
1850/51 assessed in absence of return £50; exempt.
1851/52-1852/53 assessed in absence of return £75; exempt.
1853/54 assessed in absence of return £75; reduced to £50.
1854/55-1856/57 assessed in absence of return £50.
1857/58 returned £15; assessed £50.
1858/59-1859/60 assessed in absence of return £50.

1846/47-1852/53 beerhouse keeper; 1853/54-1859/60 beerhouse keeper etc.

116 GIDDINGS, William, beerhouse keeper.

1846/47 assessed in absence of return £50; exempt.

POTTERNE

117 ADAMS, Thomas, miller.

1846/47-1849/50 assessed in absence of return £50; exempt.

118 ARMSTRONG, John.

1846/47 marked "? E Return".

Name only entered 1846/47.

119 BAKER, William, miller.

1851/52-1852/53 assessed in absence of return £100; exempt.
1853/54 returned £100 but no assessment made.

1853/54-1854/55 marked "charged in Worton".
Cross reference: Baker, William, miller, mealman, Worton.

120 BIGGS, E., miller.

1847/48-1848/49 assessed in absence of return £60; exempt.

1849/50 marked "Chandler late Biggs, miller".
Cross references: Butcher, William, miller, Potterne; Chandler, Thomas, miller, Potterne; Weeks, James, miller, Potterne.

121 BUTCHER, Mary, shopkeeper.

1842/43 returned and assessed £10; exempt.
1846/47-1848/49 assessed in absence of return £10; exempt.

122 BUTCHER, William, miller.

1857/58-1858/59 assessed in absence of return £100; income proved at £50; exempt.
1859/60 assessed in absence of return £75; exempt.

1857/58 [Weeks, James] marked "now William Butcher, miller".
Cross references: Biggs, E., miller, Potterne; Chandler, Thomas, miller, Potterne; Weeks, James, miller, Potterne.

123 CHANDLER, Thomas, miller.

1849/50-1850/51 assessed in absence of return £100; exempt.
1852/53 assessed in absence of return £100; exempt.
1853/54-1854/55 assessed in absence of return £100.

1849/50 George Chandler entered but deleted; Thomas Chandler substituted; marked "Chandler late Biggs".
1851/52 Name and occupation entered but deleted.
1853/54-1854/55 marked "now Weekes,(sic) miller"; assessment on Weeks not made until 1855/56.
Cross references: Biggs, E., miller, Potterne; Butcher, William, miller, Potterne; Weeks, James, miller, Potterne.

124 CLARKE, J. or P.C., foreign securities.

1849/50 returned and assessed £50.

125 COLEMAN, Samuel, innkeeper, Crown.

1849/50 recorded but no assessment made.
1850/51-1855/56 assessed in absence of return £60; exempt.
1856/57-1858/59 recorded; no assessments made; exempt.

1858/59 Crown noted.

126 COX, Daniel, baker.

1858/59-1859/60 recorded; no assessments made; exempt.

127 DYER, Andrew, surgeon.

1842/43 assessed in absence of return £150.

128 FAY, William, maltster & innkeeper.

1842/43 returned £70; assessed £120; exempt.

129 FRANKLIN, John, bricklayer.

1842/43 returned £30; assessed £60; exempt.
1846/47-1847/48 assessed in absence of return £75; exempt.
1848/49 assessed in absence of return £30; exempt.
1849/50 returned and assessed £25; exempt.

130 GLASS, Robert, miller.

1853/54 assessed in absence of return £75.
1854/55 assessed in absence of return £100.

1855/56 Glass, Robert deleted, Hitchens, John, miller, substituted.
Cross reference: Hitchens, John, miller, Potterne.

131 GODDEN, John, baker.

1852/53-1853/54 assessed in absence of return £50; exempt.

132 HIBBERD, John, miller, innkeeper. [by comparison, George] [also HIBBERD, Ann]

Year	Amount returned £	Commissioners' estimate £	Income proved £	Final assessment £
1846/47	–	60	60	–
1847/48	–	100	100	–
1848/49	60	100	100	–
1849/50	100	–	100	–
1850/51	–	100	100	–
1851/52	50	100	100	–
1852/53	–	100	100	–
1853/54	50	100	75	13.10.0
1854/55	–	75	–	75
1855/56	60	75	–	75
1856/57	60	75	–	–

1846/47-1855/56 John Hibberd; 1856/57 Ann Hibberd.
1846/47 miller; 1847/48-1856/57 innkeeper.
1847/48 miller deleted; tax on £13 (interest) left in charge.
1853/54 marked "pays interest"; no appeal noted.
1856/57 assessment deleted.
1857/58 marked "now Lenard, Benjamin".
Cross reference: Lenard, Benjamin Cooksey, plumber, innkeeper, Potterne.

133 HITCHENS, John, miller.

1855/56 returned and assessed £75; exempt.
1856/57-1859/60 recorded; no assessments made; exempt.

1855/56 Glass, Robert deleted, Hitchens, John, miller, substituted.
1856/57 [Bromham] marked "now removed to Potterne".
Cross references: Glass, Robert, miller, Potterne; Hitchens, John, miller, Bromham.

134 HOLLOWAY, Nathaniel, innkeeper, Kings Arms.

1859/60 assessed in absence of return £100.

1859/60 marked "Rose, John, innkeeper, Crown now Holloway" but Kings Arms noted on assessment.
Cross references: Rose, John, innkeeper, Potterne; Watts, Mary, innkeeper, Potterne.

135 HOWELL, Benjamin, tailor.

1842/43 returned and assessed £20; exempt.
1846/47 assessed in absence of return £20; exempt.

1847/48-1848/49 assessed in absence of return £40; exempt.
1849/50 returned and assessed £40; exempt.

136 LENARD, Benjamin Cooksey, plumber, innkeeper, George.

1853/54 returned and assessed £50; exempt.
1854/55-1855/56 assessed in absence of return £50; exempt.
1856/57 assessed in absence of return £50 but no assessment made.
1857/58-1859/60 recorded; no assessments made; exempt.

1853/54-1857/58 Benjamin Lenard; 1858/59-1859/60 Benjamin Cooksey Lenard.
1853/54-1856/57 plumber; 1857/58-1859/60 innkeeper.
1857/58 marked "late Hibberd, innkeeper"; "Hibberd, Ann now Lenard, Benjamin".
1858/59 George noted.
Cross reference: Hibberd, John, innkeeper, Potterne.

137 LENARD, Richard, miller.

1842/43 returned £40; assessed £60; exempt.

138 LORD, Edward, property in Australia.

1849/50 returned and assessed £1000.

139 MARSHMAN, Samuel, baker & shopkeeper.

Year	Amount returned £	Commissioners' estimate £	Income proved £	Final assessment £
1848/49	60	100	100	–
1849/50	–	100	100	–
1851/52	84	–	84	–
1852/53	–	84	84	–
1853/54	105	–	–	105
1854/55	120	–	–	120
1855/56	100	120	–	120
1856/57	60	120	–	120

1850/51 no assessment made.
1851/52 separate figures of £74 and £14 returned but not described.
1857/58 marked "now Sedgfield, John, baker & grocer".
1858/59 marked "see Sedgfield, St.Mary".
Cross reference: Sedgfield, John, baker & grocer, Potterne and St.Mary.

140 MATTHEWS, William, brickmaker.

1846/47 assessed in absence of return £40; exempt.
1847/48-1848/49 assessed in absence of return £80; exempt.
1849/50 assessed in absence of return £100; exempt.

141 MEDLECOTT, Revd. Joseph.

1846/47 name entered but deleted.

142 MERRETT, Lucy.

1842/43 name entered but deleted.

143 MERRETT, Robert, cordwainer.

1842/43 returned £10; assessed £40; exempt.
1846/47-1849/50 assessed in absence of return £40; exempt.

144 MERRETT, Thomas, innkeeper, Bell. [also MERRETT, John]

1849/50 assessed in absence of return £50; exempt.
1853/54 assessed in absence of return £50; exempt.
1854/55 returned and assessed £50; exempt.
1855/56 assessed in absence of return £50; exempt.
1856/57-1859/60 recorded; no assessments made; exempt.

1849/50, 1853/54-1858/59 Thomas Merrett; 1859/60 John Merrett.
1850/51-1852/53 no assessments made.
1858/59 Bell noted.

145 MUNDAY, W.E., machine maker & innkeeper.

1848/49 returned £40; assessed £60; exempt.
1849/50 assessed in absence of return £60; exempt.

146 NORTH, John Bunce, miller.

1846/47-1848/49 assessed in absence of return £100; exempt.
1849/50 assessed in absence of return £80; exempt.
1850/51-1852/53 assessed in absence of return £60; exempt.

1853/54 returned £50; assessed £60; exempt.
1854/55 returned and assessed £60; exempt.
1855/56 assessed in absence of return £60; exempt.
1856/57-1857/58 recorded; no assessments made; exempt.

147 OLIVIER, Henry A., clergyman.

1850/51-1851/52 returned £80 but no assessments made.

148 OLIVIER, Henry Stephen, director of railway, interest.

1848/49 assessed in absence of return £133.0.9.
1849/50 returned and assessed £130.
1851/52-1853/54 returned and assessed £7.10.0.
1854/55 assessed in absence of return £7.10.0.
1855/56 assessed in absence of return £10.10.0.
1856/57-1857/58 returned and assessed £10.10.0.
1858/59-1859/60 assessed in absence of return £10.10.0.

1848/49-1849/50 director of railway; 1851/52-1859/60 interest.
1850/51 no assessment made.
Note: H.S. Olivier acted as an Additional and a General Commissioner.

149 PARRY, G. F or H., Esquire, foreign securities.

1850/51-1853/54 returned and assessed £100.
1854/55 assessed in absence of return £100.
1855/56 assessed in absence of return £170 and £140 as trustee.
1858/59 assessed in absence of return £80 but assessment increased to £100.

1850/51, 1852/53 Esquire; 1851/52, 1853/54-1854/55 Esquire, foreign securities; 1855/56-
    1858/59 foreign securities.
1849/50 name entered but no assessment made.
1854/55 marked "ask for return".
1856/57 marked "removed to Cheltenham".
1857/58 marked "gone to Cheltenham".
1858/59 entry deleted but assessment apparently made.

150 ROSE, John, innkeeper, Crown.

1856/57assessed in absence of return £100; reduced to £60 on appeal; exempt.
1857/58-1858/59 recorded; no assessments made; exempt.

1856/57 marked "Watts, Mary now John Rose".

1859/60 marked "now Holloway"; Crown noted.
Cross references: Holloway, Nathaniel, innkeeper, Potterne; Watts, Mary, innkeeper, Potterne.

151 SEDGFIELD, John, baker & grocer.

1857/58 assessed in absence of return £120; assessment reduced to £80.
1858/59 assessed in absence of return £100; income proved; exempt.
1859/60 returned nil; no assessment made.

1857/58 marked "Marshman, Samuel now Sedgfield, John, baker & grocer".
1858/59 income proved but no figure inserted; assessment discharged; marked "no profits";
    marked [Marshman] "see Sedgfield, St.Mary".
Cross references: Marshman, Samuel, baker & grocer, Potterne; Sedgefield, (sic) Edward (for
    Sedgfield, John), grocer & agent, St.Mary.

152 SMITH, J.H., innkeeper.

1846/47 assessed in absence of return £120; exempt.

153 SPRULES, Ann, carpenter.

1842/43 returned £40; assessed £70; exempt.
1846/47-1849/50 assessed in absence of return £60; exempt.

154 STEVENS, Stephen, miller, carpenter.

1846/47-1849/50 assessed in absence of return £50; exempt.
1853/54-1854/55 returned and assessed £60; exempt.
1855/56 assessed in absence of return £60; exempt.
1856/57-1859/60 recorded; no assessments made; exempt.

1846/47-1849/50 Stephens; 1853/54-1859/60 Stevens.
1846/47-1849/50, 1853/54-1858/59 miller; 1859/60 miller & carpenter.
1850/51-1852/53 no assessments made.
1859/60 marked "carpenter at Worton".

155 WATTS, Mary, publican, innkeeper. [by comparison, Crown] [also WATTS, Charlotte]

1842/43 returned and assessed £20; exempt.
1846/47 assessed in absence of return £50; exempt.
1847/48-1848/49 assessed in absence of return £60; exempt.
1849/50 assessed in absence of return £40; exempt.

1853/54 assessed in absence of return £40; exempt.
1854/55 returned and assessed £40; exempt.
1855/56 assessed in absence of return £40; exempt.

1842/43, 1846/47-1848/49 Charlotte Watts; 1849/50-1855/56 Mary Watts.
1842/43 publican; 1846/47-1855/56 innkeeper.
1850/51-1852/53 no assessments made.
1856/57 marked "now John Rose".
Cross references: Holloway, Nathaniel, innkeeper, Potterne; Rose, John, innkeeper,
    Potterne.

156 WEEKS, James, miller.

1855/56 returned £40; assessed £50.
1856/57 returned £50; assessed £100.

1853/54-1854/55 marked "Chandler, Thomas now Weekes (*sic*), miller".
1857/58 marked "now William Butcher".
Cross references: Biggs, E., miller, Potterne; Butcher, William, miller, Potterne; Chandler, Tho-
    mas, miller, Potterne.

157 WILKINS, John, baker & shopkeeper.

1842/43 returned £10; assessed £40; reduced to £10.

1842/43 no appeal noted.

ROUNDWAY

158 HAYWARD, Robert, maltster.

1842/43 returned and assessed £50.
1846/47-1847/48 assessed in absence of return £70.

1848/49 marked "late"; entry deleted.
Pigot & Co"s Directory, 1842: Robert Hayward, maltster, Roundway.

159 SLOPER, Samuel, miller.

1853/54 entry only - Sloper Samuel see Cannings, miller.
Note: no reference at either Bishop's Cannings or Allcannings, but James Sloper, miller at
    Bishop's Cannings.

ROWDE

160 ALLEN, Charles, cattle dealer.

1847/48 returned and assessed £130; exempt.
1848/49 returned and assessed £50; exempt.
1849/50 assessed in absence of return £50; exempt.

1847/48 [St.Mary] "in Rowde".
Cross reference: Allen, Charles, cattle dealer, St.Mary.

161 BARKER, W.D., surgeon.

1842/43 returned and assessed £120.

Pigot & Co"s Directory, 1842: William Barker, physician, Prospect House.

162 BARNARD, Benjamin, brickmaker.

1851/52 returned and assessed £170.
1852/53 returned and assessed £180.
1853/54 returned £170; assessed £180.
1854/55-1855/56 assessed in absence of return £200.
1856/57 returned £175; assessed £200.
1857/58 returned £170; assessed £220.
1858/59 returned £140; assessed £220.
1859/60 returned £170; assessed £220.

163 BEEK, John, tailor.

1846/47-1849/50 assessed in absence of return £40; exempt.

164 BELLIS, John, gentleman.

1847/48 entered but deleted.

165 BLACKWELL, Thomas E., engineer, civil engineer.

1842/43 returned and assessed £300.
1846/47 assessed in absence of return £350.
1847/48 assessed in absence of return £500.
1848/49 returned and assessed £600.

1849/50-1850/51 assessed in absence of return £600.

1842/43 civil engineer; 1846/47-1850/51 engineer.
1842/43, 1848/49 assessed under letter.

166 BLANCHARD, Ann, innkeeper.

1842/43 returned and assessed £50; exempt.

167 BOND, James, innkeeper. [by comparison, Fox & Hounds, Picadilly]

1855/56 assessed in absence of return £75; exempt.

1855/56 Carpenter, John deleted, Bond, James substituted.
1856/57 marked "now Solomon Long".
Cross references: Carpenter, John, innkeeper, Rowde; Long, Solomon, innkeeper, Rowde; Wild, Henry, innkeeper, Rowde.

168 BURROWS, William, newspaper proprietor, proprietor independent newspaper.

1842/43 returned and assessed £185.
1846/47 returned and assessed £180.
1847/48 assessed in absence of return £180.
1848/49 returned and assessed £185.
1849/50-1850/51 returned and assessed £180.
1851/52 returned and assessed £182.

1842/43 proprietor independent newspaper; 1846/47-1851/52 newspaper proprietor.
1852/53-1859/60 marked "charged in St.John" or "returned in St.John".
Pigot & Co"s Directory, 1842: Mr.William Burrows, gentry, Dunkirk, publisher, Wiltshire Independent, Market Place.
Cross reference: Burrows, William, newspaper proprietor, St.John.

169 BUTLER, [Edward], [by reference to Bromham, miller]

1842/43 entry only marked "assessed in Bromham".
Cross reference: Butler, Edward, miller, Bromham.

170 CARPENTER, John, innkeeper. [by comparison, Fox & Hounds, Picadilly] [also CARPENTER, William]

1842/43 returned and assessed £45; exempt.
1846/47 assessed in absence of return £60; exempt.

1847/48 returned £50; assessed £60; exempt.
1848/49 returned £30; assessed £60; income proved at £30; exempt.
1849/50 assessed in absence of return £60; exempt.
1851/52 returned and assessed £50; exempt.
1852/53-1853/54 assessed in absence of return £75; exempt.
1854/55 assessed in absence of return £75; income proved at £50; exempt.

1842/43, 1846/47 William Carpenter; 1847/48-1854/55 John Carpenter.
1850/51 no assessment made.
1855/56 Carpenter, John deleted, Bond, James, innkeeper substituted.
Pigot & Co"s Directory, 1842: William Carpenter, Fox & Hounds, Picadilly.
Cross references: Bond, James, innkeeper, Rowde; Long, Solomon, innkeeper, Rowde; Wild,
    Henry, innkeeper, Rowde.

171 COONEY, William, innkeeper.

1846/47 assessed in absence of return £50; exempt.
1847/48 returned £44; assessed £50; exempt.
1848/49 returned £40; assessed £50; exempt.
1849/50 assessed in absence of return £40; exempt.

172 CROCKETT, Joseph, senior, land agent.

1842/43, 1846/47-1850/51 marked "entered in St.John", "returns in St.John" or "see St.John".
Pigot & Co"s Directory, 1842: Joseph Crockett, land agent, Bellevue.
Cross reference: Crockett, Joseph & Son, auctioneers, St.John.

173 DEVERALL, Richard, carpenter, journeyman carpenter.

1842/43 assessed in absence of return £40; exempt.
1846/47-1849/50 assessed in absence of return £50; exempt.

1842/43, 1848/49-1849/50 carpenter; 1846/47-1847/48 journeyman carpenter.

174 DEVERELL, John, blacksmith. [also DEVERELL, William]

1842/43 returned and assessed £149; exempt.
1846/47-1849/50 assessed in absence of return £135.10.0; exempt.
1853/54 returned and assessed £70; exempt.
1854/55-1855/56 assessed in absence of return £70; exempt.
1856/57-1859/60 recorded; no assessments made; exempt.

1842/43, 1846/47 Deverall.
1842/43, 1846/47-1849/50 John & William Deverell, blacksmiths; 1853/54-1859/60 John

Deverell, blacksmith.
1850/51–1852/53 no assessments made.

175 DYKE, Isaac, innkeeper, George.

1859/60 recorded; no assessment made; exempt.

176 DYKE, John, innkeeper, Cross Keys.

1853/54 returned and assessed £50; exempt.
1854/55 assessed in absence of return £50; exempt.
1855/56 assessed in absence of return £75; exempt.
1856/57–1859/60 recorded; no assessments made; exempt.

1857/58 returned £60 but no assessment made.
1859/60 Cross Keys noted.

177 FERRIS, John, shopkeeper.

1846/47 entered but deleted; illegible, perhaps butcher or hatter.

178 GABRIEL, Elizabeth, interest.

1846/47 returned and assessed £56.
1849/50 returned and assessed £20; exempt.
1851/52 returned and assessed £20.

1846/47, 1849/50 Elizabeth Gabriel; 1851/52 Miss Gabriel.

179 GIBBS, Louisa.

1849/50 returned and assessed £50.

1846/47 name entered as Louise Gibbs but deleted.
No occupation recorded.

180 GOLDING, Charles, innkeeper, Queens Head, Dunkirk.

1859/60 recorded; no assessment made; exempt.

Cross references: Harding, David, innkeeper, Rowde; Liddiard, Eaben, innkeeper, Rowde;
  Smith, John, innkeeper, Rowde.

181 HARDING, David, innkeeper. [by comparison, Queens Head, Dunkirk]

1842/43 assessed in absence of return £60; exempt.
1846/47 assessed in absence of return £100; exempt.
1847/48 returned £50; assessed £80; income proved at £50; exempt.
1848/49 assessed in absence of return £50; exempt.
1849/50 assessed in absence of return £80; exempt.
1850/51 returned and assessed £50; exempt.

1850/51 marked "now E. Liddiard".
Pigot & Co"s Directory, 1842: David Harding, Queens Head, Dunkirk.
Cross references: Golding, Charles, innkeeper, Rowde; Liddiard, Eaben, innkeeper, Rowde; Smith, John, innkeeper, Rowde.

182 HAYWARD, John, land agent.

1842/43 returned and assessed £1155.
1846/47 assessed in absence of return £1155.
1847/48-1848/49 returned and assessed £830.
1849/50 assessed in absence of return £1000.
1850/51 assessed in absence of return £880.
1851/52 returned and assessed £878.
1852/53-1856/57 assessed in absence of return £878.
1857/58-1858/59 returned and assessed £878.
1859/60 assessed in absence of return £878.

1842/43, 1847/48-1854/55 assessed under letter.
Pigot & Co"s Directory, 1842: John Hayward, Browfort; possibly surveyor, New Park Street, Devizes.
Note: John Hayward acted as an Additional Commissioner.

183 HIBBARD or HUBBARD, William.

1842/43 name only entered but deleted.

184 HOOKINS, John, solicitor.

1842/43 returned and assessed £196.0.5.
1846/47-1850/51 returned and assessed £200.
1851/52 returned and assessed £100.

Pigot & Co"s Directory, 1842: John Hookins, attorney, Brow Cottage.

185 KEEPENCE, Charles, bricklayer.

1846/47–1848/49 assessed in absence of return £75; exempt.
1849/50 returned and assessed £75; exempt.
1850/51 assessed in absence of return £50; exempt.
1851/52–1853/54 assessed in absence of return £65; exempt.
1854/55 assessed in absence of return £65; income proved at £50; exempt.
1855/56 assessed in absence of return £50; exempt.
1856/57–1859/60 recorded; no assessments made; exempt.

186 KINGSLAND, Revd. William, independent minister.

1853/54 returned and assessed £175 and £25 interest.
1854/55 returned £200; assessed £175.
1855/56 returned and assessed £170.
1856/57–1859/60 returned and assessed £150 and £20 interest.

1854/55 marked "£25 income on which duty is deducted".

187 KNIGHT, Henry, collector, etc.

1853/54 returned and assessed £78; exempt.
1854/55 assessed in absence of return £78; exempt.

1855/56 marked "St.Mary's". (No entry in St.Mary)

188 LEWIS, N.H., Wesleyan Minister.

1855/56 returned £98.18.0; assessed £100.

1856/57–1857/58 marked "now John Poulton, Wesleyan Minister".
Cross reference: Poulton, Revd. John, Wesleyan Minister, Rowde.

189 LIDDIARD, Eaben, innkeeper. [by comparison, Queens Head, Dunkirk]

1851/52 returned and assessed £55; exempt.
1852/53 assessed in absence of return £55; exempt.
1853/54–1854/55 assessed in absence of return £75; exempt.

1850/51 marked "Harding, David now E.Liddiard".
1855/56 marked "Smith, John late Liddiard, innkeeper".
Cross references: Golding, Charles, innkeeper, Rowde; Harding, David, innkeeper, Rowde;
    Smith, John, innkeeper, Rowde.

190 LONG, Solomon, innkeeper, beerhouse keeper, Fox & Hounds, Picadilly and Olive Branch.

1856/57-1859/60 recorded; no assessments made; exempt.

1856/57 beerhouse keeper; 1857/58-1859/60 innkeeper.
1856/57 marked "Bond, James now Solomon Long, Fox & Hounds".
1859/60 marked "Wild Henry now Solomon Long, Olive Branch".
Cross references: Bond, James, innkeeper, Rowde; Carpenter, John, innkeeper, Rowde; Wild, Henry, innkeeper, Rowde.

191 MACK, Robert A., Town Missionary.

1848/49 assessed in absence of return £70; exempt.
1849/50 returned and assessed £70; exempt.
1850/51 assessed in absence of return £80; exempt.

192 MANNING, Revd. Alexander, chaplain of new prison, private pupils.

1842/43 returned £150 as chaplain but deleted; marked "Schedule E".
1842/43 returned and assessed £80 private pupils.

1846/47 marked "Schedule E".
Cross reference: Manning, Revd. Alexander, private tutor, St.John.

193 MAYELL, Robert, baker.

1842/43, 1846/47-1847/48 assessed in absence of return £60; exempt.
1848/49 assessed in absence of return £75; income proved at £99.9.6; exempt.
1849/50 returned and assessed £75; exempt.
1850/51 returned £102.18.3 but deleted; assessed £80; exempt.
1851/52-1852/53 assessed in absence of return £80; exempt.
1853/54 returned and assessed £80; exempt.
1854/55-1855/56 assessed in absence of return £100; income proved at £80; exempt.
1856/57 assessed in absence of return £100; reduced to £97 on appeal.
1857/58 assessed in absence of return £97; income proved at £30; exempt.
1858/59-1859/60 recorded; no assessments made; exempt.

1856/57 marked "has house property".

194 NEALE, Henry, contractor, engineer.

1851/52 returned and assessed £160.
1852/53 assessed in absence of return £160.

1853/54 returned £100; assessed £160.
1854/55-1855/56 assessed in absence of return £160.
1856/57 assessed in absence of return £175.
1857/58-1858/59 returned £160; assessed £175.
1859/60 returned £170; assessed £175.

1851/52-1858/59 contractor; 1859/60 engineer.

195 PICTON, John Owen, clergyman.

1854/55 returned £100 but deleted.
1855/56-1859/60 recorded; no assessments made; exempt.

1853/54 marked "Query licensed?"
1854/55 marked "licensed curate".

196 POULTON, Revd, John, Wesleyan Minister.

1856/57 returned £80; assessed £100; reduced to £80 on appeal; exempt.
1857/58-1858/59 recorded; no assessments made; exempt.

1856/57 marked "late Lewis Wesleyan Minister".
1858/59 marked "Query liable?"
1859/60 marked "late Wesleyan Minister".
Cross reference: Lewis, N.H., Wesleyan Minister, Rowde.

197 PRICTOR, Job, Junior, shoemaker, innkeeper.

1842/43 returned £20; assessed £50; exempt.
1846/47 assessed in absence of return £75; exempt.
1847/48 returned £80; assessed £120; exempt.
1848/49 assessed in absence of return £120; income proved at £70; exempt.
1849/50 assessed in absence of return £75; exempt.

1842/43, 1846/47 shoemaker; 1847/48 innkeeper & shoemaker; 1848/49-1849/50
    innkeeper, etc.

198 PRICTOR, William, carpenter.

1842/43 assessed in absence of return £20; exempt.
1846/47-1849/50 assessed in absence of return £40; exempt.

199 PURNELL, Thomas, carpenter. [also PURNELL, James]

1842/43 returned £70; assessed £90; exempt.
1846/47-1849/50 assessed in absence of return £70; exempt.
1851/52 returned £60; assessed 90; income proved at £91.3.0; exempt.
1852/53 assessed in absence of return £90; exempt.
1853/54 returned £60; assessed 90 and £15 interest; exempt but £15 left in charge.
1854/55 assessed in absence of return £100.
1855/56 assessed in absence of return £100; income proved at £60; exempt.
1856/57-1859/60 recorded; no assessments made; exempt.

1842/43, 1846/47-1847/48 James Purnell; 1848/49-1859/60 Thomas Purnell.
1842/43, 1846/47-1852/53, 1857/58-1859/60 carpenter; 1853/54-1856/57 carpenter, etc.
1850/51 no assessment made.

200 PYKE, John, carpenter.

1842/43 returned £70; assessed £150; income proved at £128.14.0; exempt but £22
    interest left in charge.
1846/47-1847/48 assessed in absence of return £100; exempt.
1848/49 returned £80; assessed £100; income proved at £115.15.0; exempt.
1849/50 returned £60; assessed £100; exempt.
1850/51 returned £50; assessed £70; income proved at £50; exempt.

1842/43 marked "pays £22 interest".

201 SAINSBURY, George Taylor, brickmaker, brick, tile, manure & slate merchant.

1849/50 returned and assessed £120.
1850/51 returned £100; assessed £150.
1852/53 assessed in absence of return £200.
1856/57 returned £500; assessed £600.
1857/58 returned £600; assessed £650.
1858/59 returned and assessed £800.
1859/60 returned £700; assessed £900.

1849/50-1855/56 brickmaker; 1856/57-1859/60 brick, tile, manure & slate merchant, Devizes,
    Rowde & Seend.
1849/50 marked "St.Mary's brickmaker"; assessment in St.Mary deleted.
1851/52 marked "return in St.Mary's".
1852/53 marked "see St.Mary" but assessed in Rowde.
1853/54-1854/55 marked "see St.Mary" and "returned in St.Mary".
1855/56 marked "St.Mary's".
Note: 1842/43, 1846/47-1848/49, 1851/52, 1853/54-1855/56 assessed in St.Mary.
Cross reference: Sainsbury, George Taylor, brickmaker, St.Mary.

202 SELLIFONT, J.P., minister.

1851/52 returned and assessed £70; exempt.

203 SIMPSON, George, Junior, printer, salary, annual allowance.

1852/53 returned and assessed £178.5.0.
1853/54 returned £150 and £18 interest; assessed £170.
1854/55 returned £132; assessed £197.
1855/56 returned £65; assessed £197.
1856/57 returned £65p, £100a; assessed £200.
1857/58 returned £170; assessed £220.
1858/59 returned £65, £100; assessed £220.
1859/60 returned £160; assessed £250.

Abbreviations: p, printer; a, annual allowance.
1852/53-1854/55 George Simpson; 1855/56-1859/60 George Simpson, Junior.
1852/53, 1855/56, 1856/57 printer; 1857/58 salary; 1856/57, 1858/59-1859/60 annual allowance.
1858/59 the amounts returned of £65 and £100 are not described but following 1856/57 are likely to be printer and annual allowance respectively.

204 SIMS, Thomas, innkeeper.

1842/43, 1846/47 assessed in absence of return £40; exempt.

205 SINCLAIR, David, schoolmaster.

1846/47-1849/50 assessed in absence of return £70; exempt.
1851/52 returned and assessed £70; exempt.
1852/53-1853/54 assessed in absence of return £70; exempt.
1854/55 returned and assessed £75; exempt.
1855/56 assessed in absence of return £75; exempt.
1856/57-1858/59 recorded; no assessments made; exempt.
1859/60 assessed in absence of return £100; income proved at £82; exempt.

1850/51 no assessment made.
Pigot & Co"s Directory, 1842: David Sinclair, master, British School, Northgate Street.

206 SLOPER, James, miller.

1842/43, 1846/47-1847/48 marked "returned at Bishop's Cannings".
Cross reference: Sloper, James, miller, Bishop's Cannings.

207 SMITH, John, innkeeper, Queens Head, Dunkirk.

1855/56 assessed in absence of return £75; exempt.
1856/57 assessed in absence of return £80; exempt.
1857/58-1858/59 recorded; no assessments made; exempt.

1855/56 marked "Smith, John late Liddiard".
1856/57 Queens Head noted.
Cross references: Golding, Charles, innkeeper, Rowde; Harding, David, innkeeper, Rowde;
    Liddiard, Eaben, innkeeper, Rowde.

208 SMITH, Knightley, beerseller, innkeeper.

1846/47 assessed in absence of return £60; exempt.
1847/48 returned £40; assessed £60; exempt.
1848/49 assessed in absence of return £70; income proved at £50; exempt.
1849/50 assessed in absence of return £70; exempt.

1846/47-1847/48 beerseller; 1848/49-1849/50 innkeeper.

209 STRONG, Thomas, butcher.

1842/43 returned £60; assessed £150; income proved at £60; exempt.
1846/47 assessed in absence of return £70; exempt.
1847/48 returned £50; assessed £70; exempt.
1848/49-1849/50 assessed in absence of return £70; exempt.

210 VINCENT, Revd. Edward, foreign securities, debenture Drury Lane Company, fee admission ticket.

1842/43 returned and assessed £9.6.8f, £1.13.4d, 17.6a.
1846/47 returned and assessed £9.6.8f.
1847/48-1848/49 assessed in absence of return £9.6.8.

Abbreviations: f, foreign securities; d, debenture Drury Lane Company; a, fee admission ticket.
1842/43 marked "1/3 share debenture Drury Lane Company produce last year £5.1.3 of fee
    admission ticket, Do.".
1854/55, 1857/58 entered but deleted.
1855/56 returned nil; no assessment made.
Pigot & Co"s Directory, 1842: Revd. Edward Vincent, clergy, Rowde.

211 WESTON, Stephen, tailor.

1846/47-1847/48 assessed in absence of return £40; exempt.

212 WICKHAM, Stephen, maltster.

1842/43 assessed in absence of return £30; exempt.
1846/47 returned and assessed £30; exempt.

213 WILD, Henry, innkeeper, Olive Branch.

1854/55 assessed in absence of return £75; income proved at £70; exempt.
1855/56 assessed in absence of return £70; exempt.
1856/57-1859/60 recorded; no assessments made; exempt.

1856/57 Olive Branch noted.
1859/60 marked "now Solomon Long".
Cross reference: Bond, James, innkeeper, Rowde; Carpenter, John, innkeeper, Rowde; Long, Solomon, innkeeper, Rowde.

214 WILTSHIRE, John & William, bakers, pig butchers.

1842/43 returned and assessed £80; exempt.
1846/47 returned £52; assessed £80; exempt.
1847/48 assessed in absence of return £80; exempt.
1848/49 assessed in absence of return £80; income proved at £121; exempt.
1849/50 assessed in absence of return £20; exempt.

1842/43, 1846/47 bakers & pig butchers; 1847/48 bakers; 1848/49-1849/50 bakers, etc.

215 WITTEY, Samuel, solicitor's clerk.

1846/47 assessed in absence of return £130; income proved at £146.14.0; exempt.

Cross reference: Wittey, Samuel, solicitor, St.John.

216 WOODCOCK, Mary.

1846/47 name only entered and deleted.

WEEK

217 ABRAHAMS, Moses, jeweller.

1842/43 returned and assessed £100; exempt.
1846/47-1849/50 assessed in absence of return £80; exempt.

218 BARNARD, George, toll clerk to Kennet & Avon Canal Company, canal agent, agent GWR.

1842/43 returned £100; no assessment made and marked "Schedule E".
1846/47–1847/48 assessed in absence of return £100.
1848/49–1852/53 returned and assessed £100.
1853/54 returned £75; assessed £120; reduced to £75.

1842/43 toll clerk to Kennet & Avon Canal Company; 1846/47–1852/53 canal agent;
1853/54 agent GWR.
1847/48 estimate of £130 amended to £100.
1853/54 no appeal noted.
1854/55 marked "dead".
Pigot & Co"s Directory, 1842: George Barnard, collector for Kennet and Avon Canal Company,
    Bath Road.

219 BARNARD, William, agent, agent GWR, canal clerk.

1853/54 returned and assessed £65; exempt.
1854/55 returned and assessed £100.
1855/56 assessed in absence of return £100.
1856/57 returned £100 but deleted; marked "Schedule E".

1853/54 agent GWR; 1854/55–1855/56 agent; 1856/57 canal clerk.

220 BIGGS, Charles, innkeeper & corn dealer.

1848/49 returned and assessed £50; exempt.

221 BIRCH, Mr., innkeeper.

1846/47 entry only marked "late innkeeper".

222 BLATCHLEY, Gabriel, manure merchant.

1842/43 assessed in absence of return £40; income proved at £30; exempt.

Pigot & Co"s Directory, 1842: G. Blatchley, artificial manure manufacturer, Gunes Lane.

223 BOLLAND, James, gardener.

1842/43 entry only deleted.
Pigot & Co"s Directory, 1842: James Bolland, market gardener, Pan's Lane.

224 BOX, William, engineer, ironfounder.

1842/43 assessed in absence of return £100; exempt.
1846/47 assessed in absence of return £150.
1847/48 returned £100; assessed £200; income proved at £90.5.10; exempt.
1848/49 returned and assessed 100; exempt.
1849/50 assessed in absence of return £150; reduced to £60 on appeal.
1850/51 assessed in absence of return £100; exempt.

1842/43 engineer; 1846/47-1850/51 ironfounder.
Pigot & Co"s Directory, 1842: William Box, engineer etc., Bath Road.

225 BUNCE, John S., dissenting minister, private tuition.

1842/43 returned and assessed £130.
1846/47 returned £130m, £16t, £23.15.0i but no assessment made.

Abbreviations: m, dissenting minister; t, tuition; i, interest.
1842/43 dissenting minister; 1846/47 dissenting minister & private tuition.
Pigot & Co"s Directory, 1842: Revd. John Stacy Bunce, clergy, Hilworth (sic).

226 BUTCHER, John, Relieving Officer.

1856/57 returned £89; no assessment made; marked "Schedule E"

227 CANAL COMPANY

1842/43, 1846/47-1859/60 recorded but no assessments made; marked "return made at Bath",
    "carriers, Bath" or "carrier, return at Bath".

228 CHANDLER, James, innkeeper, farrier.

1850/51 assessed in absence of return £100; exempt.

1850/51 "& farrier" entered but deleted.

229 CHANDLER, John, corndealer, maltster. [also CHANDLER, Thomas]

1848/49 returned and assessed £30 and £13 interest.
1849/50 returned and assessed £100 and £13 interest.
1850/51-1851/52 returned and assessed £150.
1852/53 assessed in absence of return £150.
1853/54 returned and assessed £150.

1854/55 returned £150; assessed £200.
1855/56 assessed in absence of return £200.
1856/57 returned £160; assessed £720; reduced to £550 on appeal.
1857/58 returned £300; assessed £750.
1858/59 returned £385; assessed £900.
1859/60 assessed £200 and £310; assessed £1050.

1848/49-1853/54 John Chandler; 1854/55-1859/60 John & Thomas Chandler.
1848/49-1849/50 corndealer; 1850/51-1852/53 corndealer & maltster;
1853/54-1858/59 maltster(s); 1859/60 retail maltsters on commission.
1852/53 [Thomas Chandler] marked "now John".
1854/55 marked "partner" with Thomas Chandler.
1856/57 £550 confirmed on appeal.
1859/60 [Marden] John & Thomas Chandler, "charged in Week".
Pigot & Co"s Directory, 1842: Thomas Chandler & Son, maltsters, Melbourne Place.
Cross references: Chandler, Charles, maltster, Marden; Chandler, John & Thomas, maltsters,
    Marden; Chandler, Thomas, maltster, Week.

230 CHANDLER, Thomas, maltster.

1842/43, 1846/47-1849/50 returned and assessed £150.
1850/51 assessed in absence of return £150.

1842/43, 1846/47 maltster, etc; 1847/48-1850/51 maltster.
1842/43 assessed under letter.
1850/51 estimate of £200 amended to £150.
1851/52 estimate of £100 deleted.
1852/53 marked "now John".
1854/55 marked "partner" with John Chandler.
Cross references; Chandler, Charles, maltster, Marden; Chandler, John, maltster, Week; Chandler,
    John & Thomas, maltsters, Marden.

231 CHIVERS, William, carpenter.

1842/43 returned and assessed £70; exempt.
1846/47-1850/51 assessed in absence of return £70; exempt.
1851/52 returned and assessed £90; exempt.
1852/53 assessed in absence of return £90; exempt.
1853/54 returned £77.10.0; assessed £150; reduced to £125.
1854/55 returned £75; assessed £125.
1855/56 assessed in absence of return £125.
1856/57 returned £80; assessed £125.
1857/58 returned £100; assessed £125.
1858/59-1859/60 recorded; no assessments made; exempt.

1842/43 "Schedule A & B" entered but deleted.
1853/54 no appeal noted.

1858/59 marked "nil".
Pigot & Co"s Directory, 1842: William Chivers, carpenter & builder, Sidmouth Street.

232 COX, Caleb, conveyancer.

1842/43 returned and assessed £147; exempt.
1846/47 assessed in absence of return £150; reduced to £147 on appeal but altered to £150.
1847/48 assessed in absence of return £147 exempt.
1848/49 returned and assessed £147; exempt.
1849/50-1852/53 assessed in absence of return £147; exempt.

1846/47 duty on £150 is extended to the tax paid column despite a reduction being recorded on appeal.
1853/54 "gratuity" substituted for "conveyancer" but no assessment made.
1854/55 marked "gone away...to Bristol".

233 COX, George, butcher.

1859/60 returned £125; assessed £175.

1859/60 original estimate of £200 amended to £175.
1859/60 [St.Mary] marked "charged in Week".
Cross reference: Cox, George, butcher, St.Mary.

234 CUNNINGTON, William, woolstapler. [also CUNNINGTON, Messrs.; CUNNINGTON, William & Co]

1842/43 returned and assessed £365.
1846/47 assessed in absence of return £365.
1847/48 returned and assessed £365.
1848/49 returned and assessed £250.
1849/50 assessed in absence of return £300.
1850/51 returned and assessed £360.
1851/52-1852/53 returned and assessed £385.
1853/54 assessed in absence of return £385.
1854/55 returned and assessed £385.
1855/56 returned and assessed £400.
1856/57 assessed in absence of return £400.
1857/58 returned and assessed £420.
1858/59 returned £380; assessed £420.
1859/60 returned and assessed £420.

1842/43, 1846/47, 1848/49-1856/57 William Cunnington; 1847/48 Messrs Cunnington; 1857/58-1859/60 William Cunnington & Co.

1855/56 marked "called for return".
Pigot & Co"s Directory, 1842: William Cunnington, woolstapler, Southgate House.
Cross reference: Cunnington, William & Sons, wine merchants, St.John.

235 DAVIS, John, plasterer.

1842/43, 1846/47-1849/50 assessed in absence of return £50; exempt.

Pigot & Co"s Directory, 1842: Davis & Son, plasterers & slaters, Nursery.

236 DOWSE, James, cattle dealer, dealer.

1853/54 returned £70; assessed £75; exempt.
1854/55-1855/56 assessed in absence of return £75; exempt.
1856/57-1858/59 recorded; no assessments made; exempt.

1853/54 dealer; 1854/55-1858/59 cattle dealer.
1859/60 marked "dead".

237 DREWE, John.

1842/43 marked "see return at Queen St. Park, Bristol".
1846/47 marked "returns at Bristol".

238 ELLEN, John, clerk in Stamp Office.

1842/43, 1846/47-1848/49 assessed in absence of return £150.
1849/50 returned and assessed £150.
1850/51-1851/52 assessed in absence of return £150.
1852/53 returned nil; assessed £150.
1853/54 returned and assessed £150.
1854/55-1856/57 assessed in absence of return £150.
1857/58 returned and assessed £150.
1858/59 assessed in absence of return £150.
1859/60 assessed in absence of return £100.

239 ERWOOD, Robert, innkeeper.

1842/43 assessed in absence of return £40; exempt.

Pigot & Co"s Directory, 1842: Robert Erwood, retailer of beer, shopkeeper & dealer in groceries & sundries, Nursery.

240 FRICKER, George, tailor.

1842/43 returned £8; assessed £50; exempt.
1846/47-1849/50 assessed in absence of return £50; exempt.

Pigot & Co"s Directory, 1842: George Fricker, tailor, Sidmouth Street.

241 GEORGE, Francis, law clerk, clerk.

1853/54 returned and assessed £98.15.0; exempt.
1854/55 returned and assessed £105.
1855/56 assessed in absence of return £105.
1856/57 returned and assessed £105.
1857/58 assessed in absence of return £105.
1858/59 returned and assessed £105.
1859/60 returned and assessed £110.

1853/54 clerk; 1854/55-1859/60 law clerk.
1853/54-1854/55 [Bedborough] entries made in absence of return £105 but deleted.
Cross reference: George, Frank (sic), clerk, Bedborough.

242 GILBERT, Henry, innkeeper. [by comparison, King's Arms]

1842/43, 1846/47-1848/49 assessed in absence of return £100; exempt.

1850/51 marked "now Truman".
Pigot & Co"s Directory, 1842: Henry Gilbert, King's Arms, Green.
Cross references: Truman, William, innkeeper, Week; Wild, Edwin, innkeeper, Week.

243 GILLMAN, Charles, reporter.

1852/53 assessed in absence of return £75; exempt.
1854/55 assessed in absence of return £100; income proved at £90; exempt.

1852/53 marked "reporter see St.John".
1853/54 marked "returned in St.John".
1855/56 marked "charged in St.John".
Cross reference: Gillman, Charles, reporter, St.John.

244 GLASS, Ann, interest.

1857/58 returned £8 but entry deleted.

245 GLASS, John, coal merchant.

1842/43 assessed in absence of return £150; income proved at £100; exempt.

Pigot & Co"s Directory, 1842: John Glass, coal merchant, Wharf.

246 GOODMAN, John, innkeeper, Artichoke.

1850/51 recorded but no assessment made.
1851/52-1852/53 assessed in absence of return £75; exempt.
1853/54 returned and assessed £80; exempt.
1854/55 assessed in absence of return £80; exempt.
1855/56 assessed in absence of return £100.
1856/57 returned £100; assessed £120.
1857/58 assessed in absence of return £120.
1858/59 returned £125; assessed £130.
1859/60 returned and assessed £130.

1850/51 marked "Phillips, George, innkeeper, now Goodman, John".
1851/52 marked "late Phillips, innkeeper".
1856/57 Artichoke noted.
Cross reference: Phillips, George, innkeeper, Week

247 HALE, James, cordwainer.

1842/43, 1846/47-1849/50 assessed in absence of return £50; exempt.

Pigot & Co"s Directory, 1842: James Hale, boot & shoe maker, Sidmouth Street.

248 HARRIS, Edward, curate.

1854/55 assessed in absence of return £80 but not completed.
1859/60 returned and assessed £100.

1854/55 assessment made by General Commissioners but no duty computed.

249 HARRIS, James, clerk agent.

1859/60 marked "from St.Mary" but no assessment made.
Cross reference: Harris, James, clerk agent, St.Mary.

250 HEALE, William, nurseryman. [also HEALE, William & Son]

1842/43 returned and assessed £180.

1846/47-1848/49 assessed in absence of return £100; exempt.
1849/50 returned and assessed £34; exempt.
1850/51 assessed in absence of return £50; exempt.

1842/43 William Heale & Son; 1846/47-1850/51 William Heale.
1842/43 nurserymen; 1846/47-1850/51 nurseryman.
Pigot & Co"s Directory, 1842: William Heale & Son, nursery & seedsmen, Wick.

251 HEEVER, Elizabeth, miller. [also HEEVER, Henry]

1842/43 assessed in absence of return £100; exempt.
1846/47-1852/53 assessed in absence of return £80; exempt.
1853/54 assessed in absence of return £100; reduced to £90.
1854/55-1855/56 assessed in absence of return £90.
1856/57 returned and assessed £100.
1857/58 assessed in absence of return £100.
1858/59-1859/60 returned and assessed £100.

1842/43, 1846/47-1855/56 Elizabeth Heever; 1856/57-1859/60 Henry Heever.
1853/54 no appeal noted.

252 HICKEY, James, schoolmaster.

1842/43 assessed in absence of return £85; exempt.

253 HILL, William, plasterer, slater.

1842/43 returned and assessed £60; exempt.
1846/47-1848/49 assessed in absence of return £60; exempt.
1849/50 assessed in absence of return £40; exempt.

1842/43 plasterer & slater; 1846/47-1849/50 plasterer, etc.
Pigot & Co"s Directory, 1842: William Hill, painter, plumber & glazier, Sidmouth Street; plasterer & slater, Back Lane.

254 HUMBY, Frederick Peter, Southbroom Brewery. [also HUMBY, Frederick & ROBBINS, Frederick]

1855/56 assessed in absence of return £150.
1856/57 returned £80; assessed £200.
1857/58 returned £120; assessed £250.
1858/59 returned £250; assessed £300.
1859/60 returned and assessed £300.

1854/55-1856/57 Frederick Peter Humby; 1857/58-1858/59 Frederick Humby;
1859/60 Frederick Humby & Frederick Robbins.
1854/55 recorded as brewer but no assessment made; 1855/56-1859/60 Southbroom Brewery.
Cross reference: Humby, Frederick Peter, innkeeper, Week & St.John.

255 HUMBY, Frederick Peter, innkeeper, Antelope.

1854/55 marked "Norton, James King now Humby".
1855/56 [St.John] innkeeper, Antelope, assessed in absence of return £50.
1857/58 [St.John] marked "now Thomas Brown" "Antelope".
1858/59 [St.John] marked "Brown, Thomas, late Humby, Antelope".
Cross references: Humby, Frederick Peter, Southbroom Brewery; Norton, James King, innkeeper, Week.

256 HUMBY, James, bank clerk.

1854/55 returned £130; assessed £150; reduced to £130.

1853/54 recorded and estimated at £150 but deleted.
Cross reference: Humby, James, bank manager, St.John.

257 LANGFORD, Peter, Supervisor of Excise.

1848/49 entry only, deleted.

258 LEWIS, David, wharfinger.

1853/54 returned and assessed £85; exempt.

259 LONG, James, innkeeper, Rising Sun.

1848/49-1849/50 assessed in absence of return £70; exempt.
1854/55-1855/56 assessed in absence of return £70; exempt.
1856/57-1857/58 assessed in absence of return £100.
1858/59 assessed in absence of return £110.
1859/60 returned £110; assessed £150.

1848/49 Packer, Samuel deleted, Long, James substituted.
1850/51-1853/54 no assessments made.
1854/55 estimate made but no assessment made.
1856/57 Rising Sun noted.
Cross references: Long, James, innkeeper, Bedborough; Packer, Samuel, innkeeper, Week.

260 MANNING, Ann.

1842/43 name only entered and deleted.

261 MARSTON, Charles Henry, Baptist minister.

1859/60 assessed in absence of return £100.

1859/60 marked "app."

262 MEAD, George, coal merchant.

1842/43 assessed in absence of return £100; exempt.

263 MULLINGS, John, basket maker.

1842/43, 1846/47-1849/50 assessed in absence of return £50; exempt.

Pigot & Co"s Directory, 1842: John Mullings, basket maker, Sidmouth Street.

264 MUSSELWHITE, John, clerk to Mr.Meek, accountant.

1858/59 assessed in absence of return £120.
1859/60 returned and assessed £120.

1859/60 accountant.
Cross reference: Meek, Alexander, solicitor, St.John.

265 NASH, Robert, shopkeeper.

1842/43 returned and assessed £75; exempt.

266 NEATE, John, innkeeper.

1846/47-1847/48 assessed in absence of return £100.

267 NISBET, Robert Parry, Esquire, property out of United Kingdom, property in British Plantations.

1842/43 returned and assessed £1000.
1846/47-1849/50 returned and assessed £750.

1850/51-1851/52 returned and assessed £250.
1852/53 returned and assessed £310.
1853/54 returned and assessed £444.
1854/55 returned and assessed £460.
1855/56 returned and assessed £450.
1856/57 assessed in absence of return £547.
1857/58 returned and assessed £244.
1858/59 returned and assessed £301.12.8.
1859/60 returned and assessed £620.

1842/43, 1846/47-1859/60 Esquire; 1853/54-1857/58 property out of United Kingdom; 1858/59-1859/60 property in British Plantations.
1854/55, 1855/56 marked "apply for return".
Pigot & Co"s Directory, 1842: Robert Parry Nisbet, gentry, Southbroom House.
Note: R.P. Nisbet acted as a General Commissioner.

268 NORTH, John, coach builder.

1856/57 assessed in absence of return £125.
1857/58 returned £105; assessed £125.
1858/59 returned and assessed £101.
1859/60 returned £102; assessed £120.

1846/47 returned £100 but deleted; marked "charged at Melksham".
1847/48-1855/56 marked "charged at" or "return at Melksham".

269 NORTON, James King, innkeeper. [by comparison, Antelope]

1851/52 estimated in absence of return £50; no assessment made.
1852/53 assessed in absence of return £50; assessment discharged on appeal but no sum recorded.
1853/54 assessed in absence of return £50; exempt.

1854/55 marked "now Humby".
Cross reference: Humby, Frederick Peter, innkeeper, Week.

270 OAKFORD, James, plasterer.

1842/43 returned and assessed £50; exempt.
1846/47-1852/53 assessed in absence of return £50; exempt.
1853/54-1855/56 assessed in absence of return £70; exempt.
1856/57-1859/60 recorded; no assessments made; exempt.

Pigot & Co"s Directory, 1842: James Oakford, plasterer & slater, Potterne Road.

271 PACKER, Samuel, innkeeper. [by comparison, Sun]

1842/43 assessed in absence of return £90; exempt.
1846/47–1847/48 assessed in absence of return £100; exempt.

1848/49 marked "Long, James, innkeeper".
Pigot & Co"s Directory, 1842: Samuel Packer, Sun, Green.
Cross reference: Long, James, innkeeper, Week.

272 PALMER, Benjamin, rent of tolls.

1851/52 assessed in absence of return £150; reduced to £100 on appeal; exempt.
1852/53 assessed in absence of return £100; reduced to nil on appeal; exempt.

1852/53 marked "gone now Commissioners of Trust".
1853/54 marked "Commissioners of T[urn] P[ike] Trust".
Cross reference: Turnpike Trust, Commissioners of, Week.

273 PEAD, George.

1842/43 name only entered and deleted.

274 PHILLIPS, George, innkeeper. [by comparison, Artichoke]

1846/47 assessed in absence of return £75; exempt.
1847/48–1848/49 assessed in absence of return £100; exempt.

1850/51 marked "now John Goodman".
Cross reference: Goodman, John, innkeeper, Week.

275 PHILLIPS, James.

1842/43 name only entered and deleted.

276 PHILLIPS, Thomas, lunatic asylum keeper. [Bellevue]

Year	Amount returned £	Commissioners' estimate £	Final assessment £
1842/43	300	500	500
1846/47	–	700	700
1847/48	500	700	700
1848/49	700	–	700

1849/50	650	–	650
1850/51	650	850	850
1851/52	600	850	850
1852/53	850	–	850
1853/54	450	550	550
1854/55	265	500	500
1855/56	–	400	400
1856/57	–	75	75
1857/58	75	–	75
1858/59	75	–	75
1859/60	–	200	200

1852/53 marked "pauper patients sent to County Asylum".
1856/57 marked "to stand over" struck out.
Pigot & Co"s Directory, 1842: Thomas Phillips, governor, Lunatic Asylum, Bellevue.

277 PLANK, Charles, builder.

1851/52 returned £200 but deleted.

Cross reference: Plank, Charles Rhodes, builder, Bedborough.

278 PLAYER, Jacob, interest.

1857/58-1859/60 returned and assessed £10.

1842/43 name only entered and deleted.

279 POOLMAN & BATT, carpenters, wheelwrights.

1842/43, 1846/47 assessed in absence of return £60; exempt.
1847/48-1849/50 assessed in absence of return £120; exempt.

1842/43 carpenters & wheelwrights; 1846/47-1849/50 carpenters, etc.
Pigot & Co"s Directory, 1842: Poolman & Batt, carpenters, builders & wheelwrights, Bath Road.

280 POULDEN, Charles, beerhouse keeper & carrier.

1854/55 assessed in absence of return £30; exempt.

281 PUGH, Samuel S., dissenting minister.

1859/60 assessed in absence of return £200.

1858/59 recorded but no assessment made; marked "late Stanford".
Cross reference: Stanford, Charles, dissenting minister, Week.

282 RIX, James, coach painter.

1842/43 returned and assessed £40; exempt.
1846/47-1847/48 assessed in absence of return £40; exempt.

283 SHIPTON, Charles B., tailor.

1842/43 returned and assessed £70; exempt.
1846/47-1849/50 assessed in absence of return £70; exempt.

1842/43 Shepton; 1846/47-1849/50 Shipton.
Pigot & Co"s Directory, 1842: Charles Shipton, tailor, Bath Road.

284 SLOPER, Edwin, innkeeper.

1842/43 assessed in absence of return £75; exempt.

Pigot & Co"s Directory, 1842: Edwin Sloper, Royal Oak, Green.

285 SPRAWSON, John, coachman.

1842/43, 1846/47-1847/48 assessed in absence of return £60; exempt.

Cross reference: Sprawson, John, coachman, St.John.

286 STANFORD, Charles, dissenting minister.

1854/55 returned and assessed £200.
1855/56 assessed in absence of return £200.
1856/57-1857/58 returned and assessed £200.
1858/59 assessed in absence of return £200.

1859/60 marked "Pugh, Samuel S., late Stanford, dissenting minister".
Cross reference: Pugh, Samuel S., dissenting minister, Week.

287 STEVENS, James, beerhouse keeper.

1842/43, 1846/47-1849/50 assessed in absence of return £30; exempt.

Pigot & Co"s Directory, 1842: James Stevens, retailer of beer, Nursery.

288 SYMES, I. or J.G., surgeon.

1853/54 returned and assessed £42.
1854/55 returned £49 but no assessment made.

1854/55 marked "gone away".

289 THURNHAM, John, superintendent County Asylum.

1852/53 marked "Schedule E".
Note: Munk's Roll gives John Thurnham, craniologist and superintendent County Asylum.

290 TRUMAN, William, innkeeper. [by comparison, King's Arms]

1849/50-1850/51 assessed in absence of return £75; exempt.

1850/51 marked "Gilbert, Henry now Truman".
1853/54 marked "Wild, Edwin, late Trueman (sic), innkeeper".
Cross references: Gilbert, Henry, innkeeper, Week; Wild, Edwin, innkeeper, Week,

291 TURNPIKE TRUST, COMMISSIONERS OF, rent of tolls.

1852/53 [Benjamin Palmer, rent of tolls] "gone now Commissioners of Trust".
1854/55-1857/58 recorded but no assessments made.
1855/56 marked "Return called for - returned under Schedule B" (in St.John deleted).
1857/58 marked "charged under A & B".
Cross reference: Palmer, Benjamin, rent of tolls, Week.

292 TYLEE, John & Thomas P., brewers.

1842/43 returned and assessed £1350.

Pigot & Co"s Directory, 1842: Tylee & Co., brewers, maltsters, Northgate Street; and East Lavington.

293 VINE, John, bailiff.

1853/54 returned £65 but no assessment made.

1853/54-1854/55 marked "Schedule E".

294 WADWORTH, William, cheese factor.

1849/50-1850/51 returned and assessed £50.

Cross reference: Wadworth, William John, baker, pig killer, St Mary.

295 WAYLEN, Edward, clergyman.

1847/48 assessed in absence of return £110; exempt.

296 WEBB, John, innkeeper.

1842/43 assessed in absence of return £60; exempt.

Pigot & Co"s Directory, 1842: John Webb, retailer of beer, Bath Road.

297 WELLS, Joseph.

1846/47 name only entered and deleted.

298 WEST, Henry, innkeeper, British Lion.

1859/60 no assessment, marked "charged in Bedborough".
Cross reference: West, Henry, innkeeper, Bedborough.

299 WHEELER, Thomas, gardener.

1842/43, 1846/47-1849/50 assessed in absence of return £50; exempt.

Pigot & Co"s Directory, 1842: Thomas Wheeler, market gardener, Pan's Lane.

300 WHITE, John, bacon factor.

1842/43 returned and assessed £20; exempt.
1846/47-1849/50 assessed in absence of return £20; exempt.

Pigot & Co"s Directory, 1842: John White, cheese & bacon factor, Green.

301 WHITE, Mary, innkeeper.

1849/50 assessed in absence of return £60; exempt.

302 WILD, Edwin, innkeeper, King's Arms.

1853/54 assessed in absence of return £100; income proved at £75; exempt.
1854/55 assessed in absence of return £75; income proved at £70; exempt.
1855/56 assessed in absence of return £70; exempt.

1856/57-1857/58 recorded; no assessments made; exempt.

1853/54 marked "late Trueman (*sic*), innkeeper.
1856/57 King's Arms noted.
1858/59 marked "Kings Arms House taken down".
Cross references: Gilbert, Henry, innkeeper, Week; Truman, William, innkeeper, Week.

303 WINTERSON, William, gardener.

1842/43, 1846/47-1849/50 assessed in absence of return £60; exempt.

Pigot & Co"s Directory, 1842: William Winterson, market gardener, Bath Road or Wick.

304 WINTERSON, William, Junior, gardener.

1842/43, 1846/47-1849/50 assessed in absence of return £80; exempt.

Pigot & Co"s Directory, 1842: William Winterson, market gardener, Bath Road or Wick.

305 WITHINGTON, W.B., Baptist Minister.

1842/43 returned and assessed £100; exempt.
1846/47-1847/48 assessed in absence of return £100; exempt.
1853/54-1855/56 assessed in absence of return £40; exempt.

1848/49-1852/53 no assessments made.
1857/58, 1858/59 marked "dead".

306 WOODMAN, John, bricklayer.

1842/43 returned £30; assessed £120; income proved at £80; exempt.

1842/43 no appeal noted.

WEST LAVINGTON

307 BAKER, George & Joseph, blacksmiths, shopkeepers. [also BAKER, George Joseph]

1842/43 returned and assessed £62.10.5; exempt.
1846/47-1848/49 assessed in absence of return £62; exempt.
1849/50 assessed in absence of return £60; exempt.

1842/43, 1846/47-1847/48 George & Joseph Baker; 1848/49-1849/50 George Joseph Baker. 1842/43, 1846/47 blacksmiths & shopkeepers; 1847/48 blacksmiths, etc; 1848/49-1849/50 blacksmith.

308 BAKER, James, beerhouse keeper, innkeeper, Wheatsheaf.

1842/43 returned and assessed £56; exempt.
1846/47-1848/49 assessed in absence of return £56; exempt.
1849/50 assessed in absence of return £50; exempt.
1853/54 assessed in absence of return £120.

1842/43, 1846/47-1849/50 beerhouse keeper; 1853/54 innkeeper.
1850/51-1852/53 no assessments made.
1852/53 marked "Hazell, John now Baker, James".
1854/55-1859/60 marked "return at" or "charged at Littleton (Pannell)".
1858/59 [1856/57 Littleton Pannell] Wheatsheaf noted.
Pigot & Co"s Directory, 1842: James Baker, retailer of beer, grocer & dealer in sundries, West Lavington.
Cross references: Baker, James, innkeeper, Littleton Pannell; Hazell, John, innkeeper, West Lavington.

309 BAKER, Joseph, grocer & mealman.

1853/54 returned and assessed £50; exempt.
1854/55-1855/56 assessed in absence of return £50; exempt.
1856/57-1859/60 recorded; no assessments made; exempt.

310 BAKER, William, mealman.

1842/43 returned £66; assessed £80; exempt.
1846/47-1849/50 assessed in absence of return £70; exempt.

Pigot & Co"s Directory, 1842: William Baker, mealman, Littleton.

311 BLAKE, Christopher, grocer, builder, carpenter, assistant overseer. [also BLAKE, Robert]

1852/53 returned £35gb, £16a; assessed £51; income proved at £83; exempt.
1853/54 returned and assessed £51gb; exempt.
1854/55-1855/56 assessed in absence of return £60; exempt.
1856/57-1859/60 recorded; no assessments made; exempt.

Abbreviations: a, assistant overseer; gb, grocer & builder.
1852/53-1854/55 Robert Blake; 1855/56-1859/60 Christopher Blake.
1852/53-1853/54 grocer & builder, assistant overseer; 1854/55 grocer & builder;

1855/56-1859/60 grocer & carpenter.
1855/56 Robert Blake deleted, Christopher Blake substituted.

312 BLAKE, William, carpenter.

1842/43 returned and assessed £20; exempt.
1846/47-1849/50 assessed in absence of return £50; exempt.

Pigot & Co"s Directory, 1842: William Blake, carpenter & wheelwright, West Lavington.

313 BLAKEMORE, Frederick, innkeeper, Churchill Arms.

1849/50 assessed in absence of return £60; exempt.

1849/50 marked "Blakemore, Frederick late Rumble (*sic*) innkeeper".
1850/51 marked "Staples, John late Rumbold innkeeper.
Cross references: House, Sarah, innkeeper, West Lavington; Rumbold, William, innkeeper, West
    Lavington; Staples, John, innkeeper, West Lavington.

314 BOX, John, maltster.

1842/43 returned and assessed £30; exempt.
1846/47-1849/50 assessed in absence of return £30; exempt.

315 BUTCHER, George, mealman [by comparison, Cornbury Mill].

1842/43 returned and assessed £80; exempt.
1846/47-1850/51 assessed in absence of return £80; exempt.
1851/52-1852/53 returned and assessed £80; exempt.
1853/54 returned £76; assessed £100.
1854/55 returned £75; assessed £100.

1855/56, 1856/57 marked "now Joseph Webb, mealman".
[1856/57 Webb, Joseph noted at Cornbury Mill]
Pigot & Co"s Directory, 1842: George Butcher, miller, Cornbury Mill, West Lavington.
Cross reference: Webb, Joseph, miller, West Lavington.

316 BUTCHER, Thomas, miller.

1852/53 assessed in absence of return £150 but deleted.

317 CAMERON, Revd. J[onathan] H. L[ovett], private tutor.

1847/48-1851/52 returned and assessed £150.

1850/51 marked "to be written to".

318 CASWELL, -, Revd.

1846/47 name only entered and deleted.
Pigot & Co"s Directory, 1842: Revd. Robert Casewell, clergy, West Lavington.

319 CHAPMAN, John & William, millers, Garretts Mill. [also CHAPMAN, John]

Partnership

1842/43 returned and assessed £52.10.0 each; exempt.
1846/47 returned and assessed £51.15.0 each; John Chapman exempt.
1847/48 returned and assessed £60 each; John Chapman exempt.
1848/49 returned and assessed £70 John Chapman; exempt; assessed in absence of re-
    turn £70 William Chapman; exempt.
1849/50 returned and assessed £72 John Chapman; exempt; assessed in absence of re-
    turn £70 William Chapman; exempt.
1850/51 assessed in absence of return £70 each; exempt.
1851/52 returned and assessed £70 John Chapman; exempt; assessed in absence of re-
    turn £70 William Chapman; exempt.

John Chapman sole

1852/53 returned and assessed £70; exempt.
1853/54 returned and assessed £82; exempt.
1854/55 returned £40; assessed £100.
1855/56 assessed in absence of return £100.
1856/57 assessed in absence of return £150; reduced to £120 on appeal.
1857/58 assessed in absence of return £120.
1858/59 returned £100; assessed £120.
1859/60 returned £100; assessed £120.

1852/53 William Chapman deleted; John Chapman marked "who carried on business".
1853/54 marked "Garretts Mill".

320 COLEMAN, Mary, innkeeper. [by comparison, Black Dog] [also COLEMAN, Robert]

1842/43 returned and assessed £60; exempt.
1846/47-1847/48 assessed in absence of return £60; exempt.

1848/49-1849/50 assessed in absence of return £60; income proved at £80; exempt.
1851/52 assessed in absence of return £60; income proved at £110; exempt.
1852/53-1853/54 assessed in absence of return £60; exempt.

1842/43 Robert Coleman; 1846/47-1849/50 Mrs.Coleman; 1851/52-1853/54 Mary
    Coleman.
1850/51 no assessment made.
1854/55 marked "Whatley, Stephen late Coleman".
Pigot & Co"s Directory, 1842: Robert Coleman, Black Dog, West Lavington.
Cross reference: Whatley, Stephen, innkeeper, West Lavington.

321 DRAPER, Philip, grocer & baker.

1853/54 returned £50; assessed £120; reduced to £70.
1854/55 returned £55; assessed £120.
1855/56 assessed in absence of return £120.
1856/57 returned £70; assessed £120.
1857/58 returned £62; assessed £120.
1858/59 returned £60; assessed £120.
1859/60 returned £90; assessed £120.

1853/54 no appeal noted.
1859/60 marked "life insurance £36".

322 DUNFORD, William & James, brickmakers. [also DUNFORD, Thomas]

Sole

1842/43 assessed in absence of return £150.
1846/47 returned £60; assessed £130; reduced to £90 on appeal.
1847/48 returned £65; assessed £90.
1848/49 returned £50; assessed £90; exempt.
1849/50-1852/53 assessed in absence of return £90; exempt.
1853/54 assessed in absence of return £110; exempt.

Partnership

1854/55-1855/56 assessed in absence of return £75 each; James Dunford exempt.
1856/57 assessed in absence of return £75 James Dunford; exempt on appeal; returned
    £50 William Dunford; assessed £75.
1857/58-1859/60 James Dunford recorded; no assessments made; exempt.
1857/58 returned £70 William Dunford; assessed £75.
1858/59-1859/60 returned and assessed £75 William Dunford.

1842/43, 1846/47-1852/53 Thomas Dunford; 1853/54 James Dunford; 1854/55-1859/60
    William & James Dunford.

1853/54 entry reads Thomas (deleted) William (deleted) & James Dunford.
1854/55 composite assessment on partnership deleted; assessments made on individuals (1857/58 bracketed together).
1854/55-1855/56 Durnford.
Cross reference: Dunford, Thomas, brickmaker, Cheverell Magna.

323 FARMER, James, butcher.

1851/52 returned £50 but entry deleted.

324 GIDDINGS, James, shopkeeper.

1842/43, 1846/47-1849/50 assessed in absence of return £30; exempt.

Pigot & Co"s Directory, 1842: James Giddings, grocer & dealer in sundries.

325 GILES, James, harness maker.

1842/43 returned and assessed £40; exempt.
1846/47-1849/50 assessed in absence of return £40; exempt.

Pigot & Co"s Directory, 1842: James Giles, saddler, Littleton.

326 HAZELL, John, innkeeper, Wheatsheaf.

1842/43 returned and assessed £40; exempt.
1846/47-1847/48 assessed in absence of return £80; exempt.
1848/49-1850/51 assessed in absence of return £100; exempt.
1851/52 assessed in absence of return £150; reduced to £100; exempt.
1852/53 returned and assessed £120; assessment discharged on appeal but no sum recorded.

1851/52 no appeal noted (Statutorily an appeal had to be made to displace an assessment of £150).
1852/53 marked "Hazell, John now Baker, James".
Pigot & Co"s Directory, 1842: John Hazell, innkeeper, Wheat Sheaf, Littleton.
Cross reference: Baker, James, innkeeper, West Lavington.

327 HITCHCOCK, Charles, lunatic asylum. [Fiddington House]

1851/52 returned and assessed £1000.
1852/53 returned £500; assessed £1000.
1853/54 returned and assessed £750.

1854/55 returned £377.2.3; assessed £750.
1855/56 returned £500; assessed £600.
1856/57 returned £310; assessed £600; reduced to £380 on appeal.
1857/58 returned £155; assessed £250.
1858/59 returned and assessed £312.11.0.
1859/60 returned £320.12.0; assessed £400.

1851/52-1852/53 marked "late Willett, lunatic asylum".
Note: Between 1853/54 and 1857/58 Hitchcock was also assessed separately in West Lavington on profits as a surgeon. This related to a partnership in Market Lavington where the other partners were assessed. Hitchcock, however, had to be assessed at his place of residence, seemingly in West Lavington. But in order to reflect the integrity of the medical partnership his assessments as a surgeon have been recorded in Market Lavington.
Cross references: Hitchcock, Charles, surgeon, Market Lavington; Willett, Robert, lunatic asylum, West Lavington.

328 HOUSE, Sarah, innkeeper, [by comparison, Churchill Arms].

1842/43 returned and assessed £45; exempt.
1846/47 assessed in absence of return £45; exempt.

Pigot & Co"s Directory, 1842: Sarah House, Churchill Arms, West Lavington.
Cross references: Blakemore, Frederick, innkeeper, West Lavington; Rumbold, William, innkeeper, West Lavington; Staples, John, innkeeper, West Lavington.

329 HOWELL, Thomas, tailor & draper.

1853/54-1855/56 assessed in absence of return £50; exempt.
1856/57-1859/60 recorded; no assessments made; exempt.

1853/54-1854/55 Howle; 1855/56-1859/60 Howell.

330 INGRAM, James, baker.

1842/43 returned and assessed £50; exempt.
1846/47-1849/50 assessed in absence of return £50; exempt.

Pigot & Co"s Directory, 1842: James Ingram, baker, West Lavington.

331 KELSEY, Edw[ard] Edm[und] Peach, land agent.

1856/57 assessed in absence of return £240; reduced to £170 on appeal.

1856/57 F.James Kelsey entered but deleted; Edw. Edm. Peach Kelsey substituted.
1857/58 marked "pays in Salisbury".

1858/59-1859/60 marked "returns at Salisbury".
Cross reference: Kelsey, F.James, land agent, West Lavington.

332 KELSEY, F. James, land agent.

1851/52 returned and assessed £240.
1852/53 returned and assessed £220.
1853/54 returned £267.15.6 less £64.8.4 life insurance; estimated at £400 but reduced to £203.7.2.
1854/55 assessed in absence of return £400; reduced to £267.15.6.
1855/56 returned and assessed £240.

1853/54-1854/55 no appeal noted.
1856/57 entry deleted and Edw. Edm. Peach Kelsey substituted.
Pigot & Co"s Directory, 1842: F.J.Kelsey, land agent, West Lavington (H)ouse.
Cross reference: Kelsey, Edward Edmund Peach, land agent, West Lavington.

333 MEAD, Daniel, maltster & beerhouse keeper.

1842/43 returned and assessed £55; exempt.
1846/47-1847/48 assessed in absence of return £55; exempt.
1848/49-1849/50 assessed in absence of return £55; income proved at £40; exempt.

Pigot & Co"s Directory, 1842: Daniel Mead, retailer of beer, West Lavington.

334 MEAD, Edmund, maltster.

1842/43 returned and assessed £45; exempt.
1846/47-1849/50 assessed in absence of return £45; exempt.

335 NEWMAN, Thomas, mealman.

1842/43 returned £100; assessed £200.

1846/47 estimate of £150 deleted.

336 OATLEY, Daniel, builder, etc.

1854/55-1857/58 assessed in absence of return £75.
1858/59 returned £50; assessed £75.
1859/60 returned £40; assessed £75.

Pigot & Co"s Directory, 1842: Daniel Oatley, tiler & plasterer, Littleton.
Cross reference: Oatley, Daniel, builder, Worton.

337 PRICE, William, miller.

1846/47 assessed in absence of return £50; exempt.
1847/48-1849/50 assessed in absence of return £80; exempt.

338 RUMBOLD, William, innkeeper. [by comparison, Churchill Arms]

1847/48-1848/49 assessed in absence of return £20; exempt.

1847/48 Rumble; 1848/49 Rumbold.
1849/50 marked "Blakemore, Frederick late Rumble.
Cross references: Blakemore, Frederick, innkeeper, West Lavington; House, Sarah, innkeeper,
    West Lavington; Staples, John, innkeeper, West Lavington.

339 SAINSBURY, John, timber dealer, wheelwright. [also SAINSBURY, James]

Partnership

1842/43 James Sainsbury returned £25; assessed £50; confirmed on appeal. John
    Sainsbury assessed in absence of return £50; confirmed on appeal.

John Sainsbury sole

1846/47 returned £75; reduced to £70 on appeal.
1847/48 assessed in absence of return £120.
1848/49 returned £80; assessed £120; exempt.
1849/50-1850/51 assessed in absence of return £120; exempt.

1842/43 timber dealers & wheelwrights; 1847/48 timber dealer, etc.
Pigot & Co"s Directory, 1842: James Sainsbury, timber merchant, West Lavington.

340 SHORE, Thomas, carpenter.

1846/47 returned and assessed £35; exempt.
1847/48 assessed in absence of return £35; exempt.
1848/49-1849/50 assessed in absence of return £35; income proved at £50; exempt.

341 STAPLES, John, butcher, innkeeper, Churchill Arms.

1850/51 assessed in absence of return £70; exempt.
1851/52 assessed in absence of return £70; income proved at £80; exempt.
1852/53 assessed in absence of return £70; exempt.
1853/54 assessed in absence of return £60; exempt.
1854/55 returned and assessed £40; exempt.

1855/56 assessed in absence of return £40; exempt.
1856/57 assessed in absence of return £120; reduced to £100 on appeal.
1857/58 assessed in absence of return £100.
1858/59 returned £50; assessed £100.
1859/60 returned £60; assessed £100.

1850/51-1855/56 innkeeper; 1856/57-1859/60 innkeeper & butcher.
1850/51 marked "late Rumbold, innkeeper".
1856/57 Churchill Arms noted.
Cross references: Blakemore, Frederick, innkeeper, West Lavington; House, Sarah, innkeeper, West Lavington; Rumbold, William, innkeeper, West Lavington.

342 WEBB, James, miller.

1849/50 £13.10.0 interest assessed by General Commissioners.
1850/51 returned £50; £62.13.4 and £13.10.0 interest assessed by General Commissioners; income proved at £62 and £4.10.0 interest; £9 left in charge.
1851/52 assessed in absence of return £70; income proved at £70; exempt; £13.10.0 interest left in charge.
1852/53 assessed in absence of return £90; exempt.
1853/54 assessed in absence of return £100; income proved at £90; exempt.
1854/55-1855/56 assessed in absence of return £100.

1849/50 charged by additional assessment.
1854/55 assessment later discharged; double assessment, charged in Great Cheverell.
1856/57 marked "gone to Great Cheverell".
Cross reference: Webb, James, miller, Cheverell Magna.

343 WEBB, Joseph, miller, Cornbury Mill.

1856/57 returned £40; assessed £100; reduced to £90 on appeal.
1857/58 assessed in absence of return £90; reduced to £70.
1858/59 returned £30; assessed £80.
1859/60 returned £70; assessed £100.

1856/57 Cornbury Mill noted.
1858/59 marked "Jn?".
Cross reference: Butcher, George, mealman, West Lavington.

344 WHATLEY, Stephen, innkeeper, Black Dog.

1854/55 returned £25; assessed £60; exempt.
1855/56 assessed in absence of return £60.
1856/57 returned £24; assessed £60.
1857/58 returned £20; assessed £60.
1858/59-1859/60 returned £25; assessed £60.

1854/55 marked "late Coleman".
1858/59 Black Dog noted.
Cross reference: Coleman, Mary, innkeeper, West Lavington.

345 WILKINSON, Revd.Dr.John, private tutor.

1853/54 assessed in absence of return £586.
1854/55 returned and assessed £405.11.3.

1852/53 recorded and marked "not liable till 1855".
1855/56 Revd. John Wilkinson deleted, Revd. Matthew Wilkinson substituted.
Cross references: Wilkinson, Revd. John, tutor, Worton; Wilkinson, Revd. Matthew, private tutor, West Lavington.

346 WILKINSON, Revd.Matthew, private tutor.

1855/56 returned and assessed £506.
1856/57 returned and assessed £419.
1857/58 returned and assessed £578.14.0.
1858/59 returned and assessed £316.
1859/60 returned and assessed £387.15.0.

1855/56 Revd. John Wilkinson deleted, Revd. Matthew Wilkinson substituted.
Cross reference: Wilkinson, Revd.Dr.John, private tutor, West Lavington.

347 WILLETT, Robert, professional engagements, lunatic asylum. [also WILLETT & HOOD]

1846/47 returned £500; assessed £750.
1847/48 returned £500; assessed £850.
1848/49 assessed in absence of return £850.
1849/50 returned and assessed £850.
1850/51 assessed in absence of return £1000.

1846/47-1847/48 Robert Willett; 1848/49-1849/50 Executors of Robert Willett; 1850/51 Willett & Hood.
1846/47 professional engagements; 1847/48-1850/51 lunatic asylum.
1846/47 marked "Return vide Phillips return".
1851/52 marked "Hitchcock late Willett (& Hood deleted)".
Cross references: Hitchcock, Charles, lunatic asylum & surgeon, West Lavington; Willett, Robert, asylum keeper, Market Lavington.

348 WILTON, Revd.Edward, schoolmaster, officiating minister.

1848/49 returned and assessed £259.
1849/50-1851/52 returned and assessed £244.

1852/53 returned and assessed £240.
1853/54-1854/55 assessed in absence of return £240.
1855/56 returned and assessed £240.
1856/57 assessed in absence of return £240.
1857/58 returned and assessed £240.
1858/59 assessed in absence of return £240.
1859/60 returned and assessed £240.

1848/49-1850/51 schoolmaster, etc.; 1851/52-1855/56 schoolmaster;
1856/57-1859/60 schoolmaster & officiating minister.
1858/59 £261.3.7 entered but deleted; marked "as last year".
Pigot & Co"s Directory, 1842: Revd. Edward Wilton, clergy, master, Free School, West
    Lavington.
Cross reference: Wilton, Revd.E., clergyman & schoolmaster, Littleton Pannell.

WORTON

349 BAKER, William, mealman, miller. [by comparison, Hurst Mill]

1851/52 returned and assessed £69; exempt.
1852/53 returned and assessed £76.13.0; exempt.
1853/54 returned £67.10.0; assessed 70; exempt.
1853/54 assessed in absence of return £100 as miller.

1851/52-1852/53 mealman; 1853/54 assessments made separately as mealman and miller, sug-
    gesting two different people, especially as exemption was claimed as a mealman but tax paid
    as a miller. However, a note is recorded in 1854/55 that they are the "same person".
1850/51 marked "Chandler, George now Wm.Baker".
1851/52 marked "late Chandler".
1854/55 estimate of £150 deleted, marked "gone to Malmesbury, return there".
Cross reference: Chandler, George, mealman, Worton; Nutfield, John & George, millers, Worton;
    Sainsbury, William & John, millers, Worton.

350 BIGGS, Joseph, beerhouse keeper. [also BIGGS, John]

1854/55 returned £15; assessed £50; exempt.
1855/56 assessed in absence of return £50; exempt.
1856/57 returned £15; no assessment made; exempt.
1857/58 returned £12; no assessment made; exempt.
1858/59 returned £15; no assessment made; exempt.
1859/60 recorded; no assessment made; exempt.

1854/55 John Biggs; 1855/56-1859/60 Joseph Biggs.

351 BISHOP, John, publican, innkeeper.

1842/43, 1846/47-1850/51 assessed in absence of return £40; exempt.
1851/52 assessed in absence of return £40; income proved at £101.15.0.

1842/43 publican; 1846/47-1851/52 innkeeper.

352 BISHOP, Vincent, farmer, innkeeper, Royal Oak.

1852/53 returned £5; assessed £40; income proved at £95.
1853/54 returned £5; assessed £50; exempt.
1854/55 returned £5; assessed £50.
1855/56 assessed in absence of return £50.
1856/57 returned £20; assessed £50.
1857/58 returned £30; assessed £50.
1858/59 returned £40; assessed £50.
1859/60 returned £20; assessed £50.

1852/53-1857/58 Vincent Bishop; 1858/59-1859/60 Vince Bishop.
1852/53-1856/57 innkeeper & farmer; 1857/58-1859/60 innkeeper.
1858/59 Royal Oak noted.

353 BRIGGS, George, corn dealer.

1842/43 returned £100; assessed £200; income proved at £100; no appeal noted.

354 CHANDLER, George, mealman, Hurst Mill.

1842/43 returned and assessed £150.
1846/47-1848/49 returned £150; assessed £175.
1849/50 assessed in absence of return £175.
1850/51 returned and assessed £100; exempt.

1850/51 marked "now William Baker".
Pigot & Co"s Directory, 1842: George Chandler, miller, Hurst Mill.
Cross reference: Baker, William, mealman, Worton; Nutfield, John & George, millers, Worton; Sainsbury, William & John, millers, Worton.

355 COOPER, Isaac, innkeeper.

1851/52 assessed in absence of return £75; exempt.
1852/53 returned £20; assessed £75; exempt.

1851/52 marked "late Wise".
Cross reference: Wise, James, innkeeper, Worton.

356 DOWSE, George, mealman.

1842/43 returned and assessed £110.
1846/47 returned £130; assessed £150.
1847/48 returned £150; assessed £225.
1848/49 returned £100; assessed £225.
1849/50–1850/51 assessed in absence of return £350.
1851/52 assessed in absence of return £150; reduced to £100 on appeal; exempt.
1852/53 assessed in absence of return £100; exempt.
1853/54 returned £100; assessed £120.
1854/55 assessed in absence of return £120.

1855/56 marked "q. who now occupies".

357 DOWSE, Philip, baker, maltster.

1842/43 returned and assessed £80; exempt.

1842/43 baker; 1846/47 baker & maltster entered but deleted.

358 GOODALL, Hezekiah, brickmaker.

1857/58 returned £13; assessed £25.
1858/59 estimated £25 but deleted.
1859/60 recorded; no assessment made; exempt.

359 HOOKS, Joseph, miller.

1859/60 returned £77; assessed £120.

360 MASON, Robert Monck, tutor, allowance.

1852/53 returned and assessed £75 tutor, £25 allowance.

1852/53 marked "gone to Clapham?".
1853/54 tutor only noted; no assessment made.
1854/55 marked "gone away".

361 NUTFIELD, John & George, millers, Hurst Mill.

1858/59 John Nutfield assessed in absence of return £100.
1858/59 George Nutfield returned £40; assessed £100.
1859/60 John Nutfield returned £40; assessed £100.

1859/60 George Nutfield assessed in absence of return £100.

1858/59 marked "Sainsbury, William & John now Nutfield, John & George, millers".
1858/59 marked re George Nutfield "claims separate assessment".
1859/60 Nutland.
Note: in Pigot & Co's Trade Directory of 1842 the occupier of Hurst Mill was George Chandler.
Cross references: Baker, William, miller, Worton; Chandler, George, miller, Worton; Sainsbury, William & John, millers, Worton.

362 OATLEY, Daniel, builder.

1853/54 assessed in absence of return £40; exempt.

1854/55 marked "charged before".
Cross reference: Oatley, Daniel, builder, West Lavington.

363 PARRY, G.H., Esquire.

1850/51 name entered and deleted.

364 ROSE, Job, maltster, innkeeper, Rose & Crown.

1853/54 returned £42.12.6; assessed £80; exempt.
1854/55 assessed in absence of return £60; exempt.
1856/57 returned £50; assessed £67.
1857/58 returned £30; assessed £67.
1858/59-1859/60 assessed in absence of return £67.

1853/54-1855/56 maltster; 1856/57-1859/60 maltster & innkeeper.
1855/56 no assessment made; marked "returned in Marston".
1858/59 Rose & Crown noted.
Cross references: Rose, Job, beerhouse keeper & maltster, Marston; Smith, Knightley, innkeeper, Marston.

365 SAINSBURY, William & John, millers, Hurst Mill.

1854/55 returned £100; assessed £200.
1855/56 returned £85; assessed £200.
1856/57 returned £100; assessed £200.
1857/58 assessed in absence of return £200.

1854/55 Hurst Mill noted.
1857/58 marked "left 24 June 1857".
1858/59 marked "now Nutfield, John & George, millers".

Note: in Pigot & Co's Trade Directory of 1842 the occupier of Hurst Mill is George Chandler. Cross references: Baker, William, miller, Worton; Chandler, George, miller, Worton; Nutfield, John & George, millers, Worton.

366 SMITH, Knightley, innkeeper. [by comparison, Rose & Crown]

1853/54 returned and assessed £43.10.0; exempt.
1854/55-1855/56 assessed in absence of return £43; exempt.

1856/57-1857/58 marked "now Rose".
Cross reference: Rose, Job, innkeeper, Worton.

367 STAPLES, William, innkeeper, butcher, beerhouse keeper, builder, carpenter. [also STAPLES, John]

1853/54 returned and assessed £60; exempt.
1854/55-1855/56 assessed in absence of return £60; exempt.
1856/57-1859/60 recorded; no assessments made; exempt.

1853/54 John Staples; 1854/55-1859/60 William Staples.
1853/54-1854/55 innkeeper & butcher; 1855/56 innkeeper & builder; 1856/57-1859/60 beerhouse keeper & carpenter.

368 WILKINSON, Revd. John. tutor.

1853/54 returned £526.1.3 but no assessment made.

Cross reference: Wilkinson, Revd.John, private tutor, West Lavington.

369 WISE, James, innkeeper.

1842/43 returned and assessed £100; exempt.
1846/47-1848/49 assessed in absence of return £90; exempt.
1849/50-1850/51 assessed in absence of return £80; exempt.

1851/52 Isaac Cooper substituted; marked "late Wise".
Cross reference: Cooper, Isaac, innkeeper, Worton.

DEVIZES ST. JOHN

370 A [illeg], W.J.B.

1848/49 name only entered.

371 ABRAHAM, George, hair dresser.

1846/47-1849/50 assessed in absence of return £50; exempt.

372 ALEXANDER, Alfred, New Prison.

1854/55-1855/56 noted as assessed under Schedule E.

Cross reference: Haywood, Thomas, Governor of New Prison, St.John.

373 ANDERSON, Thomas Watson, solicitors clerk.

1853/54-1855/56 returned and assessed at £120.
1856/57 returned £99, assessed £100, reduced to £99 on appeal; exempt.

1857/58 marked "gone".
1856/57 is an example of an early form of tax avoidance. On incomes of £100, tax was payable
on the whole amount. Incomes below this sum were eligible to be wholly relieved on a
claim for exemption. By agreeing with the employer to fix the salary at £99, the taxpayer
would be better off by £3.15.10. (following evidence taken before the Select Committee
on the Income and Property Tax, House of Commons. Parliamentary Papers. (1852) ix
qq.3019, 3235).
1852/53 marked "removed to Southampton".
Cross reference: (similar instance of early legal tax avoidance) Thorp, Thomas Glossop, surveyor's
clerk, Bedborough; Coxhead, W.P., schoolmaster, St. John.

374 ANSTIE, George Washington, farmer.

1842/43 entered and deleted.

Cross reference: Anstie, George Washington, solicitor, St. Mary.

375 ANSTIE, PAUL & EDWARD, tobacco & snuff manufacturers. [also ANSTIE, Benjamin]

Year	Amount returned £	Commissioners' estimate £	Final assessment £
1842/43	562	562	562
1846/47	1026	1026	1026
1847/48	1026	1026	1026
1848/49	1353	1353	1353
1849/50	1403	1403	1403
1850/51	1522	1522	1522
1851/52	2039	2039	2039
1852/53	2026	2026	2026
1853/54	1931	1931	1931
1854/55	1473	1473	1473
1855/56	1235	1235	1235
1856/57	1309	1309	1309
1857/58	1604	1604	1604
1858/59	2064	2064	2064
1859/60	2868	2868	2868

1842/43 Benjamin & Paul Anstie assessed.
Pigot & Co's Directory, 1842: Benjamin & Paul Anstie, tobacco & snuff manufacturers, Market Place.

376 ANSTIE, Thomas Brown, surgeon, etc., apothecary

1848/49 returned and assessed £305
1849/50 returned and assessed £355
1850/51 returned and assessed £360
1851/52 returned and assessed £320
1852/53 returned and assessed £350 + £20 interest

1848/49 surgeon & apothecary.
1853/54-1855/56 marked "returned in St. Mary".
Cross reference: Anstie, Thomas Browne (sic), surgeon, St. Mary.

377 BALL, James, tea dealer, etc. [also BALL, Thomas]

1842/43 returned and assessed £240.
1846/47-1848/49 returned £200 but assessed at £240.
1849/50 assessed in absence of return £240.

1849/50 Thomas Ball assessed.
1850/51 marked "Simpson late Ball, grocer".

Pigot & Co's Directory, 1842: James Ball, grocer & tea dealer, Brittox.
Cross reference: Simpson, Edward, grocer, St.John.

378 BARLOW, George, corndealer.

1853/54 returned and assessed £80.
1854/55-1855/56 returned £80 but assessed at £100.
1856/57-1859/60 returned and assessed £100.

379 BARRY, Henry George, innkeeper, spirit merchant, Dolphin. [also BARRY, William H]

Year	Amount returned	Commissioners' estimate	Income proved	Final assessment
	£	£	£	£
1850/51	–	50	50	–
1851/52	–	75	96.6.11	–
1852/53	91.12.8	–	105	–
1853/54	82.13.0	91.12.8	91.12.8	–
1854/55	–	100	–	100
1855/56	–	100	–	100
1856/57	100	–	–	100
1857/58	100	120	–	120
1858/59	100	120	–	120
1859/60	100	120	–	120

1850/51 William H Barry assessed.
1850/51-1855/56 innkeeper.
1856/57 Dolphin noted.
1856/57-1859/60 spirit merchant.

380 BARTON, Henry, shopkeeper & baker.

1842/43 returned and assessed £140; exempt.
1846/47-1848/49 assessed in absence of return £140; exempt.
1849/50 assessed in absence of return £40; exempt.

Pigot & Co's Directory, 1842: Henry Barton, baker, Bridewell Street.

381 BASTER, William, Sack Office keeper, saddler, etc. [also BASTER, Elizabeth]

1842/43 assessed in absence of return £150; reduced on appeal to £94; exempt.
1846/47-1853/54 assessed in absence of return £60; exempt.

1854/55 assessed in absence of return £50; exempt.
1855/56-1859/60 recorded; no assessments made; exempt.

1842/43 Sack Office keeper & saddler.
1855/56-1859/60 Elizabeth Baster.
Pigot & Co's Directory, 1842: William Baster, saddler & harness maker, officer Sack Office,
St.John Street.

382 BATT, Moses, horse dealer.

1846/47-1848/49 assessed in absence of return £50; exempt.

383 BAYES, Frederick William, surgeon, officer.

1856/57 returned £110, assessed at £50.
1857/58 returned and assessed £120.

1856/57 marked "Schedule E", assessment reduced to £50.
1857/58 marked "Schedule E".
1858/59 marked "now Thornley, Robert".
Cross reference: Thornley, Robert, surgeon, St.John.

384 BAYLEY, John Raikes, solicitor.

Year	Amount returned £	Commissioners' estimate £	Final assessment £
1848/49	720	720	720
1849/50	730	730	730
1850/51	450	450	450
1851/52	Special Commissioners		
1852/53	Special Commissioners		
1853/54	No assessment made		
1854/55	–	400	370
1855/56	400	400	400
1856/57	–	200deleted	–

1848/49-1850/51, 1852/53, Bayley; 1851/52, 1853/54-1856/57 Bailey, but Bayley in St. Mary.
1848/49, 1850/51 assessed under letter.
1854/55 marked "qq Special Commissioners (last year ?)"
1856/57 marked "now MacDonald & Olivier".
Pigot & Co's Directory, 1842: Bayly & Bayly (sic), attorneys, John Raikes Bayly (sic), agent to
Scottish Union Fire Office, High Street.
Cross references: MacDonald, Alexander & Olivier, Alfred, solicitors, St.John; Bayley, J R, solicitor, St.Mary, 1842/43, 1846/47-1849/50 name entry.

385 BENNETT, William, broker, dealer.

1847/48 returned and assessed £50; exempt.
1848/49–1849/50 assessed in absence of return £50; exempt.
1850/51–1852/53 no entries made.
1853/54 returned £52; estimate made at £62 deleted.
1854/55–1855/56 assessed in absence of return £50; exempt.
1856/57 recorded; no assessments made; exempt.
1857/58 returned £40; estimate made at £50; exempt.
1858/59–1859/60 recorded; no assessments made; exempt.

1847/48–1849/50 broker; 1853/54–1859/60 dealer.

386 BIGGS, James, grocer. [also BIGGS, Thomas]

Year	Amount returned £	Commissioners' estimate £	Final assessment £
1842/43	140	–	140
1846/47	130	150	150
1847/48	150	–	150
1848/49	150	–	150
1849/50	150	175a	150
1850/51	156	–	156
1851/52	175	–	175
1852/53	180	–	180
1853/54	200	250	201.17.3
1854/55	192	–	192
1855/56	200	–	200
1856/57	–	200	200
1857/58	210	–	210
1858/59	225	–	225
1859/60	225	–	204.12.6

1842/43 Thomas Biggs assessed.
1853/54 no appeal noted.
1859/60 assessment reduced by life assurance relief of £20.7.6
Pigot & Co's Directory, 1842: Thomas Biggs, grocer, agent to Phoenix Fire Office, Long Street.

387 BIGGS, John, tea dealer.

1842/43 assessed in absence of return £40; exempt.
1846/47–1847/48 assessed in absence of return £100; exempt.

Pigot & Co's Directory, 1842: John Biggs, tea dealer, Brittox.

388 BIGGS, Richard William, schoolmaster, interest on securities, possessions in Ireland. [also BIGGS, Richard, Senior]

Year	Amount returned £	Commissioners' estimate £	Final assessment £
Partnership			
1842/43			
Biggs, R	150	150	150
Biggs, R W	150	150	150

1842/43 marked re Richard Biggs Senior "a quarter year only".

R.W.Biggs sole

Year	Amount returned £	Commissioners' estimate £	Final assessment £
1846/47	200s 30i	–	230
1847/48	102s 10i 24bp	–	136
1848/49	70s 8i 25pI	120	153
1849/50	140s 25pI	–	165
1850/51	166s,pI	–	166
1851/52	178s 22i	–	200
1852/53	216s 42i	–	258
1853/54	223s,i	258	258
1854/55	177s,i	258	258
1855/56	130s	200	200
1856/57		200	200
1857/58	113s 16i	–	129
1858/59	75s 16i	100 –	100 16
1859/60	56s 14i	100 16	116

Abbreviations: s, schoolmaster; i, interest on securities; pI, possessions in Ireland; bp British possessions.

Richard Biggs, occasionally Richard William or Williams, Junior.

Pigot & Co's Directory, 1842: Richard W Biggs, (boarding) school, Long Street

389 BIRCH, William, horse breaker.

1842/34 returned and assessed £118; exempt.
1847/48 returned and assessed £60; exempt.
1848/49 assessed in absence of return £60; exempt.
1849/50 assessed in absence of return £60; exempt.

Pigot & Co's Directory, 1842: William Birch, livery-stable keeper, Long Street.

390 BISHOP, Thomas, plumber, glazier.

1842/43 assessed in absence of return £100; exempt.
1846/47-1848/49 assessed in absence of return £89; exempt.
1849/50 assessed in absence of return £90; exempt.
1850/51-1851/52 assessed in absence of return £120; exempt.
1852/53 returned £70; estimated at £120; assessed at £70; income proved at £116.6.0; exempt.
1853/54-1855/56 assessed in absence of return £80; exemption not claimed.
1856/57-1859/60 recorded; no assessments made; exempt.

1842/43, 1846/47-1847/48 plumber & glazier; 1848/49-1850/51 plumber, etc.;
1851/52-1859/60 plumber.
Pigot & Co's Directory, 1842: Thomas Bishop, painter, plumber & glazier, High Street.

391 BOURNE, Richard, innkeeper.

1842/43 returned and assessed £182.

Pigot & Co's Directory, 1842: Richard Bourne, White Swan, Market Place.
Cross references: Frayling, Edward, innkeeper, St.John; Jenkins, David, innkeeper, St.John; Wells, Joseph, innkeeper, St.John.

392 BOWDEN, James, butcher.

1842/43 entry only.
Pigot & Co's Directory, 1842: J. Bowden, butcher, Long Street.

393 BOWSHER, Alfred, ironmonger.

1858/59-1859/60 returned £60; estimated at £100.

1858/59 marked "in business 5 months in July".

394 BRAMBLE, J.R., surveyor.

Year	Amount returned £	Commissioners' estimate £	Final assessment £
1848/49	150	–	150
1849/50	–	200	200
1850/51	50	100	100
1851/52	120	–	120
1852/53	120	–	120
1853/54	90	–	90
1854/55	50	–	50
1855/56	10	–	10

1856/57-1858/59 marked "dead".
Pigot & Co's Directory, 1842: James Roger Bramble, agent-land, &.; Roger Bramble, surveyor, Northgate Street.
Cross reference: Bramble, J.R., land surveyor, St.Mary, 1842/43, 1846/47-1847/48.

395 BRAND, Thomas, coachman, coachmaker, coachmaster.

1849/50 recorded but no assessment made.
1852/53 returned and assessed £125; exempt.
1853/54 estimated in absence of return £125; assessed at £100.
1854/55 returned and assessed £100.
1855/56 estimated in absence of return £150, amended to £100.
1856/57 assessed in absence of return £100.
1857/58 returned and assessed £100.

1849/50 coachman; 1852/53 coachman and lodger; 1853/54-1855/56 coachman, etc.; 1856/57-1857/58 coachmaster.
1857/58 marked "gone away".

396 BRIDGES, Fitzherbert, chemist.

No assessment made. Mentioned only in notes as successor to Bayntun Johnstone, and predecessor of Henry Cripps, 1852/53.
Cross references: Cripps, Henry, chemist, St.John; Hayward, Robert, chemist, St.John; Johnstone, Bayntun, chemist, St.John.

397 BROWN, Thomas, innkeeper, Antelope.

1857/58 by note "McEwen late see Thomas Brown".
1857/58 by note "Humby, Frederick Peter, Antelope, now Thomas Brown".
1858/59 marked "late Humby, Antelope".
No assessments made.

Cross references: Humby, Frederick Peter, innkeeper, St.John; McEwin, Edwin, innkeeper, St.John; Ransom, William, innkeeper, St.John.

398 BUCKLAND, Maria Grace, schoolmistress.

1853/54-1855/56 assessed in absence of return £50; exempt.
1856/57-1859/60 recorded but no assessment made; exempt.

399 BULL, Edwin, victualler, Duke of Wellington. [also BULL, Margaret]

1847/48 returned and assessed £40; exempt.
1848/49 returned and assessed £60; exempt.
1849/50-1852/53 assessed in absence of return £60; exempt.
1853/54 returned £50; estimated at £60 but no assessment made.
1854/55-1855/56 assessed in absence of return £60; exempt.
1856/57-1859/60 recorded; no assessments made; exempt.

1856/57 noted "Duke of Wellington".
1847/48-1858/59 Edwin Bull; 1859/60 Margaret Bull.

400 BULL, Henry, bookseller, printer.

1842/43 returned and assessed £150.
1846/47-1847/48 returned £150; assessed at £200.
1848/49 assessed in absence of return £200.
1849/50 returned £150; assessed at £200.
1850/51 assessed in absence of return £200; on appeal assessment discharged but no figure recorded; exempt.
1851/52 assessed in absence of return £150.
1852/53-1859/60 returned and assessed £150.

1849/50-1850/51 bookseller, etc.; 1851/52-1855/56 bookseller; 1842/43, 1846/47-1848/49, 1856/57-1859/60 bookseller & printer.
Pigot & Co's Directory, 1842: Henry Bull, bookseller, stationer & printer, library, St.John Street.

401 BULL, Mary & Fanny, milliners & dressmakers.

Year	Amount returned	Commissioners' estimate	Income proved	Final assessment
	£	£	£	£
1842/43	200	–	–	200
1846/47	150	–	–	150
1847/48	150	–	–	150
1848/49	–	150	–	150

1849/50	150	–	–	150
1850/51	–	150a	150	–
1851/52	–	150	75	75
1852/53	150	–	75	75
1853/54	100	150	75	75
1854/55	75	150	75	75
1855/56	100	–	–	100
1856/57	50	100	–	100
1857/58	100	–	50	50
1858/59	70	100	50	50
1859/60	50	100	–	50

1842/43, 1846/47–1849/50 Fanny & Mary Bull; 1850/51–1859/60 Mary &Fanny Bull.
1842/43, 1846/47–1849/50 milliners & dressmakers; 1850/51–1855/56 milliners etc.;
1856/57–1859/60 milliners.
1851/52 marked "Miss Bull relieved on appeal".
1852/53 marked against claim for exemption "Miss Bull".
Pigot & Co's Directory, 1842: M & F Bull, milliners & dressmakers, Wine Street.

402 BURGE, James, hatter.

1842/43 entry only.
Pigot & Co's Directory, 1842: James Burdge, hatter (manufacturer), Market Place.

403 BURROWS, William, newspaper proprietor.

Year	Amount returned	Commissioners' estimate	Final assessment
	£	£	£
1852/53	180	–	180
1853/54	180	250	250
1854/55	200	–	200
1855/56	–	200	200
1856/57	–	250	250
1857/58	–	250	250
1858/59	180	250	250
1859/60	180	250	250

Pigot & Co's Directory, 1842: William Burrows, Wiltshire Independent, Market Place.
Cross reference: Burrows, William, newspaper proprietor, Rowde 1842/43, 1846/47–1851/52.

404 BURT, Joseph, ironmonger.

1842/43, 1846/47–1849/50 returned and assessed £230.
1850/51–1852/53 returned and assessed £200.

1853/54 returned £230; estimated at £350; assessed at £300.
1854/55–1856/57 returned and assessed £300.
1857/58 returned and assessed £321.
1858/59 returned £320; assessed £300.
1859/60 returned £320; assessed £299.17.0.

1853/54 no appeal noted.
1859/60 assessment reduced by life assurance relief of £20.3.0.
Pigot & Co's Directory, 1842: Joseph Burt, ironmonger, brazier & tinman, St.John Street.

405 BUSH, William Robert, toyman, toy warehouse, stationer. [also BUSH, Jane]

1842/43, 1846/47 assessed in absence of return £100; exempt.
1847/48–1848/49 assessed in absence of return £60; exempt.
1849/50 returned and assessed £80; exempt.
1850/51–1851/52 assessed in absence of return £60; exempt.
1852/53 returned and assessed £135; exempt.
1853/54 returned £65; assessed £135.
1854/55–1855/56 returned and assessed £135.
1856/57–1859/60 assessed in absence of return £135.

1842/43, 1846/47–1849/50 toyman; 1850/51–1851/52 toy warehouse; 1853/54–1855/56 sta-
    tioner & toy warehouse, etc; 1852/53, 1856/57–1859/60 stationer & toy warehouse.
1842/43, 1846/47–1847/48 William Robert Bush; 1848/49–1856/57 Mrs Bush; 1857/58–
    1859/60 Mrs Jane Bush.
Pigot & Co's Directory, 1842: William R. Bush, agent to Atlas Fire Office, Brittox.

406 BUSHELL, Ann, innkeeper [by comparison, Pelican]

1846/47–1850/51 assessed in absence of return £100; exempt.
1851/52 returned and assessed £70; exempt.
1852/53 returned £70; assessed £84; exempt.

1852/53 marked "now House (sic)".
Cross references: Howse, John, innkeeper, St.John; Joyce, William, innkeeper, St.John.

407 BUTCHER, Henry, agent to Sun Fire Office.

1842/43 returned and assessed £55.
1846/47–1847/48 returned and assessed £59.10.0.
1848/49 returned £56.9.11 marked "See Schedule E".
1849/50–1850/51 marked "under Schedule E".
1851/52 returned and assessed £62.
1852/53–1855/56 marked "Schedule E".

Note: income from public offices and employments was assessable under Schedule E.
Pigot & Co's Directory, 1842: Mr.Henry Butcher, gentry, agent to Sun Fire Office, St.John Street.

408 BUTCHER, Henry, Junior, assistant secretary to North Wilts Friendly Society.

1848/49 returned and assessed £50.
1849/50-1851/52 marked "Schedule E".

1851/52 Junior added.

409 CADBY, Robert, toyman.

1842/43 returned £26; assessed £50; exempt.
1846/47 assessed in absence of return £50; exempt.

Pigot & Co's Directory, 1842: Robert Cadby, toy dealer, Brittox.

410 CALF, Henry, bank clerk.

1852/53 returned and assessed £100; exempt.
1853/54 returned £97.14.6; assessed at £100; income proved at £98; exempt.
1854/55 assessed in absence of return £100; income proved at £90; exempt.
1855/56 no assessment made. [see Nursteed]
1856/57 assessed in absence of return £110.
1857/58 returned and assessed £126.13.4.
1858/59 returned £143.6.8; assessed £160.9.8.
1859/60 returned and assessed £150 and £15.

1852/53 marked "Knight, Henry now Calf, bankers clerk".
1858/59 marked "Query Schedule E agent".
Cross references: Calf, Henry, bank clerk, Nursteed; Knight, Henry, bank clerk, St.John.

411 CANNING, George Barnes, attorney, solicitor.

1842/43 recorded but entry deleted.
1846/47 returned and assessed £250.
1847/48-1848/49 assessed in absence of return £250.
1849/50 estimated at £150 but no assessment made.
1850/51 assessed in absence of return £120; exempt.

1842/43 attorney; 1846/47-1850/51 solicitor.
1842/43 assessed as partner with William Tanner.

1850/51 Cannings.
Cross reference: Tanner, William & Canning, George Barnes, solicitors, St.John.

412 CHANDLER, Henry, grocer.

1842/43 returned and assessed £170.
1846/47 returned and assessed £160.

1847/48 marked "late".
Pigot & Co's Directory, 1842: Henry Chandler, grocer & tea dealer, Market Place.

413 CHANDLER, John, innkeeper. [by comparison, White Hart]

1842/43 returned and assessed £140.
1846/47 assessed in absence of return £140.
1847/48 assessed in absence of return £75.

1847/48 marked "newly King".
1848/49 marked "now George King".
Pigot & Co's Directory, 1842: John Chandler, White Hart, Market Place.
Cross reference: King, George, innkeeper, St.John.

414 CLARK, John, veterinary surgeon.

1856/57-1857/58 recorded; no assessments made; exempt.

1855/56 marked "Hart, Thornton gone now Clarke (sic)".
1858/59 marked "left".
Cross references: Hart, Thornton, veterinary surgeon, St.John; Vincent, J.P., veterinary surgeon,
    St.John.

415 CLARK, William & Isaac, butchers. [also CLARK, Jacob]

Year	Amount returned	Commissioners' estimate	Final assessment
	£	£	£
1846/47	300	–	300
1847/48	–	300	300
1848/49	200	300	250
1849/50	250	300a	250
1850/51	250	–	250
1851/52	250	300	300
1852/53	250	300	200
1853/54	250	300	300

1854/55	250	300	300
1855/56	200	300	300
1856/57	300	–	300
1857/58	300	–	300
1858/59	300	–	300
1859/60	–	300	300

1842/43 Clarke
1842/43 Jacob Clarke recorded marked "return in St.Mary".
1848/49, 1852/53 no appeal noted.
1855/56-1859/60 Isaac Clark assessed sole.
Pigot & Co's Directory, 1842: Jacob Clark, butcher, Maryport Street and Brittox.
Cross reference: Clark, Jacob, butcher, St.Mary.

416 CLARKE, Charles, Professor of Music.

Year	Amount returned £	Commissioners' estimate £	Income proved £	Final assessment £
1849/50	–	150a	124.12.0	–
1850/51	125	–	125	–
1851/52	–	125	125	–
1852/53	120.2.0	–	120.2.0	–
1853/54	105	120	–	120
1854/55	108	120	–	120
1855/56	112	–	–	112
1856/57	120	–	–	120
1857/58	132	–	–	132
1858/59	130	–	–	130
1859/60	132	150	–	150

1852/53 includes assessment on lodger.

417 CLARKE, Henry Matthew, Esquire, foreign securities, furnished house, interest, New Jersey Bank.

Year	Amount returned £	Commissioners' estimate £	Final assessment £
1850/51	75	–	75
1851/52	75	–	75
1852/53	75NJ 40i	115	115
1853/54	75f	85	85
1854/55	9.19.4f	–	9.19.4
1855/56	9.18.0f	–	9.18.0
1856/57	14.10.4f	–	14.10.4

1857/58	12f	–	16.10.0
	4.10.0f		
1858/59	–	16.10.0f	56.16.0
		40h	
1859/60	16.16.0	56.16.0fh	56.16.0

Abbreviations: NJ, New Jersey Bank; i, interest; f, foreign securities; h, furnished house.
1848/49 marked "returns made in St.James, London".
1849/50-1851/52 marked "returns made in London".
Note: Henry Matthew Clarke served as Additional Commissioner.

418 CLARKE, Robert, chemist.

1842/43 returned and assessed £290.
1846/47-1847/48 returned and assessed £280.
1848/49 returned and assessed £270.
1849/50 returned and assessed £260.
1850/51 assessed in absence of return £260.
1851/52 returned and assessed £262.
1852/53-1855/56 returned and assessed £265.
1856/57 returned and assessed £260.
1857/58 returned and assessed £270.
1858/59 returned and assessed £265.
1859/60 assessed in absence of return £300.

1842/43, 1846/47-1849/50 Clark; 1850/51-1859/60 Clarke.
Pigot & Co's Directory, 1842: Robert Clark (sic), chemist & druggist, agent to Family Endow-
    ment Society, Market Place.

419 COOK, Charles, solicitor.

1846/47 entry only; marked "left town".

420 COOK, Mary, milliner.

1842/43 returned and assessed £100; exempt.
1846/47 assessed in absence of return £100; exempt.

Pigot & Co's Directory, 1842: Mary Cook, milliner & dressmaker, Market Place.

421 COOMBES, John, auctioneer. [also COOMBES & BRACHER; COOMBES & ELLEN]

1851/52-1852/53 assessed in absence of return £400.
1853/54-1855/56 returned and assessed £300.

1856/57-1859/60 assessed in absence of return £350.

1850/51 marked "Crockett, Joseph & Son, auctioneers, etc., now Coombes".
1851/52-1852/53 Coombes & Ellen; 1853/54-1855/56 John Coombes.
1856/57-1859/60 John Coombes & Bracher.
1854/55 "& Bracher" entered but deleted.
Cross reference: Crockett, Joseph & Son, auctioneers, St. John.

422 COOPER, Revd. James, clerk.

1858/59-1859/60 returned and assessed £100.

423 COPEMAN, W.W., bank manager.

1842/43 returned and assessed £150.
1846/47 returned £200; assessed £250.
1847/48 assessed in absence of return £250.

1847/48 marked "King late Copeman".
Pigot & Co's Directory, 1842: W.W.Copeman, manager, North Wilts Bank.
Cross reference: King, Edward, bank manager, St.John.

424 COUZENS, George, rope maker, manure merchant, brush warehouse.

Year	Amount returned £	Commissioners' estimate £	Income proved £	Final assessment £
1849/50	100	–	100	–
1850/51	100	–	100	–
1851/52	–	100	90	–
1852/53	100	–	100	–
1853/54	90	100	90	–
1854/55	90	–	90	–
1855/56	100m	–	–	100
1856/57	100	–	–	100
1857/58	120	150	–	150
1858/59	–	100	80	–
1859/60	–	100	71	–

1849/50-1854/55, 1856/57 rope maker; 1855/56 manure merchant; 1857/58-1859/60 rope maker & brush warehouse.
1855/56 initially returned £70 as rope maker and estimated at £90 but this assessment discharged and replaced by an assessment as manure merchant(m).
1856/57 [Notton, R.J., hatter] marked "now Couzens, brush warehouse"; 1857/58 marked "now Couzens, G.".
Cross reference: Notton, R.J., hatter, St.John.

425 COWARD, Thomas & Richard, grocers. [also COWARD, Charles]

1842/43 returned £160; assessed £200.
1846/47 assessed in absence of return £200; exemption claimed as partnership.

1842/43 Charles Coward assessed.
1847/48 marked "now Perry".
Pigot & Co's Directory, 1842: Charles Coward, grocer & tea dealer, High Street.
Cross reference: Perry, John & Co., grocers, St.John.
Note: Both Thomas and Richard Coward were eligible to claim exemption for 1846/47 since
  their share of the assessment was £100 each and thus below the tax threshold.

426 COX, Jasper, ironmonger.

1842/43 assessed in absence of return £80; exempt.

Pigot & Co's Directory, 1842: Jasper Cox, ironmonger & cutler, Little Brittox.

427 COXHEAD, William Palmer, schoolmaster.

1856/57 assessed in absence of return £100; income proved at £99.6.8; exempt.
1857/58-1859/60 recorded; no assessments made; exempt.

This is an example of an early form of tax avoidance. On incomes of £100, tax was payable on
  the whole amount. Incomes below this sum were eligible to be wholly relieved on a claim
  for exemption. By agreeing with the employer to fix the salary at £99.6.8, no tax would be
  payable. (Following evidence taken before the Select Committee on the Income and Property Tax, House of Commons. Parliamentary Papers. (1852) ix qq.3019, 3235).
Cross references: (similar instance of early legal tax avoidance) Anderson, T.W., solicitor's clerk,
  St.John; Thorp, T.G., surveyor's clerk, Bedborough.

428 CRIPPS, Henry, chemist.

Year	Amount returned £	Commissioners' estimate £	Income proved £	Final assessment £
1853/54	72	–	–	–
1854/55	–	100	72	–
1855/56	–	72	72	–
1856/57	–	–	–	–
1857/58	–	110	–	–
1858/59	120	–	–	120
1859/60	130	–	–	130

1853/54 marked "late Bridges, chemist".
1858/59 marked "under letter Query".

1853/54, 1857/58 no assessment made; 1856/57 marked "exempt".
Cross references: Bridges, Fitzherbert, chemist, St.John; Hayward, Robert, chemist, St.John; Johnstone, Bayntun, chemist, St.John.

429 CROCKETT, Joseph & Son, auctioneers, appraisers.

1842/43 returned and assessed £500.
1846/47–1849/50 assessed in absence of return £400.
1850/51 returned £200; assessed £400; reduced to £200 on appeal.

1850/51–1851/52 marked "now Coombes".
Pigot & Co's Directory, 1842: Joseph Crockett, agent-land, &c., Bellevue; auctioneers, agent to Argus Life Office, Norwich Union Fire Office, Market Place.
Cross reference: Coombes, John, auctioneer, St.John.

430 CROOK, William, innkeeper. [by comparison Hare & Hounds]

1846/47 assessed in absence of return £100; exempt.
1847/48–1848/49 assessed in absence of return £150.
1849/50–1850/51 returned and assessed £151.

1850/51 marked "now Millwaters" by 11 October or 30 November 1850.
Cross references: Kite, Thomas, innkeeper, St.John; Millwaters, Nathaniel, innkeeper, St.John.

431 CRUDGE, William, painter & glazier.

1858/59 returned nil; no assessment made.
1859/60 returned £82.14.2; assessed £100; income proved at £82; exempt.

Cross reference: Crudge, William, painter & glazier, St.Mary.

432 CUNNINGTON, William & Sons, wine merchants.

Year	Amount returned	Commissioners' estimate	Final assessment
	£	£	£
1842/43	270	–	270
1846/47	250	–	250
1847/48	–	250	250
1848/49	290	–	290
1849/50	–	250	250
1850/51	250	–	250
1851/52	275	–	275
1852/53	320	–	320

1853/54	–	400	400
1854/55	–	400	400
1855/56	385	–	385
1856/57	520	–	520
1857/58	540	–	540
1858/59	540	–	540
1859/60	540	–	540

1842/43, 1846/47 William Cunnington & Sons; 1847/48-1850/51 William Cunnington;
    1851/52-1855/56 Messrs Cunnington; 1856/57-1857/58 Messrs William Cunnington &
    Sons; 1858/59-1859/60 Messrs William Cunnington & Co.
1859/60 "Bottle" noted but substituted by "Old Town Hall".
Pigot & Co's Directory, 1842: William Cunnington & Sons, wine & spirit merchants, Wine
    Street.
Cross reference: Cunnington, William, woolstapler, Week.

433 DANGERFIELD, Isaiah, fishmonger.

Year	Amount returned £	Commissioners' estimate £	Income proved £	Final assessment £
1842/43	90	150	100	–
1846/47	65	90	–	90
1847/48	65	100	–	100
1848/49	70	100	–	100
1849/50	70	100	–	100
1850/51	50	120a	–	100
1851/52	40	100	–	100
1852/53	50	80	–	80
1853/54	50	100	–	100
1854/55	40	100	–	100
1855/56	40	100	–	100
1856/57	40	100	–	100
1857/58	50	100	–	100
1858/59	50	100	–	100
1859/60	40	100	–	100

1842/43 no appeal noted.
1856/57 marked "& innkeeper" but deleted.
Pigot & Co's Directory, 1842: Isaiah Dangerfield, fishmonger, Brittox.

434 DAVIES, Elizabeth, innkeeper, Bear. [also DAVIES, Edward]

1842/43, 1846/47-1849/50 returned and assessed £150.
1850/51 assessed in absence of return £150.
1851/52 returned and assessed £150.

1852/53 returned £150; assessed £200.
1853/54-1855/56 returned and assessed £200.
1856/57 returned £200; assessed £260.
1857/58-1858/59 returned and assessed £260.
1859/60 returned £260; assessed £400.

1842/43, 1846/47-1850/51 Edward Davies; 1851/52-1859/60 Elizabeth Davies.
1842/43 Davis.
Bear recorded 1856/57.
Pigot & Co's Directory, 1842: Edward Davies, Bear (posting house), Market Place.

435 DAVIS, Arthur, printer. [later DAVIS GILLMAN]

1852/53 estimated £80 but no assessment made.
1853/54 returned £50; assessed £70.
1854/55 returned and assessed £100.
1855/56 recorded but no assessment made.

1851/52 marked "C.E.Sartain now Davis, A., printer".
1852/53 marked "late Sartain".
1855/56 Davis Gillman.
Cross reference: Sartain, C.E., printer, St.John.

436 DERHAM, James, shoemaker.

1842/43 entry only.
Pigot & Co's Directory, 1842: James Derham, boot & shoe maker, Little Brittox.

437 DEVIZES IMPROVEMENT COMMISSIONERS

1847/48 recorded but no assessment made.

438 DEVIZES TURNPIKE

1847/48 recorded but no assessment made.

439 DODMAN, John, shopman.

1842/43, 1846/47-1848/49 assessed in absence of return £85; exempt.
1849/50 assessed in absence of return £80; exempt.
1850/51-1852/53 assessed in absence of return £50; exempt.

Pigot & Co's Directory, 1842: possibly Martha Dodman, toy dealer, Little Brittox.
1853/54 marked "gone".

440 DOWSE, Thomas, miller.

1849/50 assessed in absence of return £75; exempt.
1850/51 returned £50; assessed £60; exempt.

1849/50 Douse (sic) Thomas, miller, written above Haines, Daniel, miller.
1850/51 marked "Dowse, Thomas late Haines, miller".
Cross reference: Haines, Daniel, miller, St.John.

441 DREDGE, Joseph R & S., brewers, maltsters. [also DREDGE, R & S]

1842/43 returned £382; assessed £360.
1846/47-1847/48 returned and assessed £382.

1846/47-1847/48 R & S Dredge assessed.
1846/47-1847/48 brewers.
Pigot & Co's Directory, 1842: Joseph Dredge & Co., brewers, maltsters, Bridewell Street.

442 DRING, George, clerk.

1842/43 assessed in absence of return £120; exempt.
1846/47 returned and assessed £139; exempt.
1847/48 returned and assessed £148; exempt.
1848/49 assessed in absence of return £140; exempt.
1849/50-1852/53 returned and assessed £140.
1853/54 returned and assessed £135.18.3.
1854/55 returned and assessed £136.
1855/56-1859/60 returned and assessed £140.

1853/54 marked "£140 less £4.1.9 insurance".
1854/55-1855/56 assessments include interest.
Pigot & Co's Directory, 1842: George Dring, agent to Reliance Fire Office, Registrar of Marriages, St.John Street.

443 DROVER, John, shopman.

1842/43 assessed in absence of return £100; income proved £135; exempt.
1846/47-1850/51 assessed in absence of return £100; exempt.

444 DYMOND, Thomas, tailor.

Year	Amount returned	Commissioners' estimate	Final assessment
	£	£	£
1842/43	200	275	275
1846/47	205	275	275

1847/48	195	275	275
1848/49	160	275	170
1849/50	160	180	200
1850/51	175	200	200
1851/52	170	200	200
1852/53	170	200	200
1853/54	160	200	200
1854/55	165	200	200
1855/56	170	200	200

1848/49 no appeal noted.
1849/50 £180 estimated by Additional Commissioners; increased to £200 by General Commissioners; no appeal noted.
1856/57-1857/58 marked "now Gibbs" or "see Gibbs".
Pigot & Co's Directory, 1842: Thomas Dymond, tailor & draper, High Street.
Cross reference: Gibbs, Decimus, tailor, St.John.

445 EDMOND, Thomas, pork butcher.

1852/53 returned and assessed £100; exempt.
1853/54 returned £77.8.0; assessed £100; income proved £78; exempt.
1854/55 returned £100; income proved £90; exempt.
1855/56-1856/57 returned and assessed £100.
1857/58 assessed in absence of return £100; income proved £60; exempt.
1858/59-1859/60 recorded; no assessments made; exempt.

446 EDMONDS, R & W, French teachers, schoolmasters.

1846/47-1847/48 assessed in absence of return £106.11.9; exempt.
1850/51 assessed in absence of return £100; exempt.
1851/52 assessed in absence of return £95 each; income proved £194.13.4; exempt.
1852/53 returned and assessed £201.15.2; exempt.
1853/54 recorded but no assessment made.

1846/47-1847/48 R.Edmonds; 1850/51-1853/54 R & W Edmonds.
1848/49 marked "See St.James".
1854/55 marked "gone".
Pigot & Co's Directory, 1842: E.Edmonds, mistress, Infants' School, Sheep Street.
Cross references: Edmonds, R, French teacher, St.Mary, 1842/43;
Edmonds, Richard, teacher of French, Bedborough, 1848/49-1849/50.

447 ELLIOTT, Revd. Richard, schoolmaster, dissenting minister. [also ELLIOTT, Frances]

1842/43, 1846/47 returned and assessed £500.
1847/48-1848/49 returned and assessed £400.

1849/50-1850/51 assessed in absence of return £400.
1851/52 returned and assessed £400.
1852/53 returned and assessed £300.
1853/54 returned and assessed £50 school and £40 interest; assessment deleted.

1842/43, 1846/47-1850/51 schoolmaster & dissenting minister; 1851/52-1852/53 school-master.
1852/53 marked "dead".
1853/54 Frances Elliott, schoolmistress, assessed.
Pigot & Co's Directory, 1842: Revd. Richard Elliott, Long Street.
Pigot & Co's Directory, 1842: Fanny Elliott, boarding school, Long Street.

448 ELLIS, Edward, wine merchant's clerk.

1855/56-1856/57 entry only; 1857/58 marked "gone".

449 ELLIS, George Hackett, wine merchant's clerk.

1853/54 estimate £70 entered but no assessment made.
1854/55 returned and assessed £70; exempt.
1855/56 assessed in absence of return £70; exempt.
1856/57 recorded; no assessment made; exempt.

1857/58 marked "see Giddings & Ellis".
Cross reference: Giddings, Edwin & Ellis, George, wine merchants, St.John.

450 ERLE, Rebecca, haberdasher. [also EARLE, Henry]

1842/43, 1846/47-1848/49 assessed in absence of return £130; exempt.
1849/50 returned and assessed £100' exempt.
1850/51-1851/52 assessed in absence of return £100; 1851/52 income proved £120; exempt.
1852/53 returned and assessed £140; exempt.
1853/54 returned £120; assessed £150.
1854/55 returned and assessed £150.
1855/56 returned £95; assessed £150.
1856/57-1859/60 assessed in absence of return £150.

1842/43 Henry Earle; 1846/47-1859/60 Rebecca Erle.
1842/43 shopkeeper; 1846/47-1859/60 haberdasher.
Pigot & Co's Directory, 1842: Rebecca Earle, haberdasher & baby linen, Wine Street.

451 EVANS, George, schoolmaster.

Year	Amount returned	Commissioners' estimate	Income proved	Final assessment
	£	£	£	£
1842/43	149	150	77.6.6	–
1846/47	130	–	130	–
1847/48	–	200	130	–
1848/49	–	120	120	–
1849/50	130	–	130	–
1850/51	–	130	130	–
1851/52	–	130	135	–
1852/53	130	–	130	–
1853/54	125	–	–	125
1854/55	125	–	–	125
1855/56	68	100	–	100
1856/57	–	100	–	100
1857/58	100	–	–	100
1858/59	96	–	–	96
1859/60	96	–	–	96

Pigot & Co's Directory, 1842: George Evans, Bridewell Street.

452 EVERETT, Dr William Giffard, physician.

1853/54-1859/60 returned and assessed £500.

Pigot & Co's Directory, 1842: William G. Everett, physician, Albion Place.
Cross reference: Everett, William Giffard, physician, St.Mary, prior to 1853/54.

453 EVERINGHAM, Henry, clerk.

1842/43 assessed in absence of return £100; exempt.
1846/47-1847/48 assessed in absence of return £125; exempt.

454 FALKNER, Richard, bank manager.

1842/43, 1846/47-1859/60 returned and assessed £400.

455 FERRIS, John, clothes cleaner.

1842/43, 1846/47-1848/49 assessed in absence of return £80; exempt.
1849/50 assessed in absence of return £50; exempt.

456 FOSTER, Misses, schoolmistresses.

1842/43, 1846/47-1849/50 assessed in absence of return £40; exempt.

1846/47-1849/50 Miss Foster assessed sole.
Pigot & Co's Directory, 1842: S.Foster, day school, Long Street.
Pigot & Co's Directory, 1842: Eliza Foster, milliner & dressmaker, Long Street.

457 FOX, John James & Co., drapers.

Year	Amount returned	Commissioners' estimate	Final assessment
	£	£	£
1842/43	410	–	420
1846/47	350	–	350
1847/48	–	350	350
1848/49	–	350	350
1849/50	350	–	350
1850/51	300	–	300
1851/52	300	–	300
1852/53	300	–	300
1853/54	350	–	350
1854/55	300	350	300
1855/56	–	300	150
1856/57	–	300a	150
1857/58	200	–	200
1858/59	200	300	300
1859/60	200	300	300

1842/43 returned £507 including rent £55; profits computed at £465 less rent £55; apparent
   arithmetical error in assessment.
1854/55, 1855/56 no appeal noted.
Pigot & Co's Directory, 1842: John James Fox & Co., linen & wool drapers, manufacturers of
   striped linseys and blankets, agent to Alliance Fire Office, St.John Street.

458 FRANCIS, Thomas, cordwainer.

1842/43, 1846/47-1849/50 assessed in absence of return £40; exempt.

Pigot & Co's Directory, 1842: Thomas Francis, cordwainer, Chequer.

459 FRANCIS, William, tailor.

1842/43, 1846/47-1849/50 assessed in absence of return £100; exempt.

Pigot & Co's Directory, 1842: William Francis, tailor, St.John Street.

460 FRASER, William, tailor.

1855/56-1856/57 returned and assessed £100.
1857/58 assessed in absence of return £150.
1858/59-1859/60 returned £100; assessed £150.

461 FRAYLING, Edward, innkeeper, White Swan.

1846/47-1849/50 assessed in absence of return £100; exempt.

1849/50 marked "now Wells, innkeeper, White Swan".
Cross references: Bourne, Richard, innkeeper, St.John; Jenkins, David, innkeeper, St.John; Wells, Joseph, innkeeper, St.John.

462 GIBBS, Decimus, tailor.

1856/57 returned £172; assessed £200.
1857/58-1858/59 returned £175; assessed £200.
1859/60 returned £170; assessed £250.

1856/57-1857/58 marked "late Dymond, tailor.
Cross reference: Dymond, Thomas, tailor, St.John.

463 GIBBS, John.

1842/43 name only entered.

464 GIDDINGS, George, grocer, chemist, bookseller. [also GIDDINGS, Edwin]

Year	Amount returned £	Commissioners' estimate £	Income proved £	Final assessment £
1842/43	81.16.6	–	–	81.16.6
1846/47	100	–	–	100
1847/48	95	–	–	95
1848/49	95	–	–	95
1849/50	100	–	–	100
1850/51	95	–	–	95
1851/52	100	–	–	100
	–	50c	50	–
1852/53	100	–	–	100
	–	50c	50	–
1853/54	35.17.2	100	–	100
1854/55	150	200	–	125

| 1855/56 | – | 150 | – | 150 |
| 1856/57 | 147 | 150 | – | 150 |

Abbreviations: c, chemist.
1842/43, 1846/47-1852/53 George Giddings; 1853/54-1856/57 Edwin Giddings.
1851/52-1852/53 Giddings, chemist, assessed and exemption claimed; seemingly Edwin Giddings by comparison with 1853/54 entry.
1842/43, 1846/47-1852/53 grocer; 1853/54-1854/55 grocer & chemist; 1855/56 grocer, chemist & bookseller; 1856/57 grocer & chemist.
1857/58-1858/59 marked "business given up".
Note: Edwin Giddings set up business with George Ellis, a wine merchant's clerk to form the wine merchants business of Giddings & Ellis.
Pigot & Co's Directory, 1842: George Giddings, wine & spirit merchant, grocer & tea dealer, Brittox.
Cross reference: Giddings & Ellis, wine merchants, St.John.

465 GIDDINGS, Edwin, & ELLIS, George, wine merchants.

1857/58-1858/59 returned £250; assessed £300.
1859/60 returned £300; assessed £350.

[Mackrell, Henry] 1856/57 marked "now Giddings & Ellis".
Note: Edwin Giddings set up business with George Ellis, a wine merchant's clerk to form the wine merchants business of Giddings & Ellis.
Cross references: Giddings, George [for Edwin], grocer & chemist, St.John; Ellis, George Hackett, wine merchant's clerk, St.John; Mackrell, Henry, wine merchant, St.John.

466 GILBERT, Henry, horse breaker.

1852/53 returned and assessed £64; exempt.
1853/54 returned £60; assessed £80 but no assessment made; exempt.
1854/55-1855/56 assessed in absence of return £80; exempt.
1856/57-1859/60 recorded; no assessments made; exempt.

467 GILBERT, Henry, solicitor.

1842/43 returned and assessed £100.

Pigot & Co's Directory, 1842: Henry Gilbert, attorney, St.John Street.

468 GILBERT, William, ironmonger.

1842/43 returned £100; assessed £200.
1846/47 returned £52; assessed £100; exempt.

1847/48 assessed in absence of return £100; exempt.
1848/49 returned and assessed £86; exempt.

1848/49 marked "Gilbert, William late now W.Hayward, ironmonger".
Pigot & Co's Directory, 1842: William Gilbert, ironmonger, Market Place.
Cross reference: Hayward, William, ironmonger, St.John.

469 GILLMAN, Charles, reporter, bookseller, printer, dissenting preacher.

1854/55 returned £95; assessed £100; income proved £95; exempt.
1855/56-1858/59 assessed in absence of return £100.
1859/60 assessed in absence of return £120.

1854/55 reporter & dissenting preacher; 1855/56 reporter; 1856/57 reporter & bookseller; 1857/58-1859/60 bookseller.
1854/55 marked "charged in Week".
1854/55 Gillman was also assessed in Week on £100 proving income at £90.
Cross reference: Gillman, Charles, reporter, Week.

470 GRANTHAM, Henry, schoolmaster. [also GRANTHAM, Mary, schoolmistress]

1842/43 returned and assessed £50 (Henry Grantham).
1842/43 assessed in absence of return £100; exempt (Mary Grantham).
1846/47-1849/50 assessed in absence of return £100; exempt (Henry Grantham).

Pigot & Co's Directory, 1842: Henry David Grantham, boarding school, Long Street.
Pigot & Co's Directory, 1842: Mary Grantham, ladies' boarding school, Long Street.

471 GREEN, William, auctioneer.

1842/43 assessed in absence of return £50; exempt.
1846/47 assessed in absence of return £130; exempt.
1847/48 estimated in absence of return £150 but entry deleted.

1847/48 marked "see St.Mary".
Cross reference: Green, William, auctioneer, St.Mary.

472 GREENLAND, Robert, bricklayer.

1842/43 returned £25; assessed £50; exempt.
1846/47-1849/50 assessed in absence of return £50; exempt.

Pigot & Co's Directory, 1842: Robert Greenland, bricklayer, Bridewell Street.

473 GRIFFIN, John, printer.

1842/43 assessed in absence of return £150; income proved at £141.14.0; exempt.

Pigot & Co's Directory, 1842: John Griffin, bookseller, stationer & printer, music seller, library, agent to Equitable Life Office, Brittox.

474 GUY, Edward Evans, watchmaker.

Year	Amount returned £	Commissioners' estimate £	Income proved £	Final assessment £
1842/43	–	100	100	–
1846/47	–	100	100	–
1847/48	–	100	100	–
1848/49	–	100	100	–
1849/50	–	80	80	–
1850/51	–	80	80	–
1851/52	–	80	102	–
1852/53	100	–	102.10.0	–
1853/54	85.6.8	100	85.6.8	–
1854/55	–	85	85	–
1855/56	–	85	85	–
1856/57	–	–	–	–
1857/58	–	100	–	100
1858/59	–	100	–	100
1859/60	80	100	–	100

1842/43, 1846/47-1859/60 watchmaker (tinman entered but deleted 1842/43).
1856/57 no assessment made; exempt.
Pigot & Co's Directory, 1842: Bush & Guy, watch & clock makers, Brittox.

475 GUY, John, ironmonger, etc.

1853/54 returned £77.7.0 but no assessment made; exempt.
1854/55-1855/56 assessed in absence of return £70; exempt.
1856/57-1859/60 recorded; no assessments made; exempt.

Pigot & Co's Directory, 1842: John Guy, brazier & tinman, St.John Street.

476 HADOW, James Remington, property out of Great Britain, interest.

1858/59 returned and assessed £1500p, £150i.
1859/60 returned and assessed £850p, £185i.

Abbreviations: p, property out of Great Britain; i, interest.

477 HAINES, Daniel, miller, carpenter, builder.

1842/43 returned and assessed £140.
1846/47 returned and assessed £150.
1847/48 assessed in absence of return £150.
1848/49 assessed in absence of return £50.

1842/43 builder; 1846/47-1847/48 carpenter & miller; 1848/49 miller & farmer.
1850/51 marked "Dowse, Thomas late Haines, miller".
Pigot & Co's Directory, 1842: Daniel Haines, carpenter & builder, timber merchant, Long Street.
Cross reference: Dowse, Thomas, miller, St. John.

478 HANCOCK, Samuel, dyer.

1842/43 returned £25; assessed £50; exempt.

479 HANN, Thomas B., commission agent, hop merchant.

1853/54 returned and assessed £80.15.0; exempt.
1854/55-1855/56 assessed in absence of return £100.
1856/57 returned and assessed £100.
1857/58-1858/59 assessed in absence of return £100.
1859/60 returned and assessed £100.

1853/54-1855/56 commission agent; 1856/57-1859/60 commission agent & hop merchant.

480 HARRISON, John.

1842/43 name only entered.

481 HART, Samuel, watchmaker.

1842/43 returned and assessed £230.
1846/47-1849/50 returned £150; assessed £210.
1850/51-1855/56 returned £150; assessed £200.
1856/57 returned £150; assessed £260.
1857/58-1859/60 returned £200; assessed £275.

Pigot & Co's Directory, 1842: Samuel Hart, watch & clock maker, Brittox.

482 HART, Thornton, veterinary surgeon.

1852/53-1854/55 returned and assessed £150.

1852/53 marked "late Vincent".
1855/56 marked "gone now Clarke (sic)".
Cross references: Clark, John, veterinary surgeon, St.John; Vincent, J.P., veterinary surgeon, St.John.

483 HAYWARD, John Edward, solicitor.

1848/49-1849/50 returned and assessed £200.
1850/51 returned and assessed £170.
1851/52-1854/55 returned and assessed £100.
1855/56 returned £100; assessed £200.
1856/57 returned and assessed £150.
1857/58 returned and assessed £160.
1858/59-1859/60 returned and assessed £200.

484 HAYWARD, Robert, chemist.

1842/43 returned and assessed £110.
1846/47 returned £50; assessed £100.
1847/48 assessed in absence of return £100.
1848/49 returned and assessed £100; exempt.

1848/49 marked "now Johnstone, Baynton (sic), chemist".
Pigot & Co's Directory, 1842: Robert Hayward, chemist & druggist, St.John Street.
Cross references: Bridges, Fitzherbert, chemist, St.John; Cripps, Henry, chemist, St.John; Johnstone, Bayntun, chemist, St.John.

485 HAYWARD, William, ironmonger.

1849/50 recorded but no assessment made.
1850/51 assessed in absence of return £120.
1851/52 assessed in absence of return £120; income proved at £100; exempt.
1852/53 returned and assessed £100.
1853/54 returned £96 and £40 interest (latter deleted); assessed £100; income proved at £136 but assessment made £136.
1854/55 returned £100; assessed £150; reduced by General Commissioners to £125.
1855/56 -1856/57 returned £100; assessed £125.
1857/58-1859/60 returned and assessed £125.

1848/49 marked "Gilbert, William late now W.Hayward, ironmonger".
Cross reference: Gilbert, William, ironmonger, St.John.

486 HAYWOOD, Thomas, governor of new prison.

1854/55 entry only marked "dead".

Pigot & Co's Directory, 1842: Thomas Haywood, Governor, House of Correction, Bath Road. Cross reference: Alexander, Alfred, Governor of New Prison, St.John.

487 HAZELAND, Abraham, coal merchant, trustee.

1842/43 returned and assessed £500.

1842/43 assessed as coal merchant and trustee for Jemima, Adam, Matthew and John surviving children of the late Matthew Hazeland.
Pigot & Co's Directory, 1842: Abraham Hazeland, salt & coal merchant & dealer, New Park Street.

488 HILL, John, plasterer.

1842/43, 1846/47-1849/50 assessed in absence of return £50; exempt.

1849/50 Hills.
Pigot & Co's Directory, 1842: John Hill, plasterer & slater, Long Street.

489 HILL, Richard, painter.

1858/59 returned nil; no assessment made.
1859/60 returned £75 but entry deleted.

1858/59 marked "query trade painter".
Cross reference: Hill, Richard, plumber, painter, St. Mary.

490 HILLIER, Martha.

1842/43 name only entered.

491 HILLS, Philip George, writing clerk, attorney's clerk.

1842/43 returned and assessed £70; exempt.
1846/47-1848/49 assessed in absence of return £70; exempt.
1849/50 assessed in absence of return £80; exempt.

1842/43, 1846/47-1847/48 writing clerk; 1848/49-1849/50 attorney's clerk.

492 HITCHMAN, James, hatter.

1842/43 assessed in absence of return £75; exempt.

Pigot & Co's Directory, 1842: James Hitchman, hatter & hosier, Brittox.

493 HOARE, George, chemist.

1842/43 returned £107; assessed £150; income proved at £107; exempt.

Pigot & Co's Directory, 1842: George Hoare, chemist, apothecary & surgeon, Market Place.

494 HOBBS, William, draper.

1842/43 assessed in absence of return £122; exempt.
1846/47 returned and assessed £170.
1847/48 returned and assessed £165.
1848/49 returned £150; assessed £165.

1849/50 marked "Lenthall & Co., late Hobbs".
Cross references: Lenthall, James & Co., drapers, St.John; Pope, John, linen draper, St.John.

495 HONEYWELL, William, shopkeeper. [also HONEYWELL, Mrs.]

1842/43 assessed in absence of return £150; income proved at £129; exempt.

1846/47 Mrs.Honeywell entered but deleted.
Pigot & Co's Directory, 1842: William Honywill, clothes dealer, linen & woollen draper, hatter, Brittox.

496 HOOK, Charles, confectioner, glass dealer.

1842/43 returned £185; assessed £200.
1846/47 returned and assessed £200.
1847/48 assessed in absence of return £200.

1842/43, 1846/47 confectioner; 1847/48 confectioner & glass dealer.
1848/49 marked "now Misses".
Pigot & Co's Directory, 1842: Charles Hook, baker, confectioner, china, glass, etc., dealer, Brittox
Cross reference: Hook, Eliza and Emma, confectioners, etc., St.John.

497 HOOK, Eliza & Emma, schoolmistresses, confectioners, glass dealers, Berlin wool.

Year	Amount returned £	Commissioners' estimate £	Income proved £	Final assessment £
Partnership				
1842/43				
Eliza	113.16.9	–	113.16.9	–
Emma	113.16.9	–	113.16.9	–
1846/47				
Eliza	100	–	100	–
Emma	100	–	100	–
1847/48				
Composite	–	–	–	–
1848/49				
Composite	175	250	250	–
1849/50				
Composite	200	–	200	–
1850/51				
Composite	–	200	200	–
1851/52				
Eliza	75	–	75	–
Emma	75	–	75	–
1852/53				
Eliza	75	–	–	75
Emma	75	–	–	75

1842/43 schoolmistresses; 1846/47 no occupation recorded; 1847/48 marked "Berlin wool"; 1848/49-1850/51 confectioners & glass dealers; 1851/52 confectioners; 1852/53 confectioners, etc.; 1847/48 recorded but no assessment made. Berlin wool work was a kind of tapestry. [1848/49-1849/50 Eliza & Emma Hook were assessed as worsted warehouse in St.Mary].
1848/49 marked "Charles now Misses Hook, confectioners & glass dealers".
1853/54 "Misses" deleted, Miss (Eliza) Hook assessed sole.

Eliza Hook sole

1853/54-1859/60 returned and assessed £150.

1853/54-1855/56 Miss Hook; 1856/57-1859/60 Miss Eliza Hook.
Pigot & Co's Directory, 1842: Eliza Hook, day school, St.John Street
Cross references: Hook, Eliza & Emma, worsted warehouse, St.Mary; Hook, Charles, confectioner, glass dealer, St.John.

498 HOOK, Mary & Theodosia, china warehouse.

1842/43 entry only.
1846/47 Mary Hook, sole entry deleted.

499 HOOPER, ———, grocer, etc.

1859/60 assessed in absence of return £150.

1859/60 marked "late Lyne, grocer".
Cross references: Lavington, Samuel, grocer, St.John; Long, John, grocer, St.John; Lyne, Thomas
    William, grocer, St.John.

500 HOPKINS, Thomas, linen draper.

1851/52 assessed in absence of return £119.10.0; exempt.
1852/53 returned £114; assessed £150; income proved below £150 but no sum dis-
    closed; exempt.
1853/54 returned £107; assessed £150.
1854/55-1855/56 returned and assessed £150.
1856/57 returned £120; assessed £150.
1857/58-1858/59 returned and assessed £150.
1859/60 assessed in absence of return £150.

501 HOUSE, Robert, grocer.

1848/49-1849/50 assessed in absence of return £120; 1848/49 exempt.
1851/52 assessed in absence of return £115; exempt.
1853/54 returned £109.6.0; assessed £120.
1854/55 assessed in absence of return £120.
1855/56 returned £93.5.0; assessed £120.
1856/57 assessed in absence of return £120.
1857/58 returned and assessed £170.
1858/59-1859/60 returned £135; assessed £170.

1850/51, 1852/53 not recorded
1852/53 Howse.

502 HOWITT, George Armstrong, clerk of works, etc.

1852/53 returned and assessed £136.10.0 and £5 interest; exempt.
1853/54 returned and assessed £130.

1854/55 assessed in absence of return £130; income proved £77; exempt.
1855/56 assessed in absence of return £77; exempt.
1856/57 assessed in absence of return £100; reduced to £90 on appeal; exempt.

1857/58 marked "gone".

503 HOWSE, John, innkeeper, Pelican.

1852/53 returned £70; income proved £84; exempt.
1853/54 returned £82; exempt.
1854/55 returned £150.
1855/56 returned £100; assessed £150.
1856/57-1869/60 returned £100; assessed £160.

1852/53 marked "Bushell, Ann now House (*sic*)".
1853/54 marked "John Howse late Bushell".
Cross references: Bushell, Ann, innkeeper, St.John; Joyce, William, innkeeper, St.John.

504 HUBAND, John, shopkeeper.

1842/43, 1846/47-1849/50 assessed in absence of return £120; exempt.

Pigot & Co's Directory, 1842: John Huband, haberdasher, Market Place.

505 HULBERT, Henry Hale, attorney. [also HULBERT, Charles]

1842/43 returned £210; assessed £300.
1846/47-1849/50 returned and assessed £250.
1850/51-1852/53 returned and assessed £260.
1853/54-1856/57 returned and assessed £270.
1857/58 returned and assessed £300.
1858/59-1859/60 returned and assessed £350.

1842/43 Charles and Henry Hale Hulbert; 1846/47-1859/60 Henry Hale Hulbert.
1842/43 attornies; 1846/47-1859/60 attorney.
Pigot & Co's Directory, 1842: Charles & Henry Hale Hulbert, attorneys, St.John Street.

506 HUMBY, Frederick Peter, innkeeper, Antelope.

1855/56 assessed in absence of return £50.

1857/58 marked "now Thomas Brown", "Antelope".
Cross references: Brown, Thomas, innkeeper, St. John; Humby, Frederick Peter, Southbroom Brewery, Week; McEwin, Edwin, innkeeper, St.John. Ransom, William, innkeeper, St.John;

507 HUMBY, James, bank clerk, bank manager. [by comparison, North Wilts Bank]

1852/53 returned £120; assessment wholly discharged on appeal.
1853/54 assessed in absence of return £130.
1856/57 returned £220; no assessment made, Schedule E.
1857/58-1858/59 Schedule E.

1852/53-1853/54 bank clerk; 1856/57-1858/59 bank manager.
1854/55 marked "returned in Week (see assessor's note)".
1857/58 by note under Edward King, manager of North Wilts Bank, insurance commission transferred to Mr.Humby on King's removal in 1856/57.
1859/60 marked "gone".
Cross reference: Humby, James, bank clerk, Week; King, Edward, bank manager, St.John.

508 HUTCHINS, James, town crier.

1848/49-1849/50 assessed in absence of return £80; exempt.

509 JENKINS, David, innkeeper, White Swan.

1854/55 assessed in absence of return £100; income proved at £50; exempt.
1855/56-1858/59 assessed in absence of return £100.
1859/60 returned and assessed £100.

1854/55 marked "Wells, Joseph now Jenkins innkeeper".
Cross references: Bourne, Richard, innkeeper, St.John; Frayling, Edward, innkeeper, St.John; Wells, Joseph, innkeeper, St.John.

510 JENKINS, Mrs Jane, confectioner.

1849/50-1852/53 assessed in absence of return £60; exempt.
1853/54 returned and assessed £85; exempt.
1854/55 assessed in absence of return £85; exempt.

1849/50-1850/51 marked "late White, confectioner".
1855/56 marked "Taylor, Robert late Jenkins, confectioner".
Cross references: Taylor, Robert, confectioner, St.John; White, George, confectioner, St.John.

511 JOHNSTONE, Bayntun, chemist.

1849/50-1852/53 assessed in absence of return £100; exempt.

1849/50 marked "late Robert Hayward, chemist".
1852/53 marked "now Bridges, chemist".
Cross references: Bridges, Fitzherbert, chemist, St.John; Cripps, Henry, chemist, St.John; Hayward, Robert, chemist, St.John.

512 JONES, John, schoolmaster.

1859/60 returned £99; assessed £100.

513 JONES, S.H., draper.

1842/43 returned and assessed £164.5.8.
1846/47-1847/48 returned and assessed £170.

Pigot & Co's Directory, 1842: S.H.Jones, linen & wool draper, Brittox.

514 JONES, William Blackwell, law stationer, innkeeper, Crown.

Year	Amount returned £	Commissioners' estimate £	Final assessment £
1842/43	173	–	173
1846/47	86	–	86
1847/48	90	–	90
1848/49	80	–	80
1849/50	45	–	45
1850/51	42	–	42
1851/52	44	–	44
1852/53	72	–	72
1853/54	89	–	89
1854/55	84	–	84
1855/56	82	–	82
	200i	–	200
1856/57	68	–	68
	200i	–	200

Abbreviations: i, innkeeper.
1855/56 marked "W.B.Jones late Palmer innkeeper".
1856/57 marked "Crown".
1857/58 marked "dead" "innkeeper Crown now Charles Rhodes Plank".
Pigot & Co's Directory, 1842: William B. Jones, law stationer & accountant, agent to Clerical, Medical & General Life Office, St.John Street.
Cross references: King, George, innkeeper, St.John; Palmer, Benjamin, innkeeper, St.John; Plank, Charles Rhodes, innkeeper, St.John.

515 JOYCE, William, innkeeper, [by comparison, Pelican]

1842/43 assessed in absence of return £150.

Assessment made under letter.
Pigot & Co's Directory, 1842: William Joyce, innkeeper, Pelican, Market Place.
Cross reference: Bushell, Ann, innkeeper, St.John; Howse, John, innkeeper, St John.

516 KERSLEY, -, curate.

1855/56 entry only; marked "gone".

517 KING, Edward, bank manager, commission on insurance agency. [by comparison, North Wilts Bank]

1848/49 estimate in absence of return £250 deleted and marked "returned under Schedule E".
1850/51 returned £230 but noted Schedule E.
1851/52-1852/53 recorded and noted Schedule E.
1853/54 returned and assessed £42 commission.
1854/55 returned and assessed £30 commission.
1855/56 assessed in absence of return £30 commission.

1848/49 marked "King late Copeman, bank manager".
1849/50 no entry.
1856/57 marked "removed to Pall Mall"
1857/58 marked "transferred to Mr Calf and Mr Humby".
Note: Copeman was manager of the North Wilts Bank and was succeeded by King. The level of salary is consistent with other branch managers in Devizes. The transfer of the insurance agency to Henry Calf and James Humby denotes that both were employees of the same bank, Humby succeeding King as manager. Employees of public concerns were assessed under Schedule E.
Cross references: Calf, Henry, bank clerk, St.John; Copeman, W.W., bank manager, St.John; Humby, James, bank manager, St.John.

518 KING, George, innkeeper, corndealer, coachmaster, Crown and White Hart. [also KING, Elizabeth Gale]

1842/43 returned and assessed £350.
1846/47 assessed in absence of return £350.
1847/48-1849/50 returned and assessed £425.
1850/51 assessed in absence of return £425.
1851/52 returned and assessed £350.
1852/53-1853/54 returned and assessed £300.

1842/43, 1846/47-1851/52 George King; 1852/53-1853/54 Elizabeth Gale King.
1842/43, 1846/47-1849/50 innkeeper, corndealer, coachmaster; 1850/51 innkeeper;
1851/52-1852/53 innkeeper & coach proprietor; 1853/54 innkeeper, etc.

1847/48-1851/52 Crown and White Hart.
1847/48 marked "Chandler, John, newly King".
1848/49 marked "Chandler, John, now George King".
1854/55 marked "Palmer, Benjamin, late Mrs King, innkeeper".
Pigot & Co's Directory, 1842: George King, Crown, St.John Street; corn & seed dealer, maltster, Market Place.
Cross references: Chandler, John, innkeeper, St.John; Jones, William Blackwell, innkeeper, St.John; Palmer, Benjamin, innkeeper, St.John; Plank, Charles Rhodes, innkeeper, St.John.

519 KING, Robert, baker, provision dealer.

1842/43, 1846/47-1848/49 assessed in absence of return £80; exempt.
1849/50 assessed in absence of return £70; exempt.
1852/53 returned and assessed £98; exempt.
1853/54 returned and assessed £80; exempt.
1854/55 returned and assessed £88.8.0; exempt.
1855/56 assessed in absence of return £100; income proved at £90; exempt.
1856/57 assessed in absence of return £100.
1857/58-1859/60 assessed in absence of return £100.

1842/43, 1846/47-1853/54 baker; 1854/55-1859/60 baker & provision dealer.
1850/51-1851/52 no assessments made.
Pigot & Co's Directory, 1842: Robert King, baker, Long Street.

520 KING, William, baker, confectioner.

1842/43 returned and assessed £110; exempt.
1846/47-1848/49 assessed in absence of return £100; exempt.
1849/50 assessed in absence of return £70; exempt.
1853/54 returned and assessed £80; exempt.
1854/55-1855/56 assessed in absence of return £80; exempt.
1856/57-1859/60 recorded; no assessments made; exempt.

1850/51-1852/53 no assessments made.
Pigot & Co's Directory, 1842: William King, baker, Little Brittox.

521 KINGDON, William, schoolmaster, lodgings.

1857/58 assessed in absence of return £100; income proved at £78; exempt.
1858/59 returned nil; no assessment made.
1859/60 returned and assessed £66.

522 KITE, Edward, grocer.

1842/43 assessed in absence of return £130; income proved at £120; exempt.
1846/47-1851/52 assessed in absence of return £100; exempt.

1852/53–1853/54 returned and assessed £110.
1854/55–1855/56 returned and assessed £100.
1856/57 returned £90; assessed £100.
1857/58 returned and assessed £94.
1858/59–1859/50 returned and assessed £75.

Pigot & Co's Directory, 1842: Edward Kite, grocer & tea dealer, St.John Street.

523 KITE, Thomas, innkeeper. [by comparison, Hare & Hounds]

1842/43 returned and assessed £150.

Pigot & Co's Directory, 1842: Thomas Kite, innkeeper, Hare & Hounds, Bridewell Street.
Cross references: Crook, William, innkeeper, St.John; Millwaters, Nathaniel, innkeeper, St.John.

524 KITE, Thomas, yeoman.

1847/48 entry only.

525 KNEE, Nathaniel, schoolmaster, clerk, commercial traveller, baby linen warehouse.

Year	Amount returned £	Commissioners' estimate £	Income proved £	Final assessment £
1852/53	–	100s	87	–
1853/54	–	100s	90	–
1854/55	–	100s	87	–
1855/56	–	87c	87	–
1856/57	–	100c	–	100
1857/58	70c	–	73.9.0 3.9.0b	–
1858/59	100c	–	110 10b	–
1859/60	120ct 20b	–	120 20	120 20

Abbreviations: s, schoolmaster; c, clerk; ct, commercial traveller; b, baby linen warehouse.

526 KNIGHT, Henry, auctioneer, etc.

1842/43 assessed in absence of return £122; income proved at £122.12.2; exempt.

Pigot & Co's Directory, 1842: Henry Knight, auctioneer, Brittox.

527 KNIGHT, Henry, Junior, bankers clerk, insurance office agent.

Year	Amount returned £	Commissioners' estimate £	Final assessment £
1846/47	150b 18a 7i	–	175
1847/48	150b	–	150
	17i&a	–	17
1848/49	–	167	167
1849/50	–	167	167
1850/51	167	–	167
1851/52	182	–	182

Abbreviations: b, bankers clerk; a, insurance agency; i, interest.
1852/53 marked "now Calf, bankers clerk"; Junior deleted.
Pigot & Co's Directory, 1842: Henry Knight, agent to Royal Exchange, Brittox.
Cross reference: Calf, Henry, bank clerk, St.John.

528 KNIGHT, Jeremiah.

1848/49 name only entered.

529 LAMBERT, Revd. Richard U., curate.

1856/57 assessed in absence of return £100.

1857/58 marked "left Devizes".

530 LAVINGTON, Samuel, grocer, etc.

1842/43 returned and assessed £295.
1846/47 returned and assessed £175.
1847/48-1848/49 assessed in absence of return £250.
1849/50 returned £200; assessed £250.

1850/51 marked "Lyne late Lavington, Samuel, grocer".
Pigot & Co's Directory, 1842: Samuel Lavington, grocer & tea dealer, High Street.
Cross references: Hooper, -, grocer, St.John; Long, John, grocer, St.John; Lyne, Thomas William, grocer, St.John.

531 LAVINGTON & NEATE, auctioneers. [also LAVINGTON, Thomas]

1842/43 returned and assessed £100.
1846/47 returned £250; assessed £300.

1847/48 assessed in absence of return £350.
1848/49 returned £240; assessed £300.
1849/50 returned £220; assessed £300.
1850/51 returned £100 but deleted.

1842/43, 1846/47-1849/50 Lavington & Neate; 1850/51 Thomas Lavington.
1850/51 marked "return in Poulshott", "late Lavington & Neate".
Pigot & Co's Directory, 1842: Lavington & Neate, auctioneers, Lovington (*sic*) & Neate, agents
to Farmers' & General Fire Office, High Street.

532 LEACH, Robert V[alentine], mealman.

1842/43 returned and assessed £90.14.7.

533 LEACH & BOX, corn merchants.

1842/43 returned and assessed £869.8.2¾.

Pigot & Co's Directory, 1842: Leach & Box, corn & seed dealers, manure merchants, New Park
Street.

534 LENTHALL, James & Co., drapers.

1849/50 assessed in absence of return £80; exempt.
1850/51 assessed in absence of return £150; income proved at £97.9.0 on appeal;
exempt.
1851/52 assessed in absence of return £120; income proved at £98; exempt.
1852/53 returned and assessed £95; exempt.
1853/54 returned and assessed £115.
1854/55 assessed in absence of return £115.
1855/56 assessed in absence of return £150.

1849/50 Lenthall & Co; 1850/51-1851/52 James Lenthall; 1852/53-1855/56 James N.
Lenthall.
1849/50 marked "late Hobbs".
1856/57 marked "now John Pope", "Pope, John, late Lenthall, linen draper".
1857/57 marked "now Pope".
Cross references: Hobbs, William, draper, St.John; Pope, John, linen draper, St. John.

535 LEWIS, David, corn dealer.

1857/58 returned and assessed £74; exempt.

1858/59 marked "left Devizes".

536 LOCKE, Francis Alexander Sydenham, Treasurer under Devizes Improvement Act.

1850/51-1851/52 returned and assessed £208.
1852/53 returned and assessed £172.
1853/54 returned £128; no assessment made.
1854/55 returned and assessed £164.
1855/56 returned and assessed £184.
1856/57-1857/58 assessed in absence of return £184.
1858/59 returned £184; no assessment made.
1859/60 assessed in absence of return £184.

1857/58 assessment on Treasurer under Devizes Improvement Commissioners.
1850/51 marked "late Saunders, interest".
1856/57 marked "Query".
1858/59 marked "chargeable under Schedule E, an office".
Cross reference: Saunders, Henry, Treasurer under Devizes Improvement Act, St.John.

537 LOCKE, OLIVIER & TUGWELL, bankers. [also HUGHES, LOCKE & CO; LOCKE, OLIVIER & SAUNDERS]

Year	Amount returned £	Commissioners' estimate £	Final assessment £
1842/43	2090.6.8	–	2090.6.8
1846/47	775.14.1	–	775.14.1
1847/48	864.17.3	–	864.17.3
1848/49	584.6.7	–	584.6.7
1849/50	732.4.4	–	732.4.4
1850/51	993	–	993
1851/52	1666	–	1666
1852/53	1492.13.6	–	1492.13.6
1853/54	1151.15.10	–	1151.15.10
1854/55	944.3.10	–	944.3.10
1855/56	1125.17.6	–	1125.17.6
1856/57	1054.16.10	–	1054.16.10
1857/58	870.14.9	–	870.14.9
1858/59	815.9.1	–	815.9.1
1859/60	871.4.0	–	871.4.0

1842/43, 1846/47-1847/48 Hughes, Locke & Co; 1848/49-1850/51 Locke, Olivier & Saunders;
1851/52-1859/60 Locke, Olivier & Tugwell.
Pigot & Co's Directory, 1842: Hughes, Locke & Co., (draw on Lubbock & Co., London).

538 LONG, John, grocer.

1856/57 assessed in absence of return £150.
1857/58-1858/59 returned and assessed £150.

1856/57-1857/58 marked "late Lyne, grocer".
1859/60 marked "Hooper, late Long, grocer".
Cross references: Hooper, -, grocer, St.John; Lavington, Samuel, grocer, St. John; Lyne, Thomas William, grocer, St.John.

539 LONG, William, corn factor.

1851/52-1853/54 returned and assessed £150.
1854/55 assessed in absence of return £200.
1855/56 returned £204, £150 substituted; assessed £250.
1856/57-1857/58 returned £250; assessed £300.
1858/59 assessed in absence of return £300.
1859/60 returned £300; assessed £400.

1851/52 [St.Mary] marked "King, George now Long, maltster".
1851/52 marked "Long, W., late King, G., corn factor".
Cross reference: King, George, maltster, St.Mary.

540 LOTT, Thomas, gunsmith.

1853/54-1855/56 assessed in absence of return £60; exempt.
1856/57-1859/60 recorded; no assessments made; exempt.

541 LOWE & SIBREE, Misses, schoolmistresses.

1842/43, 1846/47-1849/50 assessed in absence of return £65; exempt.

Pigot & Co's Directory, 1842: Low (sic) & Sibree, preparatory school, Market Place.

542 LYNE, Thomas William, grocer, etc.

1850/51 assessed in absence of return £120.
1851/52-1855/56 returned and assessed £150.

1850/51-1851/52 grocer; 1852/53-1855/56 grocer, etc.
1850/51 marked "Lyne late Lavington, Samuel, grocer".
1856/57 marked "Long, John late Lyne, grocer".
Cross references: Hooper, -, grocer, St.John; Lavington, Samuel, grocer, St. John; Long, John, grocer, St.John.

543 MACCORMICK, Revd. Joseph, curate.

1853/54 assessed in absence of return £100; income proved at £96; exempt.

1853/54 MacCormic; 1854/55 by note, MacCormick.
1854/55 marked "gone".

544 MACDONALD, Alexander and OLIVIER, Alfred, solicitors.

1856/57 assessed in absence of return £200.
1857/58 returned and assessed £72.

[Bayley, John Raikes] 1856/57 "now MacDonald & Olivier".
1857/58 Alexander MacDonald assessed sole.
1858/59 marked "assessed by Special Commissioners".
1859/60 marked "returns at Pewsey".
Cross reference: Bayley, John Raikes, solicitor, St. John.

545 MCEWIN, Edwin, innkeeper, Antelope.

1854/55 assessed in absence of return £100.
1855/56 assessed in absence of return £50.

1854/55 McEwan; 1855/56-1856/57 McEwin; 1857/58 McEwen.
1856/57 marked "McEwin late, now Humby, F.P."
1857/58 marked "McEwen late see Thomas Brown.
Cross references: Brown, Thomas, innkeeper, St.John; Humby, Frederick Peter, innkeeper, St.John; Ransom, William, innkeeper, St.John.

546 MACKRELL, Henry, wine merchant. [also MACKRELL, James]

1846/47 returned and assessed £250.
1847/48-1849/50 assessed in absence of return £250.
1850/51-1855/56 returned and assessed £250.
1856/57 assessed in absence of return £250.

1846/47-1849/50 James Mackrell; 1850/51-1856/57 Henry Mackrell.
1856/57 marked "now Giddings & Ellis".
Cross references: Ellis, George Hackett, wine merchant's clerk, St.John; Giddings & Ellis, wine merchants, St.John.

547 MANNING, Revd. Alexander, private tutor.

Year	Amount returned £	Commissioners' estimate £	Final assessment £
1849/50	35	–	35
1850/51	25	–	25

1851/52	45	–	45
1852/53	30	–	30
1853/54	37	–	37

1855/56 marked "given up to his son".
1857/58 marked "Schedule E"
Cross reference: Manning, Revd. Alexander, chaplain of new prison and private pupils, Rowde;
Manning, Alexander, private tutor, St.John.

548 MANNING, Alexander, private tutor.

1857/58–1859/60 assessed in absence of return £50.

1855/56 marked "Manning, Revd. Alexander, private tutor, given up to his son".
Cross reference: Manning, Revd. Alexander, private tutor, St.John.

549 MARSHMENT, Samuel, artist in photography.

1859/60 assessed in absence of return £150; reduced to £55 on appeal; exempt.

550 MARTIN, Thomas, draper.

1842/43 returned and assessed £200.
1846/47–1847/48 returned £200; assessed £300.
1848/49 returned £180; assessed £300.
1849/50 returned £100; assessed £200.
1850/51 returned and assessed £200.
1851/52–1852/53 returned £150; assessed £175.
1853/54 assessed in absence of return £175.

1853/54 marked "now Tyrell, draper".
Pigot & Co's Directory, 1842: Thomas Martin, linen & wool draper, agent to Guardian Fire
Office, Market Place.
Cross reference: Tyrell, William, linen draper, St.John.

551 MARWIN, William, innkeeper, Lamb.

1852/53 returned and assessed £100; exempt.
1853/54 returned £31.1.10; assessed £100; income proved at £75; exempt.
1854/55 returned and assessed £100.
1855/56 assessed in absence of return £150; reduced to £125.
1856/57 returned £100; assessed £120.
1857/58–1859/60 returned and assessed £110.

1852/53 marked "late Winkworth".
1854/55 Lamb Inn noted; 1856/57 Lamb noted.

1854/55 marked "£200 for 1855".
Cross reference: Winkworth, William, innkeeper, St.John.

552 MASLEN, Louisa, dressmaker.

1842/43, 1846/47 assessed in absence of return £20; exempt.

Pigot & Co's Directory, 1842: Louisa Mazlen (sic), milliner & dressmaker, New Park Street.

553 MASLEN, Maria, shoemaker. [also MASLEN, William]

1842/43 returned and assessed £75; exempt.
1846/47-1848/49 assessed in absence of return £80; exempt.
1849/50-1850/51 assessed in absence of return £100; exempt.
1851/52 assessed in absence of return £130; exempt.
1852/53 returned and assessed £130; exempt.
1853/54 returned and assessed £125.
1854/55-1858/59 returned and assessed £130.
1859/60 returned £130; assessed £150.

1842/43 William Maslen, Maria entered but deleted; 1846/47 William Maslen;
1847/48-1859/60 Maria Maslen.
Pigot & Co's Directory, 1842: William Andrews Maslen, boot & shoe maker, Brittox.

554 MASLEN, Michael, baker & grocer.

1856/57 returned £60; no assessment made; exempt.
1857/58 recorded; no assessment made; exempt.
1858/59 returned £40; no assessment made; exempt.
1859/60 recorded; no assessment made; exempt.

555 MATTHEWS, R.D., clerk.

1856/57 returned and assessed £115.
1857/58 assessed in absence of return £115.

1856/57 marked "from Bedborough".
1858/59 [Bedborough] marked "dead".
Cross reference: Matthews, R.D., clerk, Bedborough.

556 MAYSMOR, Richard, bank manager, Wilts & Dorset Bank.

1846/47 returned and assessed £250.
1847/48 assessed in absence of return £250.

1848/49 marked "See Schedule E".
1849/50 no entry.
1850/51 returned £250; no assessment made; marked "E".
1851/52–1858/59 marked "Schedule E".
1859/60 recorded; no assessment made.

1846/47–1851/52 Maysmore.
1858/59 Wilts & Dorset Bank noted.
Cross reference: Scott, H.L., bank manager, St.John.

557 MEEK, Alexander, solicitor, agent, Treasurer for Wilts interest on borrowed money for militia store.

Year	Amount returned £	Commissioners' estimate £	Final assessment £
1846/47	–	150ag	150
1847/48	–	150ag	150
1848/49	150ag	–	150
1849/50	–	150ag	150
1850/51	–	150ag	150
1851/52	150ag	–	150
1852/53	150ag	–	150
	1500s	–	1500
1853/54	150ag	–	150
	1450s	–	1450
1854/55	1450s	–	1450
1855/56	1250s	–	1250
1856/57	1250s	–	1250
1857/58	–	1250s	1250
1858/59	325t	1250s	325
			1250
1859/60	325t	1250s	325
			1250

Note: Alexander Meek was a partner in the firm of Tugwell & Meek until 1851/52. He was also clerk to the General Commissioners of income tax.
Abbreviations: ag, agent; s, solicitor; t, treasurer for Wilts on money borrowed for militia stores.
Pigot & Co's Directory, 1842: Tugwell & Meek, attorneys, St.John Street; Alexander Meek, town clerk and clerk to the magistrates, St.John Street.
Cross reference: Tugwell & Meek, solicitors, St.John.

558 MILLWATERS, Nathaniel, innkeeper & mail contractor, Hare & Hounds.

1851/52 returned and assessed £180.16.0.
1852/53 returned £150 as innkeeper, £10 as mail contractor; assessed £200.
1853/54–1855/56 returned £150; assessed £200.

1856/57 assessed in absence of return £220.
1857/58-1859/60 returned £150; assessed £230.

1851/52 marked "late Crook".
1856/57 Hare & Hounds noted.
Cross references: Crook, William, innkeeper, St.John; Kite, Thomas, innkeeper, St.John.

559 MILSOM, Robert, shopkeeper, leather cutter.

1842/43, 1846/47-1849/50 assessed in absence of return £80; exempt.
1851/52 returned and assessed £127.3.6; exempt.
1852/53 assessed in absence of return £100; exempt.
1853/54 returned £87.2.6; assessed £100; income proved at £97; exempt.
1854/55 assessed in absence of return £100.
1855/56 returned and assessed £100.
1856/57-1857/58 assessed in absence of return £100.
1858/59-1859/60 returned and assessed £100.

1842/43, 1846/47-1849/50 shopkeeper; 1851/52-1859/60 leather cutter.
1850/51 no assessment made.
Pigot & Co's Directory, 1842: Robert Milsom, leather cutter, High Street.

560 MITCHELL, John, tea dealer & draper.

1842/43 returned and assessed £78; exempt.
1846/47 assessed in absence of return £80; exempt.

Pigot & Co's Directory, 1842: John Mitchell, tea dealer, linen & wool draper, Long Street.

561 MOORE, Peter Halked, curate.

1855/56-1856/57 returned and assessed £30.

1857/58 marked "now -", "left Devizes".

562 MORRIS, Charles, clothier.

1856/57 recorded; no assessment made; exempt.
1857/58 assessed in absence of return £100.
1858/59 returned and assessed £120.

563 MORRIS, William, bacon factor.

1842/43, 1846/47-1855/56 returned and assessed £150.

1856/57 returned £100; assessed £150.
1857/58 returned and assessed £150.
1858/59 returned £125; assessed £150.
1859/60 returned and assessed £150.

Pigot & Co's Directory, 1842: William Morris, cheese & bacon factor & dealer, Market Place.

564 MUDY, William, drawing & music master.

1842/43 returned and assessed £170.

Pigot & Co's Directory, 1842: William Mudy, music teacher, Chequer.

565 MULCOCK, Ann, widow.

1842/43 name only entered.

566 MULLINGS, Thomas, shoemaker.

1842/43, 1846/47-1848/49 assessed in absence of return £40; exempt.
1849/50 assessed in absence of return £80; exempt.

Pigot & Co's Directory, 1842: Thomas Mullings, boot & shoe maker, (& parish clerk), shop
   keeper & dealer in groceries and sundries, Long Street.

567 MUNDAY, James, baker.

1842/43, 1846/47-1849/50 assessed in absence of return £30; exempt.

Pigot & Co's Directory, 1842: James Munday, confectioner, High Street.

568 MUSSELWHITE, Thomas, saddler. [also MUSSELWHITE, George & Henry]

1842/43 assessed in absence of return £140; exempt.
1846/47-1851/52 assessed in absence of return £100; exempt.
1852/53 returned and assessed £125; exempt.
1853/54 returned £125; assessed £150.
1854/55 assessed in absence of return £130.
1855/56 returned and assessed £130.
1856/57 returned £125; assessed £130.
1857/58 returned and assessed £130.
1858/59 returned £0; assessed £150.
1859/60 returned £125; assessed £150; exemption claimed by each partner.

1842/43, 1846/47-1858/59 Thomas Musselwhite; 1859/60 Thomas Musselwhite & Sons (George & Henry).
Pigot & Co's Directory, 1842: Thomas Musselwhite, saddler & harness maker, St.John Street.

569 NEATE, Ann, innkeeper. [by comparison, Elm Tree]

1842/43 assessed in absence of return £150.

Pigot & Co's Directory, 1842: Ann Neate, Elm Tree, Long Street.
Cross reference: Sloper, Edwin, innkeeper, St.John.

570 NEATE, John, innkeeper, maltster. [by comparison, Black Horse]

1842/43 returned and assessed £210.
1846/47 returned and assessed £200.
1847/48 assessed in absence of return £250.
1848/49 returned and assessed £200.
1849/50 returned and assessed £160.
1850/51 returned and assessed £100.

1842/43 innkeeper & maltster; 1846/47-1847/48 innkeeper, etc.; 1848/49-1850/51 maltster.
1850/51 Executors of John Neate assessed.
Pigot & Co's Directory, 1842: John Neate, Black Horse, maltster, St.John Street.

571 NORMAN , John, hair dresser, hair cutter.

1842/43, 1846/47 assessed in absence of return £140; exempt.
1847/48-1848/49 assessed in absence of return £60; exempt.
1849/50 assessed in absence of return £50; exempt.
1853/54 returned and assessed £80; exempt.
1854/55 returned £100; assessed £80; exempt.
1855/56 assessed in absence of return £80; exempt.
1856/57 recorded; no assessment made; exempt.
1857/58 assessed in absence of return £100; income proved at £79; exempt.
1858/59 recorded; no assessment made; exempt.
1859/60 returned £89; no assessment made; exempt.

1850/51-1852/53 no assessments made.
Pigot & Co's Directory, 1842: John Norman, perfumer & hair dresser, St.John Street.

572 NORRIS, Henry Kent, solicitor.

1842/43 returned £149 (deleted); assessed £100; exempt.
1846/47-1849/50 returned and assessed £120.
1850/51 assessed in absence of return £170.

1851/52-1852/53 returned and assessed £120.
1853/54 returned £120; assessed £150.
1854/55 returned and assessed £150.
1855/56 returned £120; assessed £150.
1856/57 returned and assessed £160.
1857/58 returned £120; assessed £160.
1858/59 assessed in absence of return £160.
1859/60 assessed in absence of return £200.

Pigot & Co's Directory, 1842: Henry Kent Norris, attorney, Market Place.

573 NORTH WILTS BANKING COMPANY.

1842/43, 1846/47-1859/60 recorded but marked "return at Melksham".
Pigot & Co's Directory, 1842: North Wilts Banking Company, Market Place (draw on Drewett
    & Fowler, London)

574 NOTT, William, solicitor's clerk.

1858/59 returned and assessed £70.
1859/60 returned £70; reduced by life assurance relief of £1.19.2.

1858/59 marked "See Schedule E".

575 NOTTON, R.J., hatter.

1853/54 returned and assessed £80; exempt.
1854/55-1855/56 assessed in absence of return £80; exempt.

1856/57 marked "now Couzens, brush warehouse".
1857/58 marked "now Couzens, G.".
Cross reference: Couzens, George, brush warehouse, rope maker, St.John.

576 OATLEY, Cornelius, builder.

1846/47-1849/50 assessed in absence of return £100; exempt.

Cross reference: Oatley, Cornelius, carpenter, St.Mary.

577 PAGAN, Alexander, tea dealer.

1842/43 returned and assessed £80; exempt.
1846/47-1848/49 assessed in absence of return £80; exempt.

Pigot & Co's Directory, 1842: Alexander Pagan, tea dealer, linen & woollen draper, Long Street.

578 PALMER, Benjamin, innkeeper. [by comparison, Crown]

1854/55 returned and assessed £200.
1855/56 recorded but no assessment made.

1855/56 marked "now W.B.Jones".
Cross reference: Jones, William Blackwell, innkeeper, St.John; King, George, innkeeper, St.John; Plank, Charles Rhodes, innkeeper, St.John.

579 PAULING, William, fellmonger.

1842/43 returned £50; assessed £75; exempt.
1846/47-1847/48 assessed in absence of return £75; exempt.
1848/49 returned and assessed £110; exempt.
1849/50 assessed in absence of return £110; exempt.

Pigot & Co's Directory, 1842: William Pauling, fellmonger & glover, Northgate Street.

580 PEPLER, Jane, dressmaker.

1842/43, 1846/47-1849/50 assessed in absence of return £50; exempt.

Pigot & Co's Directory, 1842: Jane & Ann Pepler, milliners & dressmakers, Brittox.

581 PERRY, John & Co., grocers.

1847/48 returned £120; assessed £150; income proved at £120; exempt.
1848/49 assessed in absence of return £120; income proved at £199; exempt.
1849/50 assessed in absence of return £120; exempt.

1847/48 marked "Coward, Thomas & Richard, now Perry, grocers".
1848/49 exemption claimed as partnership.
Cross reference: Coward, Thomas & Richard, grocers, St.John.

582 PHILLIPS, Peter Pattie, draper, linen draper, warehouseman.

1851/52 returned and assessed £100; exempt.
1852/53 assessed in absence of return £150; assessment discharged but no sum recorded.
1853/54 returned £105; assessed £150.
1857/58 assessed in absence of return £100.

1858/59 assessed in absence of return £150.
1859/60 returned £130; assessed £175.

1851/52-1853/54 draper; 1857/58-1858/59 linen draper; 1859/60 warehouseman.
1854/55-1855/56 marked "gone to Australia".
1857/58 marked "late Watson, linen draper".
Cross reference: Watson, John, tea dealer & draper, St.John.

583 PHILLIPS, Thomas, shopman.

1842/43, 1846/47-1849/50 assessed in absence of return £90; exempt.

Pigot & Co's Directory, 1842: possibly Thomas Phillips, boot & shoe maker, New Park Street.

584 PHIPPS, Revd. James E., surplice fees, subscriptions for sittings.

1842/43 returned surplice fees £185 (deleted); no assessment made.
1851/52 returned and assessed subscriptions for sittings £170.
1852/53 returned and assessed subscriptions for sittings £160.

1842/43 marked "See Schedule A".
Pigot & Co's Directory, 1842: Revd. Edward James Phipps, Long Street.

585 PLANK, Charles Rhodes, innkeeper, Crown.

1857/58 assessed in absence of return £200.
1858/59 assessed in absence of return £150.
1859/60 assessed in absence of return £200.

1857/58 marked "Jones, William Blackwell, innkeeper, Crown (dead) now Charles Rhodes Plank".
Cross references: Jones, William Blackwell, law stationer, innkeeper, St.John; Plank, Charles Rhodes, builder, Bedborough; Plank, Charles, builder, Week.

586 PLANK, Sarah, glass dealer.

1842/43, 1846/47 assessed in absence of return £50; exempt.

Pigot & Co's Directory, 1842: Sarah Plank, china, glass, etc., dealer, St.John Street.

587 PLUMMER, John Alderson - see SPENCER, Thomas C & PLUMMER, John Alderson.

588 POOK, Thomas, coachman.

1842/43, 1846/47-1848/49 assessed in absence of return £80; exempt.

589 POPE, John, linen draper.

1856/57 assessed in absence of return £140; reduced to £120 on appeal.
1857/58-1858/59 returned and assessed £120.
1859/60 assessed in absence of return £150.

1856/57-1857/58 marked "late Lenthall, linen draper".
Cross references: Hobbs, William, linen draper, St.John; Lenthall, James & Co., draper, St.John.

590 PRENTIS, Charles William, chemist [also PRENTICE, J.C.].

1854/55 returned and assessed £125.
1855/56 assessed in absence of return £125.
1856/57 returned and assessed £136.
1857/58 returned £100 (deleted).

1854/55-1855/56 J.C.Prentice; 1856/57-1857/58 Charles William Prentis.
1854/55 original entry £100 deleted marked "see below".
1854/55 marked "Read now Mr or W Prentice, chemist".
1857/58 marked "now Rowland, William S., chemist".
Cross references: Read, James, chemist, St.John; Rowland, William S., chemist, St.John; Thompson, -, chemist, St.John.

591 PRICE, Andrew, innkeeper.

1846/47 entry only.

592 RANDELL, James, builder, plasterer, land and house agent.

1842/43, 1846/47-1848/49 assessed in absence of return £50; exempt.
1849/50 assessed in absence of return £80; exempt.
1853/54 returned £90; assessed £100; income proved £90; exempt.
1854/55 returned and assessed £100.
1855/56 returned and assessed £120.
1856/57 assessed in absence of return £120.
1857/58 returned and assessed £120.
1858/59 returned nil; no assessment made.
1859/60 assessed in absence of return £100.

1846/47-1849/50 Randall.

1842/43, 1846/47-1849/50 plasterer; 1853/54-1854/55 builder, etc., (land and house agent); 1855/56-1859/60 builder, etc.
1859/60 marked "app." and assessment not extended to tax paid column.
1850/51-1852/53 no assessments made.

593 RANDLE, Nathaniel Bakewell, bookseller.

1842/43, 1846/47-1858/59 returned and assessed £200.
1859/60 returned £200; assessed £250; reduced to £233 but no appeal noted.

Pigot & Co's Directory, 1842: Nathaniel Bakewell Randle, bookseller, stationer & printer, jeweller & silversmith, Market Place.

594 RANSOM, William, publican & woolstapler. [by comparison, Antelope]

1842/43 returned and assessed £130; exempt.
1846/47-1849/50 assessed in absence of return £120; exempt.

Pigot & Co's Directory, 1842: William Ransom, innkeeper, Antelope, Market Place.
Cross references: Humby, Frederick Peter, innkeeper, St.John; McEwin, Edwin, innkeeper, St.John; Ransom, William, woolstapler, Bedborough.

595 READ, James, chemist, druggist.

1846/47-1847/48 assessed in absence of return £100; exempt.
1848/49-1849/50 returned and assessed £150.
1850/51 assessed in absence of return £150.
1851/52 returned and assessed £150.
1852/53 returned £50; assessed £100; exempt.

1846/47 chemist & druggist; 1847/48-1849/50 chemist, etc.; 1850/51-1852/53 chemist.
1852/53-1853/54 marked "now Thompson, chemist".
Cross references: Prentis, Charles William, chemist, St.John; Rowland, William S., chemist, St John; Thompson, -, chemist, St.John.

596 REEVE, Jonah, upholsterer.

1842/43, 1846/47-1859/60 recorded and marked "return at Marlborough".
1857/58 marked additionally "return for both at Marlborough, see Board's letter with Mr. Cottle".
1857/58 assessment made at £200 but deleted.
Pigot & Co's Directory, 1842: Jonah Reeve, auctioneer, appraiser & cabinet maker, High Street, Marlborough.
Pigot & Co's Directory, 1842: Jonah Reeve, cabinet maker & upholsterer, Market Place and High Marlborough.

597 RENDELL, William, smith.

1853/54 returned and assessed £85; exempt.
1854/55 returned and assessed £80; exempt.
1855/56 returned and assessed £75; exempt.
1856/57 recorded; no assessment made; exempt.
1857/58 returned and assessed £75; exempt.
1858/59 returned £75; no assessment made; exempt.
1859/60 recorded; no assessment made; exempt.

1853/54-1855/56 Randell; 1856/57-1859/60 Rendell.

598 REW, Henry, hair dresser & hatter.

1842/43 returned and assessed £85 hair dresser, £25 hatter; exempt.

Pigot & Co's Directory, 1842: Henry Rew, perfumer & hair dresser, Market Place.

599 REYNOLDS, C.B., draper & tailor.

1842/43 returned £140; assessed £175.

Pigot & Co's Directory, 1842: Charles Benjamin Reynolds, tailor, Market Place.

600 RICHARDSON, George, tea dealer, etc.

1853/54 returned £90; assessed £100.

601 ROACH, Charles, hatter.

1842/43 returned £200; assessed £250.
1846/47 returned and assessed £250.
1847/48 assessed in absence of return £300.
1848/49 returned £170; assessed £300.
1849/50 returned £200; assessed £300.
1850/51 returned £200; assessed £250.
1851/52 returned £170; assessed £250.
1852/53-1853/54 returned and assessed £250.
1854/55-1856/57 returned and assessed £260.
1857/58 returned and assessed £240.
1858/59 returned and assessed £200.
1859/60 returned £200; assessed £250.

Pigot & Co's Directory, 1842: Charles Roach, straw hat maker, hatter & furrier, Brittox.

602 ROWLAND, William S., chemist.

1857/58-1859/60 returned and assessed £100.

1857/58 marked "Prentis C.W., now Rowland, William S., chemist".
Cross references: Prentis, Charles William, chemist, St.John; Read, James, chemist, St.John;
    Thompson, -, chemist, St.John.

603 RUDMAN, Joel, corn dealer.

1858/59 recorded; no assessment made; exempt.
1859/60 returned £60; assessed £100; income proved at £78; exempt.

604 SALMON, W.W., steward.

1842/43 returned and assessed £150.

Pigot & Co's Directory, 1842: Wm.W.Salmon, stamp distributor and Treasurer for the County,
    St.John Street.

605 SARTAIN, C.E., printer.

1846/47-1848/49 assessed in absence of return £70; exempt.
1850/51-1851/52 assessed in absence of return £60; exempt.

1849/50 no assessment made.
1851/52 marked "now Davis, A., printer".
Cross reference: Davis, [Gillman] Arthur, printer, St.John.

606 SAUNDERS, Henry, Treasurer under Devizes Improvement Act.

1842/43, 1846/47 returned and assessed £200.
1847/48 assessed in absence of return £160.
1848/49 returned and assessed £188.
1849/50 assessed in absence of return £188.

Cross reference: Locke, Francis Alexander Sydenham, Treasurer under Devizes Improvement Act.

607 SCORREY, -, tailor.

1853/54 estimated in absence of return £70; no assessment made; exempt.

1852/53 marked "Plummer, J.A., now Scorrey tailor".

1854/55 marked "late Plummer gone away not recorded".
Cross reference: Plummer, J.A., tailor, St.John.

608 SCOTT, H.L., bank manager. [by comparison, Wilts & Dorset Bank]

1842/43 returned and assessed £210.

Pigot & Co's Directory, 1842: H.L.Scott, bank manager, Wilts & Dorset Bank.
Cross reference: Maysmor, Richard, bank manager, St.John.

609 SEAGRAM, William Ballard, physician, visiting private lunatic asylum.

Year	Amount returned £	Commissioners' estimate £	Final assessment £
1842/43	190	–	190
	100	–	100
1846/47	200	–	285
	85p	–	–
1847/48	–	285	235(sic)
1848/49	–	235	235
1849/50	200	–	200
1850/51	180	–	180
1851/52	150	–	150
1852/53	170	–	170
1853/54	180	–	180
1854/55	120	–	120
1855/56	40L	–	40
1856/57	40L	–	40

Abbreviations: p, property outside Great Britain; L, visiting private lunatic asylum.
1842/43 an apparent partnership between W.B. and W.B. Seagram, M.Ds.
1846/47-1854/55 physician.
Assessments generally included "interest on property out of Great Britain" but deleted 1850/51 reinstated 1851/52.
1857/58 marked "left Devizes".
Pigot & Co's Directory, 1842: William B. Seagram, physician, the Ark.
Note: W.B. Seagram acted as an Additional Commissioner.

610 SHEPPARD, William.

1842/43 entry only; marked "left".
Pigot & Co's Directory, 1842: William Sheppard, carpenter & builder, Sheep Street.

611 SIMPSON, Edward, grocer, tea dealer.

Year	Amount returned £	Commissioners' estimate £	Final assessment £
1850/51	–	150	150
1851/52	220	–	220
1852/53	320	–	320
1853/54	320	–	320
1854/55	350	–	350
1855/56	270	350	350
1856/57	300	360	360
1857/58	300	360	360
1858/59	360	–	360
1859/60	350	360	360

1850/51-1853/54 grocer; 1854/55-1859/60 grocer & tea dealer.
1850/51-1851/52 marked "Simpson late Ball, grocer"
Cross reference: Ball, James, tea dealer, St.John.

612 SIMPSON, George, printer, newspaper proprietor.

1842/43 returned and assessed £540.
1846/47 returned £500; assessed £540.
1847/48-1848/49 returned and assessed £540.
1849/50-1850/51 assessed in absence of return £600.
1851/52-1855/56 returned and assessed £600.
1856/57-1857/58 assessed in absence of return £600.
1858/59 returned and assessed £600.
1859/60 assessed in absence of return £600.

1842/43, 1846/47-1853/54 printer; 1853/54-1859/60 newspaper proprietor.
Pigot & Co's Directory, 1842: George Simpson, printer, Devizes & Wiltshire Gazette, Market
    Place; agent to Alfred Life Office, Market Place.

613 SIMS, John, shoemaker.

Year	Amount returned £	Commissioners' estimate £	Income proved £	Final assessment £
1842/43	–	150	–	100
1846/47	70	100	–	100
1847/48	–	100	–	100
1848/49	50	100	100	–
1849/50	–	65	65	–
1850/51	–	150a	–	56

1851/52	56	–	–	56
1852/53	56	–	–	56
1853/54	54	–	–	–
1854/55	–	60	–	60
1855/56	50	60	–	60
1856/57	40	60	–	60
1857/58	40	60	–	60
1858/59	35	50	–	50
1859/60	40	60	–	60

1842/43 marked "statement in writing to be made". No appeal noted.
1850/51 income proved £56; income from property in addition £103.
1853/54 no assessment made.
Pigot & Co's Directory, 1842: John Sims, boot & shoe maker, St.John Street.

614 SKINNER, Joseph, tinman.

1847/48-1852/53 assessed in absence of return £90; exempt.

1847/48 [St.Mary] marked "St.John".
1854/55 marked "gone".
Pigot & Co's Directory, 1842: Joseph Skinner, brazier & tinman, Brittox.
Cross reference: Skinner, Joseph, tinman, St.Mary.

615 SLADE, Samuel, tailor, shopkeeper.

1842/43 returned and assessed £80; exempt.
1846/47-1849/50 assessed in absence of return £80; exempt.

Pigot & Co's Directory, 1842: Samuel Slade, shopkeeper & dealer in groceries & sundries, Bridewell Street.

616 SLOPER, Ann, innkeeper, Black Swan. [also SLOPER, George]

Year	Amount returned £	Commissioners' estimate £	Income proved £	Final assessment £
1842/43	270	–	–	270
1846/47	160	200	–	200
1847/48	155	200	–	200
1848/49	150	200	–	200
1849/50	–	60	100	–
1850/51	62	120	120	–
1851/52	60	120a	112.11.0	100
	52.10.0i			

1852/53	70pi	112	–	112
1853/54	60	90	–	137
	47i			
1854/55	60	105	–	152
	47i			
1855/56	109	152	–	152
1856/57	60	152	–	152
	47i			
1857/58	60	150	–	197
	47i			
1858/59	70	150	–	202.10.0
	52.10.0i			
1859/60	70	203	–	203
	55i			

Abbreviations: i, interest; pi, profits and interest.
1842/43 George Sloper; 1846/47-1847/48 Anne(sic) Sloper; 1848/49-1859/60 Ann(sic) Sloper.
1851/52 although income proved at £112.11.0, tax paid on £100.
1854/55 Black Swan noted.
Pigot & Co's Directory, 1842: George Sloper, Black Swan, Market Place.

617 SLOPER, Edwin, innkeeper, Elm Tree.

Year	Amount returned £	Commissioners' estimate £	Final assessment £
1846/47	157	–	157
1847/48	154	–	154
1848/49	154	–	154
1849/50	154	200	200
1850/51	–	200	200
1851/52	150	175	175
1852/53	150	175	175
1853/54	150	175	150
1854/55	150	–	150
1855/56	150	175	150
1856/57	150	216	216
1857/58	170	200	200
1858/59	180	200	200
1859/60	175	200	180

1853/54, 1855/56 reduced but no appeal noted.
1859/60 assessment reduced by life assurance relief of £20.
Cross reference: Neate, Ann, innkeeper, St.John.

618 SLOPER, Joseph, linen draper, worsted dealer, shoemaker.

1842/43 returned £150; estimated £175; assessment reduced to £150.
1846/47-1848/49 returned and assessed £150.
1849/50 assessed in absence of return £150.

1842/43, 1846/47-1848/49 shoemaker & worsted dealer; 1849/50 worsted dealer; 1850/51 linen draper.
1842/43 no appeal noted.
1850/51 marked "Street late Sloper, boot & shoe warehouse"; "late Sloper shoemaker".
Pigot & Co's Directory, 1842: Joseph Sloper, boot & shoe maker, Market Place.
Cross references: Sloper, Joseph, linen draper, St.Mary; Street, -, boot & shoe warehouse, St.John.

619 SLY, William, harness maker [also SLY, William, junior]

1857/58 assessed in absence of return £160.
1858/59-1859/60 returned and assessed £160.

1857/58 William Sly senior and William Sly junior.
Pigot & Co's Directory, 1842: William Sly, saddler & harness maker, Brittox.
Cross reference: Sly, William, saddler, St.Mary.

620 SMITH, Revd. A[lfred], clergyman.

1842/43 returned and assessed £30.
1847/48-1848/49 returned and assessed £25.
1849/50 assessed in absence of return £25; assessment discharged on appeal.
1852/53-1853/54 returned and assessed £24.
1854/55 returned and assessed £40.
1855/56 returned and assessed £30.
1856/57 assessed in absence of return £30.
1857/58-1858/59 returned and assessed £26.
1859/60 returned nil; no assessment made.

1842/43 marked "brickmaker".
1850/51-1851/52 no assessment made.
1852/53 marked "church at Poulshot".
1853/54-1858/59 marked "clergyman at Poulshot".
1859/60 marked "no professional income at all".
Pigot & Co's Directory, 1842: Revd. Alfred Smith, clergy, Old Park.
Note: Revd. A. Smith acted as an Additional and a General Commissioner.

621 SMITH, Elizabeth, lodging house keeper.

1842/43, 1846/47-1849/50 assessed in absence of return £60; exempt.

622 SMITH, James, currier.

1842/43, 1846/47–1849/50 assessed in absence of return £60; exempt.
1851/52 returned and assessed £126.10.0; exempt.
1852/53 returned and assessed £122.10.0; exempt.
1853/54 returned £100; assessed £122.10.0
1854/55 returned £120; assessed £122.10.0
1855/56–1857/58 returned £100; assessed £125.
1858/59 returned £110; assessed £125.
1859/60 returned £125; assessed £150.

1850/51 no assessment made.
1859/60 marked "left Devizes".
Pigot & Co's Directory, 1842: James Smith, currier & leather cutter, Brittox.

623 SMITH, Thomas B., bookseller.

1842/43 returned and assessed £100.

Pigot & Co's Directory, 1842: Thomas Burrough Smith, bookseller, printer & stationer, agent to
    Minerva Life Office, Market Place.

624 SPENCER, Thomas C & PLUMMER, John Alderson, tailors.

1842/43 assessed in absence of return £109; exempt.
1846/47 assessed in absence of return £120; exempt.
1847/48 assessed in absence of return £300; income proved at £200; exempt.
1848/49 assessed in absence of return £200; exempt.
1849/50 returned and assessed £200; exempt.
1850/51 assessed in absence of return £120; exempt.
1851/52 assessed in absence of return £120; income proved at £140.9.6; exempt.
1852/53 assessed in absence of return £80; exempt.

1842/43 Thomas Spencer, shopman's assistant; 1846/47 Thomas C Spencer, tailor;
1847/48–1849/50 Thomas C. Spencer & John Alderson Plummer, tailors;
1850/51–1852/53 John Alderson Plummer, tailor.
1852/53 marked "now Scorrey, tailor".
Exemption claimed as partnership.
Cross reference: Scorrey, -, tailor, St.John.

625 SPRAWSON, John, stage coachman, coach proprietor, coach driver.

1852/53 returned and assessed £140.15.0; exempt.
1853/54–1859/60 returned and assessed £125.

1852/53 stage coachman; 1853/54–1854/55 coach proprietor & driver;

1855/56-1859/60 coach proprietor.
Cross reference: Sprawson, John, coachman, Week.

626 STANFORD, Charles, minister.

1848/49 returned and assessed £140; exempt.
1849/50-1850/51 assessed in absence of return £140; exempt.
1851/52 assessed in absence of return £150.
1852/53 returned and assessed £140; exempt.
1853/54 returned and assessed £150.

1854/55 marked "charged in Week".
Cross reference: Stanford, Charles, dissenting minister, Week.

627 STEPHENS, William, coach proprietor.

1856/57-1858/59 recorded; no assessments made; exempt.

1857/58 margin note illegible: "114 ex. at ...."

628 STEWART. William Matthew, tea seller, commercial traveller.

Year	Amount returned £	Commissioners' estimate £	Income proved £	Final assessment £
1842/43	–	110	110	–
1846/47	–	100	100	–
1847/48	–	100	100	–
1848/49	–	100	100	–
1849/50	150 20i	–	–	170
1850/51	170	–	–	170
1851/52	170	–	–	170
1852/53	150 20i	–	–	170
1853/54	150 20i	–	–	170
1854/55	170	–	–	170
1855/56	170	–	–	170
1856/57	150 20i	–	–	170
1857/58	170 20i	–	–	190
1858/59	170 20i	–	–	190

1859/60	170	–	–	160.19.6
	20i	–	–	20

Abbreviation: i, interest.
1842/43 tea seller; 1846/47-1859/60 commercial traveller.
1847/48 assessed under letter.
1859/60 assessment reduced by relief for life assurance of £9.0.6.

629 STOCKEN, George, law clerk, school.

1852/53 returned and assessed £134.14.6; exempt.
1853/54-1857/58 assessed in absence of return £135.
1858/59-1859/60 assessed in absence of return £175.

1852/53-1856/57 law clerk, school; 1857/58-1859/60 law clerk.

630 STOCKWELL, George, beerhouse keeper.

1842/43, 1846/47-1849/50 assessed in absence of return £50; exempt.

Pigot & Co's Directory, 1842: George Stockwell, retailer of beer, shop keeper & dealer in groceries and sundries, South End.

631 STREET, -, boot & shoe warehouse.

1850/51 assessed in absence of return £100; exempt.

1850/51 marked "late Joseph Sloper, boot & shoe warehouse"; "late Sloper, shoemaker".
Cross reference: Sloper, Joseph, shoemaker, St.John.

632 TABRAM, W.M. [by comparison, clothes dealer & hatter]

1842/43 assessed in absence of return £100; exempt.

Pigot & Co's Directory, 1842: William Tabram, clothes dealer & hatter, Market Place.

633 TANNER, William & CANNING, George Barnes, solicitors.

1842/43 returned and assessed £700.

Pigot & Co's Directory, 1842: Tanner & Canning, attorneys, St.John Street; William Tanner, agent to West of England Fire Office, St.John Street.
Cross reference: Canning, George Barnes, solicitor, St.John.

634 TAYLOR, Robert, confectioner.

1855/56 assessed in absence of return £75; exempt.
1856/57 recorded; no assessment made; exempt.

1855/56-1857/58 marked "late Jenkins, confectioner"
1857/58 marked "gone".
Cross references: Jenkins, Mrs Jane, confectioner, St.John; White, George, confectioner, St.John.

635 TENNANT, William, [surveyor of taxes] interest.

1848/49 returned and assessed £28.
1849/50 returned and assessed £19.
1850/51 returned and assessed £15.

636 THOMPSON, -, chemist.

1853/54 returned £70; assessed £100; income proved at £70; exempt.

1853/54 marked "late Read chemist".
Cross references: Prentis, Charles William, chemist, St.John; Read, James, chemist, St.John; Rowland, William S., chemist, St.John.

637 THORNLEY, Robert Samuel, surgeon, etc.

1858/59 assessed in absence of return £120 (deleted) £30.
1859/60 returned £20; assessed £45; assessment reduced by relief for life assurance £6.17.4.

1858/59 marked "late Bayes".
Cross reference: Bayes, Frederick William, surgeon, St.John.

638 TUGWELL & MEEK, solicitors.

1842/43 returned and assessed £2250.
1846/47-1850/51 returned and assessed £2000.
1851/52 returned and assessed £1500.

Note: Alexander Meek continued to be assessed sole 1852/53 et seq.
Pigot & Co's Directory, 1842: Tugwell & Meek, attorneys, St.John Street.
Cross reference: Meek, Alexander, solicitor, St.John.
Note: William Edmund Tugwell acted as an Additional Commissioner; Alexander Meek was Clerk to the Commissioners.

639 TYRELL, William, linen draper.

1854/55 returned and assessed £175.
1855/56 returned £130; assessed £175.
1856/57 returned £150; assessed £175.
1857/58-1858/59 returned and assessed £175.
1859/60 returned £175; assessed £200.

1853/54 marked "Martin, Thomas now Tyrell, draper".
Cross reference: Martin, Thomas, draper, St.John.

640 VINCENT, J.P., veterinary surgeon.

1846/47 returned and assessed £156.
1847/48 assessed in absence of return £160.
1848/49 returned and assessed £154.
1849/50 returned and assessed £150.
1850/51 assessed in absence of return £150.
1851/52 returned and assessed £150.

Note: assessed in St.Mary 1842/43.
Pigot & Co's Directory, 1842: J.P.Vincent, veterinary surgeon, Northgate Street.
Cross reference: Vincent, J.P., veterinary surgeon, St.Mary.

641 WALKE, Revd. William Dewdney, curate.

1859/60 returned and assessed £80.

642 WALLACE, Hill, gentleman, income from foreign securities.

1842/43 returned and assessed £266.
1846/47 returned and assessed £289.

Pigot & Co's Directory, 1842: Captain Hill Wallace, gentry, St.John Street.
1846/47 includes income from foreign securities.

643 WARD, Isaiah, painter etc.,

1842/43 returned and assessed £130.
1846/47 assessed in absence of return £130; exempt.
1847/48-1848/49 returned and assessed £200.
1849/50 returned and assessed £122.9.0; exempt.
1850/51 assessed in absence of return £100; exempt.
1851/52-1852/53 assessed in absence of return £75; exempt.

1853/54 assessed in absence of return £100.
1854/55–1858/59 returned and assessed £100.
1859/60 returned £100; assessed £125.

1842/43, 1846/47–1850/51, 1852/53–1855/56 painter; 1851/52, 1856/57–1859/60, painter etc.
Pigot & Co's Directory, 1842: Isaiah Ward, house & ornamental painter & gilder, fancy repository & stationery, Market Place.

644 WARNE, William & Co., drapers.

1842/43 assessed in absence of return £150; assessment reduced to £120; exempt.

1842/43 no appeal noted.
Pigot & Co's Directory, 1842: William Warne, linen & wool draper, Wine Street.

645 WASTEFIELD, Andrew, music master.

1842/43 assessed in absence of return £150; assessment reduced to £125; exempt.

1842/43 no appeal noted.
Pigot & Co's Directory, 1842: Andrew Wastefield, music teacher, High Street.

646 WATSON, John, tea dealer, draper.

1848/49–1849/50 assessed in absence of return £50; exempt.
1852/53 assessed in absence of return £150.
1853/54–1854/55 returned and assessed £150.

1842/43, 1846/47–1849/50, 1852/53 tea dealer & draper; 1853/54–1854/55 draper etc.
1852/53 Charles Watson entered but deleted.
1850/51–1851/52 no assessments made.
1854/55 marked "insolvent and dead"; 1855/56 marked "dead"; 1857/58 marked "Phillips, Peter Pattie, late Watson, linen draper".
Pigot & Co's Directory, 1842: Charles Watson, tea dealer & linen & woollen draper, Green.
Cross references: Phillips, Peter Pattie, linen draper, St.John; Watson, Charles, tea dealer, Bedborough.

647 WEAVER, Henry, auctioneer & agent.

1858/59 returned £250; assessed £222.3.4.
1859/60 assessed in absence of return £300.

648 WELLS, James, innkeeper, Swan.

1850/51-1851/52 assessed in absence of return £80; exempt.
1852/53 returned £128; assessed £80; income proved £128; exempt.
1853/54 returned £53.6.8; estimated £60 but no assessment made.

1849/50 marked "Frayling, Edward now Wells innkeeper Swan".
1854/55 marked "now Jenkins, innkeeper".
Cross references: Bourne, Richard, innkeeper, St.John; Frayling, Edward, innkeeper, St.John; Jenkins, David, innkeeper, St.John.

649 WHEELER, Thomas, tailor.

1846/47-1849/50 assessed in absence of return £50; exempt.
1858/59-1859/60 recorded; no assessment made; exempt.

1858/59 marked "Qy. chd. at 90?"

650 WHITCHURCH, Samuel, ironmonger, wine merchant.

1842/43, 1846/47 returned and assessed £250.
1847/48 assessed in absence of return £250.
1848/49 returned nil; assessed £150.
1849/50-1854/55 returned and assessed £150.

1842/43, 1846/47-1848/49 ironmonger & wine merchant; 1849/50-1851/52 ironmonger etc; 1852/53-1854/55 ironmonger.
1855/56 marked "insolvent".
1856/57 marked "now Reeve, ironmonger".
Pigot & Co's Directory, 1842: Samuel Whitchurch, ironmonger, Market Place; Whitchurch & Co., wine merchants, Northgate Street.

651 WHITE, George, confectioner.

1842/43 returned £80; assessed £100; exempt.
1846/47-1847/48 assessed in absence of return £100; exempt.
1848/49 returned £60; assessed £100; exempt.

1849/50 marked "Jenkins, late White, confectioner".
Pigot & Co's Directory, 1842: George White, baker, confectioner, St.John Street.
Cross references: Jenkins, Mrs Jane, confectioner, St.John; Taylor, Robert, confectioner, St.John.

652 WILD, George, innkeeper, Three Crowns.

1856/57 marked "late Chandler 3 Crowns". No assessment made.

Cross reference: Wild, George, innkeeper, St.Mary.

653 WILTS & DORSET BANKING COMPANY.

1842/43, 1846/47-1859/60 recorded but marked "return at Salisbury" or "return at Sarum".
Pigot & Co's Directory, 1842: Wilts & Dorset Banking Company, Brittox. (draw on Williams, Deacon & Co., and the London & Westminster Bank)

654 WILTSHIRE, William Edward, saddler, harness maker [also WILTSHIRE, Mrs].

1842/43 returned and assessed £120; exempt.
1846/47-1849/50 assessed in absence of return £120; exempt.
1853/54 returned and assessed £95; exempt.
1854/55-1855/56 assessed in absence of return £95; exempt.
1856/57-1857/58 recorded; no assessments made; exempt.

1842/43, 1846/47-1848/49 possibly William & Edward Wiltshire but indistinct;
1842/43, 1846/47-1849/50 harness maker(s); 1853/54-1857/58 saddler; 1856/57 Mrs Wiltshire.
1850/51-1852/53 no assessments made.
Pigot & Co's Directory, 1842: William Wiltshire, saddler & harness maker, Market Place.

655 WINKWORTH, William, innkeeper [by comparison Lamb Inn]

1842/43 returned £80; assessed £120; income proved at £100; exempt.
1846/47-1850/51 assessed in absence of return £100; exempt.
1851/52 returned £50; assessed £100.

1852/53 marked "Marwin, William late Winkworth, innkeeper".
Pigot & Co's Directory, 1842: William Winkworth, Lamb, St.John Street.
Cross reference: Marwin, William, innkeeper, St.John.

656 WINTERSON, Joseph, gardener.

1842/43, 1846/47-1847/48 assessed in absence of return £50; exempt.

Pigot & Co's Directory, 1842: Joseph Winterson, gardener, Pan's Lane.

657 WITHINGTON, William Bamforth, watchmaker.

1858/59 returned £78.12.4; no assessment made.
1859/60 assessed in absence of return £100.

Cross references: Withington, W., watchmaker, St.Mary; Wood, John, watchmaker, St.Mary.

658 WITTEY, Samuel, solicitor, conveyancer. [also WALL, John & WITTEY, Samuel]

1853/54 returned and assessed £650.
1854/55 returned £300; assessed £650; reduced to £550.
1855/56 returned £500; assessed £600; reduced to £550.
1856/57 assessed in absence of return £600.
1857/58 returned £550; assessed £600.
1858/59 returned and assessed £600.
1859/60 returned £600; assessed £550.7.6.

1853/54 John Wall & Samuel Wittey; 1854/55-1859/60 Samuel Wittey.
1853/54 attorneys, solicitors & conveyancers; 1854/55-1857/58 solicitor etc.;
1858/59-1859/60 solicitor.
1859/60 assessment reduced by life assurance relief of £49.12.6.
Pigot & Co's Directory, 1842: John William Wall, attorney, agent to Crown Fire Office, English
    & Scottish Fire Office, St.John Street.
Cross reference: Wittey, Samuel, solicitor's clerk, Rowde.

659 WOOD, Peter Almerick Leh[eup], sittings subscriptions.

1853/54 returned and assessed £160.
1854/55 assessed in absence of return £160.
1855/56 returned and assessed £179.13.6.
1856/57 returned and assessed £186.10.0.
1857/58 returned and assessed £275.
1858/59 returned and assessed £347.18.10.
1859/60 returned £391.15.1; assessed £392.

660 WOODROFFE, William, tailor.

1842/43 assessed in absence of return £50; exempt.

Pigot & Co's Directory, 1842: William Woodroff (sic), tailor, Long Street.

661 YOUNG, John, interest.

1853/54 returned and assessed £16.16.7; income proved at £95; exempt.
1854/55-1857/58 assessed in absence of return £16.16.7; exempt 1857/58.

1857/58 marked "sunk in purchase of property last Christmas".

662 YOUNG, Joseph, innkeeper.

1858/59 returned £100; entry deleted.

1858/59 marked "assessed in St.Mary".
Cross reference:Young, Joseph Eden, innkeeper, St.Mary.

663 YOUNG, Joseph, provision dealer, carrier.

1852/53 returned and assessed £105.
1853/54 estimated £80; no assessment made.

1852/53 provision dealer; 1853/54 carrier.
1853/54 marked "given up".
Cross reference:Young, Joseph, carrier, St.Mary.

664 YOUNG & WHITE, builders [also WHITE, T.B.]

1842/43 returned £343; assessed 400; reduced to £358.
1846/47 returned and assessed £313.
1847/48 returned £295; assessed £313.
1848/49 returned £284; assessed £313.
1849/50 returned £205; assessed £350; reduced to £250 on appeal.
1850/51 returned and assessed £216.

1842/43, 1846/47-1850/51 Young & White; 1851/52 (entry only) T.B.White.
1852/53 marked "White now Mullings, Benoni, builder"; [Bedborough] marked "Mullings, Benoni late White, builder".
Pigot & Co's Directory, 1842: Young & White, carpenters & builders, Green and Bridewell Street.
Cross references: Mullings, Benoni, builder, Bedborough; White, Benoni Thomas, builder, Bedborough.

DEVIZES ST. MARY

665 ABRAHAMS, Joseph, photographic artist.

1859/60 assessed in absence of return £100; income proved at £87; exempt.

666 ADEY, John Thomas, coal merchant, tallow chandler, tallow merchant.

1849/50 assessed in absence of return £150; income proved at £120; exempt.
1850/51-1851/52 returned and assessed £180.
1852/53 returned £70; assessed £180.
1853/54-1859/60 returned and assessed £180.

1849/50, 1853/54 coal merchant & tallow chandler; 1850/51, 1852/53 tallow & coal merchant;
1851/52, 1854/55-1859/60 coal merchant; 1854/55 ironmonger deleted.

667 ADLAM, Samuel, plumber, glazier, painter. [also ADLAM, Mrs., straw bonnet maker]

Year	Amount returned £	Commissioners' estimate £	Income proved £	Final assessment £
1842/43	–	30	132.10.0	–
1846/47	100	–	–	100
1847/48	100	–	100	–
1848/49	128.7.6	153.7.6	100	–
1849/50	–	100	100	–
1850/51	81.13.1	–	81.13.1	–
1851/52	129.4.10	–	94.3.0	–
1852/53	114.6.6 20i	150	–	150
1853/54	103	150	–	150
1854/55	139	150	–	150
1855/56	67.3.6 30s	150	–	150
1856/57	136.10.0	150	–	150
1857/58	97.8.6	100	–	100
1858/59	61.10.6	100	–	100
1859/60	100	–	–	100

Abbreviations: i, interest; s, straw business.
1842/43, 1846/47-1848/49 plumber & glazier and wife as straw bonnet maker; 1849/50 plumbers (*sic*) etc; 1850/51-1852/53 plumbers (*sic*); 1853/54 plumber and millinery business; 1854/55 plumber etc; 1855/56 plumber and straw business; 1856/57-1857/58 plumber, straw business etc; 1858/59-1859/60 plumber, painter, straw business, etc.
Assessed as Samuel Adlam and wife, or Mrs. Adlam.
1848/49 no appeal noted but income proved at £100; the estimate of £25 related to the straw bonnet business.
Pigot & Co's Directory, 1842: Lydia Adlam, milliner, straw hat maker, Brittox.
Cross reference: Stockwell, Adlam & Gregory, plumbers & glaziers, St.Mary.

668 ALLEN, Charles, cattle dealer.

1842/43, 1846/47 assessed in absence of return £40; exempt.

Cross reference: Allen, Charles, cattle dealer, Rowde.

669 ANSTIE, George Washington, solicitor.

1842/43, 1846/47-1847/48 returned and assessed £500.
1848/49 returned and assessed £400.
1849/50-1850/51 returned and assessed £450.
1851/52-1859/60 returned and assessed £300.

Assessed under letter for all years.
Pigot & Co's Directory, 1842: George Washington Anstie, attorney, agent for Britannia Fire Office, Northgate Street.
Cross references: Anstie, George Washington, farmer, St.John.

670 ANSTIE, Thomas Browne, surgeon, apothecary.

1853/54-1855/56 returned and assessed £350.
1856/57 assessed in absence of return £340.
1857/58-1859/60 returned and assessed £350.

1853/54-1857/58 surgeon; 1858/59-1859/60 surgeon & apothecary.
Cross reference: Anstie, Thomas Brown (*sic*), surgeon, St.John.

671 ATTWOOD, John, linen draper.

Noted only in 1859/60 entry under Joseph Flower & Co., linen drapers: "now John Attwood".
Cross references: Flower, Joseph & Co., linen drapers, St.Mary; House, -, draper, St.Mary; Matthews, William, draper, St.Mary.

672 AYTON, Jacob, chemist, surgeon dentist.

Year	Amount returned £	Commissioners' estimate £	Income proved £	Final assessment £
1842/43	–	80	80	–
1846/47	–	100	100	–
1847/48	143.14.2	–	143.14.2	–
1848/49	–	115	115	20
1849/50	66.17.7	86.17.7	–	20
1850/51	– 20i	150a	117.18.0	20
1851/52	– 20i	100	109.2.0	20
1852/53	92.4.0 20i	–	92.4.0	20
1853/54	99.3.6	100	–	100
1854/55	–	97.8.6	97.8.6	–
1855/56	–	90	90	–
1856/57	Exempt			
1857/58	Exempt			
1858/59	Exempt			
1859/60	89.2.6	100	–	100

Abbreviations: i, interest.
1842/43, 1846/47-1847/48 chemist; 1848/49-1859/60 surgeon dentist.
1849/50 entries for profits deleted.
The sums of £20 left in charge in years where exemption otherwise claimed relates to interest.
Pigot & Co's Directory, 1842: Jacob Ayton, (operative) chemist & druggist, Northgate Street.
Cross reference: Ayton, Jacob, surgeon dentist, St.John.

673 BAKER, Thomas, watchmaker.

1842/43, 1846/47-1847/48 assessed in absence of return £120; exempt.
1848/49 assessed in absence of return £100; income proved at £90; exempt.
1849/50 assessed in absence of return £100; exempt.
1853/54 returned and assessed £95; exempt.
1854/55 returned and assessed £80; exempt.
1855/56 assessed in absence of return £80; exempt.
1856/57 recorded; no assessment made; exempt.
1857/58 returned and assessed £110.
1858/59 returned £75; assessed £110.
1859/60 returned £72; assessed £110.

1850/51-1852/53 no assessments made.
Pigot & Co's Directory, 1842: Thomas Baker, watch & clock maker, Maryport Street.

674 BARNARD, George, canal agent.

1847/48 returned £100; no assessment made; marked "charged in Week".

Cross reference: Barnard, George, canal agent, Week.

675 BARNARD, John, chemist etc.

Year	Amount returned £	Commissioners' estimate £	Final assessment £
1848/49	340	–	340
1849/50	332	–	332
1850/51	327	–	327
1851/52	315	–	315
1852/53	312	–	312
1853/54	290	–	290
1854/55	287	–	287
1855/56	275	–	275
1856/57	268	–	268
1857/58	270	–	270
1858/59	260	–	260
1859/60	250	300	300

1848/49 marked "Heard, Thomas James" deleted "Barnard, chemist etc" inserted.
1849/50 marked "Heard & Barnard now Barnard, chemist"
Cross reference: Heard, Thomas James, chemist, St.Mary.

676 BAYLEY, J[ohn] R[aikes], solicitor.

1842/43 entry only; marked "return in St.John".
1846/47-1847/48 marked "Special Commissioners".
1848/49 entry only.
Pigot & Co's Directory, 1842: Bayly & Bayly (sic) attorneys, High Street.
Cross reference: Bayley, John Raikes, solicitor, St.John.

677 BERRY, William, shopman.

1842/43 assessed in absence of return £52; income proved at £79; exempt.
1846/47-1848/49 assessed in absence of return £52; exempt.

678 BERRY & OFFER, straw bonnet makers.

1842/43, 1846/47-1849/50 assessed in absence of return £40; exempt.

Pigot & Co's Directory, 1842: Berry & Offer, straw hat makers, Maryport Street.

679 BIDWELL, Elizabeth, schoolmistress. [also BIDWELL, Anna]

1842/43 assessed in absence of return £30; income proved at £40.16.8; exempt.
1846/47-1847/48 assessed in absence of return £80; exempt.
1848/49-1849/50 assessed in absence of return £80; income proved at £70; exempt.
1851/52 assessed in absence of return £80; exempt.
1852/53 returned and assessed £100; exempt.
1853/54 returned and assessed £110.16.0.
1854/55 returned and assessed £110.4.0.
1855/56-1856/57 returned and assessed £100.
1857/58 returned and assessed £130.
1858/59 returned and assessed £180.
1859/60 returned and assessed £200.

1842/43 Anna Bidwell; 1846/47 Eliza Bidwell; 1847/48-1859/60 Elizabeth Bidwell.
1850/51 no assessment made.
Pigot & Co's Directory, 1842: Elizabeth Bidwell, boarding school, New Park Street.

680 BIGGS, George, innkeeper [by comparison, White Lion].

1846/47 returned and assessed £100; exempt.
1847/48 returned and assessed £80; exempt.
1848/49 returned £50; assessed £80; exempt.

1849/50 marked "now Truman, innkeeper".
Cross references: Thomas, George, innkeeper, St. Mary; Trueman, Richard, innkeeper, St.Mary.

681 BIGWOOD, George, shoemaker.

1846/47-1849/50 assessed in absence of return £50; exempt.
1853/54 returned and assessed £60; exempt.
1854/55-1855/56 assessed in absence of return £60; exempt.
1856/57-1858/59 recorded; no assessments made; exempt.
1859/60 returned £89; no assessment made; exempt.

1850/51-1852/53 no assessments made.
Pigot & Co's Directory, 1842: George Bigwood, boot & shoe maker, Maryport Street.

682 BLACKWELL, Elizabeth & Sarah, schoolmistresses.

Partners assessed separately 1842/43, 1846/47-1849/50

Elizabeth Blackwell

1842/43 assessed in absence of return £40; income proved at £36; exempt.

1846/47-1849/50 assessed in absence of return £40; exempt.

Sarah Blackwell

1842/43 assessed in absence of return £60; income proved at £64; exempt.
1846/47-1849/50 assessed in absence of return £60; exempt.

Misses Blackwell

1852/53 returned and assessed £126.9.0; exempt.
1853/54 returned and assessed £120; exempt.
1854/55 returned and assessed £120; income proved at £119.10.0; exempt.
1855/56 assessed in absence of return £120; exempt.
1856/57-1858/59 recorded; no assessments made; exempt.
1859/60 returned £108; no assessment made; exempt.

1850/51-1851/52 no assessments made.
1856/57 Mrs. Sarah Blackwell noted.
1857/58 assessed as school; Sarah omitted, Thomas inserted.
1858/59 Thomas deleted, Sarah inserted.
Pigot & Co's Directory, 1842: Elizabeth & Sarah Blackwell, school, Sheep Street.

683 BLENCOWE, Henry, innkeeper, Castle.

1851/52 assessed in absence of return £120; exempt.
1852/53 returned £116; assessed £130; exempt.
1853/54 returned and assessed £118.
1854/55 returned £130; assessed £150.
1855/56 returned £131; assessed £150.
1856/57 returned and assessed £150.
1857/58 returned £150; assessed £200.
1858/59 returned and assessed £150.
1859/60 returned £150; assessed £200.

1851/52 marked "late Grace".
1856/57 Castle noted.
Cross reference: Grace, William, innkeeper, St.Mary.

684 BOX, Richard, corn dealer.

1846/47-1847/48 returned and assessed £500.

Richard Box was also mentioned by name only in Market Lavington 1842/43 and Cheverell
    Parva 1846/47-1847/48.
1848/49 marked "now Glass & Ferris, corn dealers".
Cross reference: Glass, James & Ferris, Thomas, corn merchants, St. Mary.

685 BRABANT R[obert] H., gentleman.

1842/43 entry only.
Pigot & Co's Directory, 1842: Robert H. Brabant, gentry, physician, Northgate Street.

686 BRAMBLE, J.R., land surveyor.

1842/43 returned £75; assessed £150; reduced to £75.
1846/47 assessed in absence of return £200.
1847/48 returned and assessed £150.

1842/43 assessment increased on objection by surveyor but reduced; no appeal noted.
Cross reference: Bramble, J.R., surveyor, St.John.

687 BRANDFORD, James, fruit dealer, etc., journeyman, journeyman saddler.

1853/54 returned and assessed £90.10.0; exempt.
1854/55-1855/56 assessed in absence of return £60; exempt.
1856/57-1859/60 recorded; no assessments made; exempt.

1853/54-1856/57 fruit dealer, etc; 1857/58 fruit dealer & journeyman;
1858/59-1859/60 fruit dealer & journeyman saddler.
1857/58 £77 returned but no assessment made.

688 BRINKWORTH, Charles, baker, pig butcher.

1842/43 returned and assessed £130; exempt.
1846/47-1847/48 assessed in absence of return £120; exempt.
1848/49 assessed in absence of return £120; income proved at £100; exempt.
1849/50 assessed in absence of return £120; exempt.
1852/53 returned and assessed £100; income proved at £127; exempt.
1853/54 returned £61.2.9; assessed £100; income proved at £72; exempt.
1854/55 assessed in absence of return £100.
1855/56 assessed in absence of return £120.
1856/57 returned £100; assessed £120.
1857/58 returned and assessed £120.
1858/59-1859/60 returned £100; assessed £120.

1842/43, 1846/47-1849/50 baker; 1852/53-1859/60 baker & pig butcher.
1850/51-1851/52 no assessments made.
Pigot & Co's Directory, 1842: Charles Brinkworth, baker, New Park Street.

689 BRISTOW, Charles, cabinet maker.

1846/47-1848/50 assessed in absence of return £90; exempt,

690 BUNTER, G.B., chemist.

Year	Amount returned £	Commissioners' estimate £	Assessment made £	Income proved £
1847/48	–	155	150	115
1848/49	–	150	134	128.17.6
1849/50	–	150	150a	138
1850/51	133.10.0	–	133.10.0	133.10.0
1851/52	–	150	150a	130
1852/53	–	130	130	130

1847/48-1849/50 marked "Late Sainsbury".
1852/53 marked "now Madge"; assessment discharged but no sum recorded.
Cross references: Madge, James Cornelius, chemist, St.Mary; Sainsbury, G.T., chemist & brickmaker, St.Mary.

691 BURGESS, Joseph, baker, grocer.

Year	Amount returned £	Commissioners' estimate £	Income proved £	Final assessment £
1842/43	–	139.10.0	139.10.0	–
1846/47	–	140	140	–
1847/48	108.10.0	–	108.10.0	–
1848/49	80	–	80	–
1849/50	–	80	80	–
1851/52	–	80	89.5.0	–
1852/53	89.5.0	105	80 15.15.0i	–
1853/54	–	100	80	–
1854/55	–	80	80	–
1855/56	–	80	80	–
1856/57	Exempt			
1857/58	75	–	–	–
1858/59	Exempt			
1859/60	66	100	73	–

Abbreviation: i, interest.
1842/43, 1846/47-1849-50 baker & grocer; 1851/52-1859/60 baker.
1850/51 no assessment made.
Pigot & Co's Directory, 1842: Joseph Burges (sic), baker, Burgess, grocer & tea dealer, shop keeper & dealer in groceries and sundries, Monday Market Street.

692 CATLEY, Samuel, tailor, clothes seller, dissenting preacher.

1842/43, 1846/47-1849/50 assessed in absence of return £90; exempt.
1852/53 returned and assessed 100; exempt.
1853/54 returned £78; assessed £100.
1854/55-1856/57 assessed in absence of return £100.
1857/58-1858/59 returned £90; assessed £100.
1859/60 returned and assessed £100.

1842/43, 1846/47-1849/50 tailor; 1852/53-1853/54 clothes seller & dissenting preacher;
1854/55-1857/58 clothes seller; 1858/59-1859/60 tailor & clothes seller.
1850/51-1851/52 no assessments made.
Pigot & Co's Directory, 1842: Samuel Catley, clothes dealer & tailor, Maryport Street.

693 CHANDLER, James, innkeeper & brewer [by comparison, Old Crown].

1842/43 returned £150; assessed £200 but reduced to £150. Assessed under letter. No
    appeal noted.

Pigot & Co's Directory, 1842: James Chandler, Old Crown, New Park Street.
Cross references: Dyke, George, innkeeper, St.Mary; Waylen, William, innkeeper, St.Mary.

694 CHANDLER, James, innkeeper, beerhouse keeper. [by comparison Three Crowns]

1846/47-1847/48 assessed in absence of return £75; exempt.
1848/49 assessed in absence of return £75; income proved at £80; exempt.
1849/50 returned and assessed £100; exempt.
1850/51 recorded but marked "charged in Week".
1851/52 returned and assessed £120; exempt.
1852/53 returned and assessed £130; exempt.
1853/54 returned £59.10.4; assessed £130; income proved at £90; exempt.
1854/55-1855/56 assessed in absence of return £90; exempt.

1846/47-1849/50 beerhouse keeper; 1850/51-1855/56 innkeeper.
1856/57 marked "now Wild"; "Wild, George, late Chandler, Three Crowns".
Cross reference: Wild, George, innkeeper, St.Mary.

695 CHANDLER, John, innkeeper.

1846/47 assessed in absence of return £40; exempt.

696 CHANDLER, John, toll keeper & mealman.

1847/48 returned £60 and £13 interest; exempt.

697 CHAPMAN, Joseph, shopkeeper, hardware & glass warehouse.
[also CHAPMAN, Stephen]

Year	Amount returned £	Commissioners' estimate £	Income proved £	Final assessment £
1842/43	70	100	70	–
1846/47	–	100a	123	–
1847/48	–	100	–	150
1848/49	–	100	–	100
1849/50	100	–	100	–
1850/51	56	–	56	–
1851/52	–	100a	100	–
1852/53	87	–	87	–
1853/54	93.8.0	100	–	100
1854/55	138	–	–	138
1855/56	–	140	–	140
1856/57	124.16.9	200	–	200
1857/58	120	200	–	200
1858/59	160.18.8	200	–	200
1859/60	118.14.0	150	–	120

1842/43, 1846/47 Stephen Chapman; 1847/48-1859/60 Joseph Chapman.
1842/43, 1846/47-1849/50 shopkeeper; 1850/51-1859/60 hardware & glass warehouse.
1847/48 marked Chapman, Stephen now Joseph, shopkeeper; note "property St.John".
1847/48 Additional Commissioners' estimate increased to £150 by General Commissioners
1856/57 marked "Devizes and Chippenham".
1859/60 includes £5 interest; marked "Thomas Church late Chapman, hardware & glass warehouse.
Pigot & Co's Directory, 1842: Stephen Chapman, china, glass, etc., dealer, Sidmouth Street.
Cross reference: Church, Thomas, hardware & glass warehouse, St.Mary.

698 CHIVERS, William, carpenter.

1859/60 returned £52; no assessment made; exempt.

Pigot & Co's Directory, 1842: William Chivers, carpenter & builder, Sidmouth Street.

699 CHURCH, Thomas, hardware & glass warehouse.

1859/60 returned £118.14.0; assessed £150; reduced to £120 and £5 interest.

1859/60 marked "late Chapman"
Cross reference: Chapman, Joseph, hardware & glass warehouse, St.Mary.

700 CLARK, Jacob, butcher.

1842/43 returned £300; assessed £350; reduced to £300; no appeal noted.

Pigot & Co's Directory, 1842: Jacob Clark, butcher, Maryport Street & Brittox.
Cross reference: Clark, William & Isaac, butchers, St.John.

701 CLARK, William, shopkeeper, grocer.

1842/43 returned £50; assessed £70; exempt.
1846/47-1849/50 assessed in absence of return £70; exempt.
1853/54 returned and assessed £45; exempt.
1854/55-1855/56 assessed in absence of return £50; exempt.
1856/57-1859/60 recorded; no assessments made; exempt.

1842/43, 1847/48-1849/50 shopkeeper; 1846/47 no occupation noted; 1853/54-1859/60
    grocer.
1850/51-1852/53 no assessments made.
Pigot & Co's Directory, 1842: William Clark, grocer & tea dealer, New Park Street.

702 CLARK, William, surgeon.

1842/43 returned £150; assessed £200.

Pigot & Co's Directory, 1842: William Clark, surgeon, Lansdown Grove.

703 COATES, Robert, innkeeper Odd Fellows' Arms, earthenwareman, hardwareman. [also COATES, Joseph]

1842/43, 1846/47-1847/48 assessed in absence of return £75; exempt.
1848/49 assessed in absence of return £75; income proved at £120.
1849/50 returned £100; assessed £150; reduced to £117 on appeal; exempt.
1850/51 returned and assessed £120; exempt.
1851/52 assessed in absence of return £120; exempt.

1842/43 Joseph Coates innkeeper & earthenwareman; 1846/47 innkeeper & hardwareman;
    1847/48-1850/51 innkeeper etc; 1851/52 innkeeper.
1852/53 marked "& glass warehouse".
1853/54 marked "Robert Coates H.Higgins innkeeper".
Pigot & Co's Directory, 1842: Robert Coates, Odd Fellows' Arms, hardware ironmonger,
    Sidmouth Street.
Cross references: Hale, Matthew, innkeeper, St.Mary; Higgins, H., innkeeper, St.Mary.

704 COLE, Daniel, innkeeper [also COLE, Jemima; by comparsion White Horse].

1842/43 returned and assessed £150.

1842/43 marked "now Jemima".
Pigot & Co's Directory, 1842: Daniel Cole, White Horse.

705 COLLINGS, John, butcher. [also LEWIS & COLLINGS]

1842/43 returned £60; assessed £120; exempt.
1846/47-1850/51 assessed in absence of return £120; exempt.
1851/52 assessed in absence of return £150; income proved at £100; exempt.
1852/53 assessed in absence of return £100; income proved and assessment discharged but no sum recorded.
1853/54 assessed in absence of return £110; income proved at £70; exempt.
1854/55 assessed in absence of return £130.
1855/56 returned £120; assessed £150.
1856/57-1857/58 returned and assessed £150.

1842/43, 1846/47-1849/50 Lewis & Collings; 1850/51-1855/56 John Collings; 1856/57-1857/58 John Lewis Collings.
1849/50 marked "now Collings butcher".
1850/51 marked "late Lewis & Collings".
1858/59 marked "now Lewis butcher".
Pigot & Co's Directory, 1842: Lewis & Collins (sic), butchers, Northgate Street.
Cross reference: Lewis, Henry, butcher, St.Mary.

706 COLLINS, John, interest.

1852/53 returned £22.10.0; no assessment made.

1852/53 marked "charged under Schedule A".

707 COOK, Elizabeth Ann, schoolmistress.

1842/43 assessed in absence of return £46; exempt.
1846/47-1849/50 assessed in absence of return £65; exempt.

1842/43, 1846/47 Ann Elizabeth Cook.
Pigot & Co's Directory, 1842: Ann Cook, boarding school, Albion Place.

708 COX, George, butcher.

1848/49 assessed in absence of return £80; exempt.
1849/50 returned £60; assessed £80; exempt.
1850/51 returned and assessed £70; exempt.
1851/52 assessed in absence of return £70; exempt.
1852/53 returned and assessed £60; exempt.
1853/54 returned and assessed £110.
1854/55 assessed in absence of return £110.
1855/56 assessed in absence of return £125.
1856/57-1857/58 returned £110; assessed £125.
1858/59 returned £110; assessed £150.

1859/60 marked "charged in Week".
Cross reference: Cox, George, butcher, Week.

709 COXHEAD, Arthur, confectioner, baker, schoolmaster.

1846/47-1849/50 assessed in absence of return £80; exempt.
1853/54 returned and assessed £56b&c, £30; exempt.
1854/55 assessed in absence of return £86; exempt.
1855/56 assessed in absence of return £70; exempt.
1856/57 returned £4c, £40s (school income deleted marked "Schedule E"); assessed £60 confirmed on appeal.
1857/58 returned £51.12.8c, £30s (school income deleted marked "Schedule E"); assessed £70; exempt.
1858/59 returned £50; assessed £70 (marked "Schedule E"); income proved at £48; exempt.
1859/60 returned £49; no assessment made; exempt.

Abbreviations: c, confectioner; s, schoolmaster; b, baker.
1846/47-1847/48 no occupation noted; 1848/49-1849/50 baker; 1853/54 baker, confectioner & schoolmaster; 1854/55-1855/56 confectioner etc; 1856/57-1859/60 confectioner & schoolmaster.
1850/51-1852/53 no assessments made.
Cross reference: Coxhead, William Palmer, schoolmaster, St.John.

710 CRUDGE, William, painter & glazier.

1856/57-1857/58 recorded; no assessments made; exempt.

1859/60 marked "See St.John".
Cross reference: Crudge, William, painter & glazier, St.John.

711 CUMNER, Charles, baker & grocer.

1853/54 returned and assessed £78; exempt.
1854/55 assessed in absence of return £78; exempt.
1855/56 returned and assessed £70; exempt.
1856/57-1859/60 recorded; no assessments made; exempt.

1857/58-1858/59 £80 returned.

712 DANGERFIELD, Isaiah, innkeeper, White Hart.

1853/54 returned and assessed £40; exempt.
1854/55-1855/56 returned £40; assessed £60.
1856/57 returned £50; assessed £60.

1856/57 White Hart noted.
1857/58 marked "Now Joseph Young".
Cross reference: Young, Joseph Eden, innkeeper, St.Mary.

713 DANGERFIELD, Thomas, shopkeeper.

1853/54 returned and assessed £50; exempt.
1854/55-1855/56 assessed in absence of return £50; exempt.
1856/57 returned £50; no assessment made.

1856/57 marked "now -".
1857/58 marked "now Chase". (no further reference to Chase).

714 DARK, George, innkeeper, Angel.

1854/55-1855/56 assessed in absence of return £70; exempt.
1856/57-1859/60 recorded; no assessments made; exempt.

1856/57 Angel noted.

715 DAY, Ozias, bacon & cheese factor.

1842/43 assessed in absence of return £80; exempt.
1846/47-1847/48 assessed in absence of return £95; exempt.
1848/49 assessed in absence of return £80; exempt.

1848/49 marked "Day, Ozias late now -".
1849/50 marked "Day, Ozias late now Staples".
Pigot & Co's Directory, 1842: Ozias Day, cheese & bacon factor, Monday Market Street, shop
keeper & dealer in groceries and sundries, Bridewell Street.
Cross reference: Holder, Charles, grocer, St.Mary; Humphrey, Thomas & Carter, John, grocers,
St.Mary; Staples, William, grocer, St.Mary; Vines, Uriah, grocer, St.Mary.

716 DERHAM, Joseph, shoemaker.

1846/47-1849/50 assessed in absence of return £80; exempt.

717 DEW, John, mealman, salary.

1857/58 assessed in absence of return £100.
1858/59 returned and assessed £100.
1859/60 returned £100; assessed £120.

1857/58 Dewey.
1857/58 salary Glass & Ferris; 1858/59-1859/60 mealman.

718 DOWLAND, Joseph, linen draper.

1853/54 returned and assessed £80; exempt.
1854/55-1855/56 assessed in absence of return £80; exempt.
1856/57-1857/58 assessed in absence of return £100.
1858/59-1859/60 returned and assessed £100.

[Manley, Benjamin] 1852/53 marked "now Joseph Dowland, pawnbroker."
Pigot & Co's Directory, 1842: Martha Dowland, stay maker, Northgate Street.
Cross reference: Manley, Benjamin, pawnbroker, St. Mary.

719 DOWLING, David, stay maker.

1842/43 assessed in absence of return £70; exempt.
1846/47-1849/50 assessed in absence of return £50; exempt.

1842/43 Dowland.

720 DOWLING, Edward, agent.

1842/43, 1846/47-1849/50 assessed in absence of return £50; exempt.

721 DREDGE, Stephen.

1849/50 name only entered.

722 DYKE, George, innkeeper, Old Crown.

1847/48 assessed in absence of return £100; exempt.
1848/49 returned and assessed £105; income proved at £120; exempt.
1849/50 assessed in absence of return £105; exempt.
1850/51-1851/52 returned £100; assessed £120; exempt.
1852/53 assessed in absence of return £150.
1853/54-1854/55 returned and assessed £120.
1855/56 returned £100; assessed £120.
1856/57 returned £100; assessed £200.
1857/58 returned £100; assessed £190.
1858/59-1859/60 returned £100; assessed £150.

1847/48 marked "Waylen William, innkeeper now Dyke".
1852/53, 1853/54, 1856/57 Old Crown noted.
Cross references: Chandler, James, innkeeper, St.Mary; Waylen, William, innkeeper, St.Mary.

723 EADSON, Elizabeth, dressmaker, milliner.

1842/43, 1846/47-1849/50 assessed in absence of return £50; exempt.
1851/52 assessed in absence of return £60; exempt.

1842/43, 1846/47-1849/50 milliner; 1851/52 dressmaker.
1850/51 no assessment made.
Pigot & Co's Directory, 1842: E & C Eadson, milliners & dressmakers, Maryport Street.

724 EAGLESFIELD, John C., watchmaker, confectioner.

1842/43 assessed in absence of return £100; exempt.
1846/47 assessed in absence of return £75.10.0; exempt.
1847/48-1849/50 assessed in absence of return £75; exempt.

1842/43 watchmaker & confectioner; 1846/47-1849/50 watchmaker.
Pigot & Co's Directory, 1842: John Charles Eaglesfield, confectioner, Northgate Street.
Pigot & Co's Directory, 1842: possibly Charles Eaglesfield, working jeweller, New Park Street.

725 EAGLESFIELD, Thomas, coal merchant.

1842/43 assessed in absence of return £50; exempt.

Pigot & Co's Directory, 1842: Thomas Eaglesfield, coal merchant, Wharf.

726 EDEN, Eliza, milliner.

1846/47-1849/50 assessed in absence of return £50; exempt.

727 EDEN, John, cordwainer.

1842/43 assessed in absence of return £30; income proved at £22; exempt.
1846/47-1849/50 assessed in absence of return £30; exempt.

Pigot & Co's Directory, 1842: John Eden, boot & shoe maker, Sidmouth Street.

728 EDEN, Thomas, coach maker, coach builder. [also EDEN, Joseph]

1842/43 assessed in absence of return £100; income proved at £70; exempt.
1846/47-1849/50 assessed in absence of return £100; exempt.
1854/55 assessed in absence of return £100 but deleted.
1855/56 assessed in absence of return £50; exempt.
1859/60 assessed in absence of return £100.

1842/43, 1846/47-1849/50; 1854/55-1855/56 Thomas Eden; 1859/60 Joseph Eden.
1842/43, 1854/55-1855/56 coach maker; 1846/47-1849/50 coach builder; 1859/60 coach maker.
1850/51-1853/54, 1856/57-1858/59 no assessments made.
1854/55 marked "insolvent".
1856/57 recorded but no assessment made.
1857/58 marked "dead"
1858/59 marked "dead, business ceased".
1859/60 marked "Eden, Joseph late Thomas Eden coachmaker".
Pigot & Co's Directory, 1842: Thomas Eden, coachmaker, Bath Road.

729 EDMONDS, R., French teacher.

1842/43 returned £67t and £38i; assessed £100t and 38i; exempt.

Abbreviations: t, teacher; i, interest from foreign securities.
Cross references: Edmonds, R., French teacher, St.John; Edmonds, R. & W., schoolmasters, St.John; Edmonds, Richard, teacher of French, Bedborough.
Pigot & Co's Directory, 1842: E.Edmonds, schoolmistress.

730 ELDRIDGE, Rebecca, shopkeeper.

1842/43 assessed in absence of return £50; income proved at £10; exempt.
1846/47-1849/50 assessed in absence of return £50; exempt.

Pigot & Co's Directory, 1842: Rebecca Eldridge, shopkeeper, dealer in groceries & sundries, Monday Market Street.

731 ERWOOD, James, innkeeper.

1848/49-1849/50 assessed in absence of return £50; exempt.

732 EVERETT, William Giffard, physician.

1842/43 returned and assessed £300.
1846/47-1848/49 returned and assessed £400.
1848/50 returned £400; assessed £500.
1850/51-1852/53 returned and assessed £500.

1852/53 marked "assessed in St.John". (no assessment made in St.John 1852/53)
1853/54 marked "at St.John".
Pigot & Co's Directory, 1842: William Giffard Everett, physician, Albion Place.
Cross reference: Everett, Dr. William Giffard, physician, St.John.

733 FERRIS, John, cabinet maker, auctioneer.

1842/43 returned £180; assessed £200.
1846/47 returned and assessed £120.
1847/48 assessed in absence of return £150.
1848/49 returned £110; assessed £150.
1849/50 returned £90; assessed £150.
1850/51 returned £75; assessed £150.
1851/52 returned £130; assessed £150.
1852/53 returned and assessed £150.
1853/54 returned £120; assessed £200.
1854/55 returned £150; assessed £250.
1855/56 returned £200; assessed £250.
1856/57 assessed in absence of return £300.
1857/58 returned £150; assessed £300; increased by General Commissioners to £400.
1858/59 returned and assessed £400.
1859/60 assessed in absence of return £400.

1842/43, 1846/47-1859/60 cabinet maker; 1851/52, 1853/54 cabinet maker & auctioneer.
Pigot & Co's Directory, 1842: John Ferris, land, house & estate agent, cabinet maker, inspector of weights & measures, Brittox.

734 FIDLER, Thomas, innkeeper.

1842/43, 1846/47 assessed in absence of return £100.
1847/48 returned £50; assessed £100; exempt.

735 FLOWER, Joseph & Co., linen drapers.

1857/58-1859/60 returned and assessed £100.

1857/58 marked "late Matthews, linen drapers".
1859/60 marked "now John Attwood".
Cross references: Attwood, John, linen draper, St.Mary; House, -, draper, St.Mary; Matthews, William, draper, St.Mary.

736 FOWLER, William, surgeon.

1842/43 returned and assessed £400.

Pigot & Co's Directory, 1842: William Fowler, surgeon, Northgate Street.

737 FRANCIS, James, innkeeper, Royal Oak. [also FRANCIS, Mary]

1842/43, 1846/47-1847/48 returned £100; assessed £150.

1848/49-1852/53 returned £90; assessed £150.
1853/54-1854/55 returned £90; assessed £120.
1855/56 returned and assessed £120.
1856/57 returned £100; assessed £180.
1857/58 returned £120; assessed £180.
1858/59-1859/60 returned £100; assessed £150.

1842/43 marked "Mary Francis now John".
1856/57 Royal Oak noted.
Pigot & Co's Directory, 1842: Mary Francis, Royal Oak, New Park Street.

738 FRANCIS, Samuel, tailor.

1853/54 returned and assessed £50; exempt.
1854/55-1855/56 assessed in absence of return £50; exempt.
1856/57-1859/60 recorded; no assessments made; exempt.

1857/58 returned £40 but no assessment made.
Pigot & Co's Directory, 1842: Samuel Francis, tailor, Green.

739 GALE, William Dathan, marine store dealer, timber merchant.

1854/55 assessed in absence of return £100.
1855/56 returned and assessed £100.
1856/57-1857/58 assessed in absence of return £100.
1858/59 returned and assessed £100.
1859/60 assessed in absence of return £100.

1854/55 timber merchant & marine store dealer; 1855/56-1859/60 marine store dealer.

740 GANE, Edward, timber dealer.

1842/43 assessed in absence of return £150; reduced by General Commissioners to
    £100; income proved at £50; exempt.
1846/47-1847/48 assessed in absence of return £150.
1848/49 assessed in absence of return £100; exempt.

Pigot & Co's Directory, 1842: Edward Gane, timber merchant, New Park Street.

741 GERRISH, Henry, dispenser of medicine.

1858/59 returned and assessed £20.

1859/60 marked "removed to Salisbury".

742 GERRISH, John, schoolmaster, stationer, collector, general agent.

Year	Amount returned £	Commissioners' estimate £	Income proved £	Final assessment £
1842/43	–	108	122	–
1846/47	–	120	120	–
1847/48	–	120	120	–
1848/49	–	120	120	–
1849/50	139.4.0	140	139.4.0	–
1850/51	142.12.0	–	126	–
1851/52	103.17.0	–	103.17.0	–
	90	–	–	90aa
1852/53	80	–	–	80
1853/54	72.16.0	–	–	72.16.0
1854/55	70	–	–	70
1855/56	70	90	–	90
1856/57	90	–	–	90
1857/58	76.13.6	100	–	100
1858/59	80.17.9	100	–	100
1859/60	84.8.0	100	–	100

1842/43, 1846/47-1847/48 schoolmaster; 1848/49-1854/55 schoolmaster & stationer, etc;
1855/56-1856/57 schoolmaster & stationer; 1857/58 schoolmaster; 1858/59-1859/60 school-
    master, collector & general agent.
1851/52 additional assessment (aa) made in the sum of £90 on returned figure.
Pigot & Co's Directory, 1842: John Gerrish, master at the Blue Coat School, Maryport Street.

743 GLASS, Joseph, brewer.

1842/43 assessed in absence of return £100; exempt.
1846/47-1849/50 assessed in absence of return £80; exempt.
1851/52 assessed in absence of return £80; exempt.
1852/53 returned and assessed £94; exempt.
1853/54 returned £64; assessed £80.

1848/49 income proved at £97.
1850/51 no assessment made.
1852/53 marked "Gable now". (but assessments continue)
1854/55 marked "now gone".
Pigot & Co's Directory, 1842: Joseph Glass, retailer of beer, New Park Street.

744 GLASS, James & FERRIS, Thomas, corn merchants, maltsters.

1848/49-1849/50 returned and assessed £500.
1850/51 assessed in absence of return £500.

1851/52 returned £500; assessed £600.
1852/53-1855/56 returned and assessed £600.
1856/57 returned £600; assessed £900.
1857/58 returned £800; assessed £900.
1858/59 returned and assessed £900.
1859/60 assessed in absence of return £900.

1848/49-1850/51, 1853/54-1859/60 corn merchants; 1851/52-1852/53 corn merchants &
    maltsters.
1848/49 marked "Richard Box now Glass & Ferris, corn dealers".
1855/56 marked "return required, see below". (entry made at end of list)
1859/60 James Glass assessed sole.
Cross reference: Box, Richard, corn dealer, St.Mary.

745 GOLDSTONE, Edward, surgeon dentist.

1842/43 assessed in absence of return £100; exempt.

Pigot & Co's Directory, 1842: Edward Goldstone, surgeon dentist, Sidmouth Street.

746 GRACE, William, innkeeper. [by comparison, Castle]

1842/43 returned £150; assessed £200 under letter.
1846/47 assessed in absence of return £200.
1847/48 returned £152.7.0; assessed £200.
1848/49 assessed in absence of return £200.
1849/50-1850/51 assessed in absence of return £150.

1851/52 marked Blencowe, Henry late Grace.
Pigot & Co's Directory, 1842: William Grace, posting & commercial, Castle, New Park Street.
Cross reference: Blencowe, Henry, innkeeper, St.Mary.

747 GREEN, William, auctioneer.

1848/49 assessed in absence of return £100; exempt.
1849/50 assessed in absence of return £150; reduced to £100 on appeal; exempt.

748 GREENLAND, Charles, Professor of Music.

1853/54 returned £75 and £22 interest; assessed £75; exempt.
1854/55-1855/56 assessed in absence of return £75; exempt.
1856/57-1857/58 recorded; no assessments made; exempt.

749 GREENLAND, James, bricklayer.

1842/43 assessed in absence of return £100; income proved at £80; exempt.
1846/47-1847/48 assessed in absence of return £100; exempt.
1848/49 assessed in absence of return £100; income proved at £65.
1849/50 assessed in absence of return £100; exempt.
1853/54 returned £20; no assessment made; exempt.
1854/55-1855/56 assessed in absence of return £20; exempt.
1856/57-1857/58 recorded; no assessments made; exempt.

1850/51-1852/53 no assessments made.
Pigot & Co's Directory, 1842: James Greenland, bricklayer, Back Street.

750 GREGORY, George, painter.

1846/47 entry only.
Cross reference: Stockwell, Adlam & Gregory, painters & glaziers, St.Mary.

751 HALE, Matthew, innkeeper, Odd Fellows' Arms, horse dealer.

1854/55 assessed in absence of return £100; income proved at £50; exempt.
1855/56 assessed in absence of return £50; exempt.
1856/57-1859/60 recorded; no assessments made; exempt.

1854/55-1855/56 innkeeper; 1856/57-1859/60 innkeeper & horse dealer.
1854/55 Odd Fellows' Arms noted.
1857/58 returned £52, 1859/60 returned £54.3.0 but no assessments made; exempt.
Cross references: Coates, Robert, innkeeper, St.Mary; Higgins, H., innkeeper, St.Mary.

752 HAMPTON, Edward, surgeon.

1846/47-1849/50 assessed in absence of return £100; exempt.

753 HARRIS, James, clerk, agent.

1846/47-1849/50 assessed in absence of return £60; exempt.
1856/57-1857/58 assessed in absence of return £100.
1858/59 returned and assessed £100.

1846/47-1849/50 no occupation recorded; 1856/57 clerk; 1857/58 clerk, etc.;
1858/59 clerk, agent, etc.
1859/69 marked "removed to Week".
Cross reference: Harris, James, clerk, agent, etc., Week.

754 HEARD, Thomas James, chemist.

1842/43 returned and assessed £400.
1846/47 returned and assessed £344.
1847/48 returned and assessed £346.

1848/49 entry deleted; Barnard chemist etc., substituted.
1849/50 marked "Heard & Barnard now Barnard chemist".
Pigot & Co's Directory, 1842: Thomas James Heard, chemist & druggist, Brittox.
Cross reference: Barnard, John, chemist, St.Mary.

755 HIGGINS, H., innkeeper. [by comparison Odd Fellows' Arms]

1853/54 assessed in absence of return £100; income proved at £70; exempt.

1853/54 marked "Robert Coates H.Higgins innkeeper".
Cross references: Coates, Robert, innkeeper, St.Mary; Hale, Matthew, innkeeper, St.Mary.

756 HIGGS, Elijah Andrew, grocer, etc.

1857/58 assessed in absence of return £125.
1858/59 returned and assessed £125.
1859/60 returned £95; assessed £125.

1856/57 marked "Weston, John now Higgs, baker, etc".
Cross reference: Weston, John, baker, St.Mary.

757 HILL, Richard, plumber, glazier, painter. [also HILL, William]

1842/43 assessed in absence of return £100; exempt.
1846/47-1849/50 assessed in absence of return £80; exempt. (income proved at £35 1848/49).
1852/53 returned £80; assessed £120; income proved at £80; exempt.
1853/54 returned £75; assessed £120; income proved at £75; exempt.
1854/55 assessed in absence of return £76; income proved at £70; exempt.
1855/56 assessed in absence of return £70; exempt.
1856/57-1858/59 recorded; no assessments made; exempt.

1842/43, 1846/47-1849/50 William Hill; 1852/53-1858/59 Richard Hill.
1842/43, 1846/47 plumber & glazier; 1847/48-1849/50 plumber, etc; 1852/53 plumber.
1850/51-1851/52 no assessments made.
1853/54-1858/58 plumber & painter.
1858/59 marked "Query St.John".
Pigot & Co's Directory, 1842: William Hill, painter, plumber & glazier, Sidmouth Street.
Cross reference: Hill, Richard, painter, St. John.

758 HOLDER, Charles, grocer.

1856/57 assessed in absence of return £125; entry deleted.

1856/57 marked "Staples, William now Holder, grocer".
1856/57 appeals include Charles Holder assessment discharged.
Cross references: Day, Ozias, bacon & cheese factor, St. Mary; Humphrey, Thomas & Carter, John, grocers, St.Mary; Staples, William, grocer, St.Mary; Vines, Uriah, grocer, St.Mary.

759 HOLLOWAY, Joseph, whitesmith.

1842/43 returned £50; assessed £100; exempt.
1846/47-1849/50 assessed in absence of return £80; exempt.

Pigot & Co's Directory, 1842: Joseph Holloway, brightsmith, New Park Street.

760 HOOK, Eliza & Emma, worsted warehouse.

1848/49 assessed in absence of return £60; income proved at £70; exempt.
1849/50 assessed in absence of return £60; exempt.

1849/50 marked "Each" ?
Cross reference: Hook, Eliza & Emma, confectioners, etc., St.John.

761 HOUSE, -, draper.

1857/58 by way of note "Matthews, William now House, draper".
No assessment made.
Cross references: Attwood, John, linen draper, St.Mary; Flower, Joseph & Co., linen drapers, St.Mary; Matthews, William, draper, St.Mary.

762 HULL, Samuel, butcher. [also HULL, James]

1842/43 returned £120; assessed £200; reduced to £150 but no appeal noted.
1846/47 assessed in absence of return £175.
1847/48 returned £150; assessed £200.
1848/49-1849/50 returned £175; assessed £200.
1850/51 assessed in absence of return £200.
1851/52 returned £150; assessed £200.
1852/53 assessed in absence of return £200.
1853/54-1854/55 returned and assessed £200.
1855/56 returned £175; assessed £200.
1856/57-1858/59 returned and assessed £200.
1859/60 assessed in absence of return £200.

1842/43, 1846/47-1847/48 James Hull; 1848/49-1859/60 Samuel Hull.
1847/48-1848/49 marked "now Samuel".
Pigot & Co's Directory, 1842: James Hull, butcher, Brittox.

763 HUMPHREY, Thomas & CARTER, John, [by succession, grocers]

1857/58 entry only marked "Staples, William late Holder now Humphrey & Carter".
Cross references: Day, Ozias, bacon & cheese factor, St. Mary; Holder, Charles, grocer, St.Mary;
    Staples, William, grocer, St.Mary; Vines, Uriah, grocer, St.Mary.

764 HUNT, George, shoemaker, cordwainer, linen draper.

1848/49 returned £85; assessed £120.
1849/50, 1852/53 assessed in absence of return £120.
1853/54 returned £90; assessed £120.
1854/55 returned and assessed £120.
1855/56 assessed in absence of return £150.
1856/57 returned and assessed £150s, £100l.
1857/58-1858/59 assessed in absence of return £150.
1859/60 returned £150s, £100l; assessed £300.

Abbreviations: s, shoemaker, l, linen draper.
1842/43 cordwainer; 1848/49-1858/59 shoemaker; 1859/60 shoemaker & linen draper.
1842/43, 1846/47-1847/48 recorded marked "return in Bath"; 1850/51 no assessment made;
1851/52 estimated in absence of return £120 but no assessment made.
1849/50-1850/51 marked in brackets "Bath".
Pigot & Co's Directory, 1842: George Hunt, boot & shoe maker, Brittox.

765 HURST, Joseph, baker.

1842/43, 1846/47-1847/48 assessed in absence of return £100; exempt.

Pigot & Co's Directory, 1842: Joseph Hurst, baker, Sidmouth Street.

766 HUTCHINS, William, innkeeper.

1846/47-1847/48 assessed in absence of return £50; exempt.

767 JACKSON, D.D., dyer & bird stuffer.

1846/47-1848/49 assessed in absence of return £20; exempt.
1849/50 assessed in absence of return £50; exempt.

768 JEFFERIES, Charles, cabinet maker.

1846/47-1854/55 assessed in absence of return £70; exempt.
1855/56 assessed in absence of return £70; income proved at £75; exempt.

769 JEFFERIES, Cornelius, carver & gilder, painter, etc.

Year	Amount returned £	Commissioners' estimate £	Income proved £	Final assessment £
1842/43	60	125	–	125
1846/47	–	150	–	150
1847/48	–	150	120	–
1848/49	–	120	70	–
1849/50	–	120	120	–
1850/51	116.7.0	–	116.7.0	–
1851/52	–	120	104.15.0	–
1852/53	80	120	115	–
1853/54	80	100	–	100
1854/55	–	100	–	100
1855/56	60	100	–	100
1856/57	60	100	–	100
1857/58	110	–	–	110
1858/59	50	100	–	100
1859/60	–	75	–	75

1842/43 carver & gilder; 1846/47-1859/60 painter, etc.
1859/60 estimated at £100 but reduced to £75; no appeal noted.
Pigot & Co's Directory, 1842: Cornelius Jefferies, painter & gilder, Sidmouth Street.

770 JEFFERIES, Joseph, bacon factor.

1842/43, 1846/47-1855/56 assessed in absence of return £75; exempt.
1856/57-1859/60 recorded; no assessments made; exempt.

Pigot & Co's Directory, 1842: Joseph Jefferies, cheese & bacon factor, butcher, Maryport Street.

771 JEFFERIES, Priscilla, dressmaker.

1842/43, 1846/47-1849/50 assessed in absence of return £40; exempt.

Pigot & Co's Directory, 1842: Priscilla Jefferies, milliner & dressmaker, Maryport Street.

772 JEFFERIES, Samuel, shoemaker.

1842/43, 1846/47-1849/50 assessed in absence of return £50; exempt.

Pigot & Co's Directory, 1842: Samuel Jefferies, boot & shoe maker, Maryport Street.

773 KER, C., shopkeeper.

1846/47 assessed in absence of return £50; exempt.
1847/48 returned and assessed £130; income proved at £53; exempt.
1848/49 assessed in absence of return £53; exempt.
1849/50 assessed in absence of return £50; exempt.

774 KING, George, maltster.

1842/43 returned and assessed £150.
1846/47-1847/48 returned £100; assessed £150.
1848/49-1849/50 returned and assessed £150.
1850/51 assessed in absence of return £150.

1851/52 marked "now Long, maltster".
Pigot & Co's Directory, 1842: George King, corn & seed dealer, Market Place.
Cross reference: Long, William, cornfactor, St.John.

775 KING, Thomas G., corn dealer.

1848/49 assessed in absence of return £100; income proved at £88.3.0; exempt.

776 KINGSTON, William, cooper.

1842/43 returned £80; assessed £100; exempt.
1846/47-1849/50 assessed in absence of return £85; exempt.

1842/43 Kingstone.
Pigot & Co's Directory, 1842: William Kingston, cooper, New Park Street.

777 KNEE, Joseph, shoemaker.

1842/43, 1846/47-1851/52 assessed in absence of return £90; exempt.
1852/53 returned and assessed £90; exempt.
1853/54 assessed in absence of return £90; exempt.
1854/55 assessed in absence of return £90; income proved at £75; exempt.
1855/56 assessed in absence of return £50; exempt.
1856/57-1859/60 recorded; no assessments made; exempt.

778 LANSDOWN, Richard, painter, gilder, picture frame maker.

1853/54 returned £85; assessed £100; income proved at £85; exempt.
1854/55 assessed in absence of return £80; exempt.
1855/56 assessed in absence of return £100; income proved and assessment discharged,
sum not recorded.
1856/57 recorded; no assessment made; exempt.
1857/58 assessed in absence of return £90; exempt.
1858/59-1859/60 recorded; no assessments made; exempt.

1853/54 painter, gilder & picture frame maker, (glazier deleted);
1854/55-1856/57, 1859/60 painter & gilder, etc.; 1857/58-1858/59 painter & gilder.

779 LAWES, William & Co., carriers, wagon office.

1842/43 Carriers; 1846/47-1848/49 Wagon Office.
1842/43, 1846/47-1848/49 marked "return made at Chippenham".
1849/50 marked "now Perry".
Cross reference: Perry, Horatio Nelson, carrier, Bedborough (formerly agent to Lawes &
Co.)

780 LENARD, Sarah, dressmaker.

1842/43, 1846/47-1848/49 assessed in absence of return £100; exempt.
1849/50 assessed in absence of return £60; exempt.

Pigot & Co's Directory, 1842: Sarah Lenard, straw hat maker, Maryport Street.

781 LENARD, William, glazier, painter.

1842/43, 1846/47-1849/50 assessed in absence of return £40; exempt.

1842/43 glazier & painter; 1846/47 glazier; 1847/48-1849/50 glazier, etc.
Pigot & Co's Directory, 1842: William Webb Lenard, painter, plumber & glazier, Maryport
Street.

782 LENTHALL, Joseph, attorney's clerk.

1853/54 returned £90; assessed £100; income proved at £90; exempt.
1854/55 assessed in absence of return £90; exempt.
1855/56 assessed in absence of return £100; income proved and assessment discharged,
sum not recorded.
1856/57-1859/60 recorded; no assessments made; exempt.

783 LEVANDER, H.C., schoolmaster.

1859/60 assessed in absence of return £110.

Assessment made by General Commissioners; recorded on a separate page inserted into certificates of assessment.

784 LEWIS, Henry, butcher.

1858/59-1859/60 assessed in absence of return £150.

1858/59 marked "Collings, John now Lewis, butcher".
Cross reference: Collings, John, butcher, St.Mary.

785 LEWIS, Jonathan, butcher, lodgings.

1842/43 assessed in absence of return £90.
1846/47 returned and assessed £60b, £40l.
1847/48 assessed in absence of return £100; income proved at £60; duty of £1.15.0 left in charge.

Abbreviations: b, butcher; l, lodgings.
Pigot & Co's Directory, 1842: Jonathan Lewis, butcher, New Park Street.

786 MABBETT, Betty, innkeeper. [by comparison Angel]

1842/43 assessed in absence of return £50; exempt.

Pigot & Co's Directory, 1842: Elizabeth Mabbett, Angel, Sheep Street.

787 MACKLIN, James, innkeeper. [by comparison White Bear]

1842/43 returned £150; assessed £180 under letter.
1846/47 returned £180; assessed £200.
1847/48-1849/50 returned £150; assessed £200.
1850/51 assessed in absence of return £200.
1851/52 returned £140; assessed £175.
1852/53 assessed in absence of return £175.

1842/43, 1846/47-1847/48 Maklin.
1852/53 marked "now Decimus Wild".
Pigot & Co's Directory, 1842: James Macklin, White Bear, Monday Market Street.
Cross reference: Wild, Decimus, innkeeper, St.Mary; Macklin, Thomas, innkeeper, St.Mary.

788 MACKLIN, Thomas, innkeeper, White Bear.

1859/60 assessed in absence of return £300.

1859/60 marked "Wild, Decimus (deleted)".
Cross reference: Macklin, James, innkeeper, St.Mary; Wild, Decimus, innkeeper, St.Mary.

789 MADGE, James Cornelius, chemist.

1853/54 assessed in absence of return £70; exempt.
1854/55 assessed in absence of return £100; income proved at £90; exempt.
1855/56 assessed in absence of return £100.
1856/57 returned and assessed £100.
1857/58 returned £118; assessed £130.
1858/59 returned and assessed £127.
1859/60 returned and assessed £132.

1853/54 marked "late Bunter, chemist".
Cross reference: Bunter, G.B., chemist, St.Mary; Sainsbury, G.T., chemist & brickmaker, St. Mary.

790 MANLEY, Benjamin, pawn broker.

1842/43 returned £120; assessed £150; income proved at £120; exempt.
1846/47 assessed in absence of return £102; income proved at £100; exempt.
1847/48 returned and assessed £134; exempt.
1848/49 assessed in absence of return £134; exempt.
1849/50 returned and assessed £125; exempt.
1850/51 returned and assessed £130.
1851/52 assessed in absence of return £100; exempt.
1852/53 assessed in absence of return £80; exempt.

1852/53 marked "now Joseph Dowland, pawnbroker". (note: Dowland assessed as linen draper)
Pigot & Co's Directory, 1842: Benjamin Manley, pawnbroker, Maryport Street.
Cross reference: Dowland, Joseph, linen draper, St.Mary.

791 MANNINGS, Mary, dressmaker.

1855/56 returned and assessed £70; exempt.
1856/57-1859/60 recorded; no assessments made; exempt.

792 MANNINGS, Michael, woolstapler.

1853/54 returned £90; exempt.
1854/55 recorded; no assessment made; exempt.

793 MARTEN, -, linen draper.

1850/51 assessed in absence of return £100; exempt.

1849/50 marked "Overy, Alfred now Marten linen draper".
1850/51 marked "Marten late now Walker linen draper".
Pigot & Co's Directory, 1842: Thomas Martin (sic), linen & woollen draper, Market Place.
Cross reference: Overy, Alfred, linen draper, St.Mary; Walker, John, linen draper, St.Mary.

794 MASLEN, David, grocer, etc.

1856/57 assessed in absence of return £93; reduced to £80 on appeal.
1857/58 returned £52; assessed £80.
1858/59 returned £50; assessed £80.
1859/60 returned and assessed £80.

795 MASLEN, Ellen Ann, milliner, dressmaker.

1842/43 returned and assessed £100; exempt.
1846/47-1847/48 assessed in absence of return £75; exempt.

1842/43 milliner & dressmaker; 1846/47-1847/48 milliner.
1848/49 marked "now Mrs.J.Perry" "milliner".
Pigot & Co's Directory, 1842: Ellen Ann Mazlen (sic), milliner & dressmaker, Brittox.

796 MATTHEWS, William, draper.

1842/43, 1846/47 assessed in absence of return £120; exempt.
1847/48 returned and assessed £100; exempt.
1848/49 assessed in absence of return £100; income proved at £116.18.9; exempt.
1849/50 assessed in absence of return £150; reduced to £112 on appeal; exempt.
1850/51 returned and assessed £120; exempt.
1851/52 returned £116; no assessment made; exempt.
1852/53 assessed in absence of return £120.
1853/54-1854/55 returned and assessed £102.
1855/56 returned and assessed £100.
1856/57 returned and assessed £102.

1857/58 marked "now House".
Pigot & Co's Directory, 1842: William Mathews (sic), linen & woollen draper, New Park
    Street.
Cross references: Attwood, John, linen draper, St.Mary; Flower, Joseph & Co., linen drapers,
    St.Mary; House,-, draper, St.Mary.

797 MAYSMORE, Richard, bank manager.

1856/57-1858/59 marked "Schedule E".
1859/60 name and occupation recorded but no assessment made.

Cross reference: Maysmor(sic), Richard, bank manager, St.John.

798 MEAD, James, coal merchant.

1842/43 assessed in absence of return £100; income proved at £80; exempt.
1846/47-1847/48 assessed in absence of return £53; exempt.

Pigot & Co's Directory, 1842: George Mead, coal merchant, Wharf.

799 MEDLAND, William Thomas, baker, grocer.

Year	Amount returned £	Commissioners' estimate £	Income proved £	Final assessment £
1842/43	–	150	130	–
1846/47	–	117	117	–
1847/48	–	117	117	–
1848/49	–	117	130	–
1849/50	125	150a	135.13.4	–
1850/51	–	135	135	–
1851/52	–	135a	129.16.0	–
1852/53	84.18.0	100	138	–
1853/54	54.8.0	100	–	100
1854/55	100	–	–	100
1855/56	–	100	–	100
1856/57	100	–	–	100
1857/58	–	100	–	100
1858/59	100	–	–	100
1859/60	100	–	–	100

1842/43 baker & grocer; 1846/47-1859/60 grocer, etc.
Pigot & Co's Directory, 1842: William T.Medlam (sic), grocer & tea dealer, Maryport Street.

800 MONTGOMERY, Ronald, surgeon, visitor private lunatic asylum.

Year	Amount returned £	Commissioners' estimate £	Final assessment £
1846/47	180	–	180

1847/48	206	–	206
1848/49	170	–	170
1849/50	186	–	186
1850/51	295	–	295
1851/52	233.5.9	–	233.5.9
1852/53	252	–	252
1853/54	250	–	250
1854/55	265.10.0	–	265.10.0
1855/56	256.16.6	–	256.16.6
1856/57	266.10.8	–	266.10.8
1857/58	256.18.10	–	256.18.10
1858/59	222.7.6	–	222.7.6
1859/60	202.17.11	–	202.17.11

1859/60 additional entry as visitor private lunatic asylum deleted.

801 MORGAN, Mary, dressmaker & fancy repository.

1842/43 returned £30; assessed £50; income proved at £47; exempt.
1846/47-1848/49 assessed in absence of return £50; exempt.
1849/50 recorded but no assessment made.

Pigot & Co's Directory, 1842: Mary Morgan, fancy repository, Sidmouth Street.

802 MULLINGS, Benoni, cabinet maker.

1842/43 assessed in absence of return £90; exempt.

Pigot & Co's Directory, 1842: Benoni Mullings, cabinet maker, Northgate Street.

803 MULLINGS, John, cordwainer, grocer.

1842/43, 1846/47-1849/50 assessed in absence of return £50; exempt.

Pigot & Co's Directory, 1842: John Mullings, boot & shoe maker, Maryport Street.

804 MUNDY, A.B., tailor.

1846/47-1847/48 assessed in absence of return £50; exempt.

1848/49 marked "late tailor".

805 NOYES, Edwin, cooper.

1853/54 returned and assessed £75; exempt.

1854/55-1855/56 assessed in absence of return £75; exempt.
1856/57-1857/58 recorded; no assessments made; exempt.

1857/58 marked "dead" but remains in list for 1858/59 and 1859/60 as if exempt.

806 OAKFORD, Edward, tiler & plasterer.

1846/47 assessed in absence of return £80; exempt.
1848/49-1849/50 assessed in absence of return £80; exempt.

1847/48 entry deleted.
Pigot & Co's Directory, 1842: Edward Oakford & Son, plasterers & slaters, New Park Street.

807 OAKFORD, T.D. Junior, tiler & plasterer.

1842/43 returned and assessed £35; exempt.
1846/47-1849/50 assessed in absence of return £80; exempt.

Pigot & Co's Directory, 1842: Edward Oakford & Son, plasterers & slaters, New Park Street.

808 OATLEY, Samuel, carpenter. [also OATLEY, Cornelius]

1842/43, 1846/47-1852/53 assessed in absence of return £100; exempt.
1853/54 assessed in absence of return £100; income proved at £80; exempt.
1854/55 assessed in absence of return £80; exempt.

1842/43 Cornelius Oatley; 1846/47-1854/55 Samuel Oatley.
Pigot & Co's Directory, 1842: Cornelius Oatley, carpenter & builder, Sheep Street.
Cross reference: Oatley Cornelius, builder, St.John.

809 OFFER CHARITY or OFFER, Charity.

1846/47-1849/50 assessed in absence of return £50; exempt.

810 ORAM, James, brewer.

Year	Amount returned £	Commissioners' estimate £	Income proved £	Final assessment £
1842/43	–	150	130	–
1846/47	–	200a	–	150
1847/48	150	200	–	200
1848/49	200	–	–	200

1849/50	200	–	–	200
1850/51	200	–	–	200
1851/52	200	–	–	200
1852/53	200	250	–	250
1853/54	250	300	–	300
1854/55	225	300	–	300
1855/56	250	300	–	300
1856/57	300	450	–	450
1857/58	400	600	–	600
1858/59	500	600	–	600
1859/60	500	700	–	700

Pigot & Co's Directory, 1842: James Oram, brewer, Northgate Street.

811 OVERTON, John, dissenting minister.

1846/47 entry only.

812 OVERY, Alfred, linen draper.

1842/43 returned and assessed £150.
1846/47-1847/48 assessed in absence of return £175.
1848/49 returned £150; assessed £175.
1849/50 assessed in absence of return £175; assessment discharged on appeal but no
    figure recorded.

1849/50 marked "now Marten linen draper".
Pigot & Co's Directory, 1842: Alfred Overy, linen & woollen draper, Maryport Street.
Cross references: Marten, -, linen draper, St.Mary; Walker, John, linen draper, St. Mary.

813 PARADISE, John, orange dealer.

1846/47-1848/49 assessed in absence of return £30; exempt.

814 PARKER, Sarah Jane, straw bonnet maker.

1842/43, 1846/47-1848/49 assessed in absence of return £20; exempt.
1849/50 assessed in absence of return £50; exempt.

Pigot & Co's Directory, 1842: Sarah Jane Parker & Co., straw hat maker, Maryport Street.

815 PEACOCK, Mary & Samuel, carriers.

1842/43, 1846/47 entries only marked "return at Bath".
1842/43 Mary & Samuel John Peacock; 1846/47 M & S Peacock.

816 PERRETT, Charlotte, coal dealer.

1859/60 returned and assessed £100.

817 PERRETT, George, coal merchant, shopkeeper.

Year	Amount returned £	Commissioners' estimate £	Income proved £	Final assessment £
1842/43	–	115	115	–
1846/47	120	–	–	120
1847/48	120	–	–	120
1848/49	–	120	–	120
1849/50	132	150a	132	–
1850/51	135	–	135	–
1851/52	–	135	135	–
1852/53	80	135	129.2.0	–
1853/54	118.10.0	–	–	118.10.0
1854/55	116.3.6	–	–	116.3.6
1855/56	100	–	–	100
1856/57	100	–	–	100
1857/58	120	–	–	120
1858/59	100	120	–	120
1859/60	–	120	–	120

1842/43, 1846/47-1857/58 George Perrett; 1858/59-1859/60 James Phipp as Executor of
    George Perrett.
1842/43, 1846/47 shopkeeper, etc; 1847/48-1850/51 coal merchant & shopkeeper;
1851/52-1857/58 coal merchant.
Pigot & Co's Directory, 1842: George Perrett, shopkeeper & dealer in groceries & sundries,
    New Park Street.

818 PERRETT, Reuben, boat owner, coal merchant.

Year	Amount returned £	Commissioners' estimate £	Income proved £	Final assessment £
1842/43	80	–	80	–
1846/47	–	80	80	–
1847/48	–	80	80	–
1848/49	–	80	103.10.0	–
1849/50	95	–	95	–
1850/51	30	–	30	–
1851/52	–	95	94	–
1852/53	50	95	124	–
1853/54	25	100	–	100

1854/55	–	100	–	100
1855/56	100	–	–	100
1856/57	42	100	–	100
1857/58	65	100	–	100
1858/59	100	–	–	100
1859/60	100	–	–	100

1842/43, 1846/47-1852/53 boat owner; 1853/54-1859/60 coal merchant.

819 PHILLIPS, George, boat owner, coal merchant.

1842/43, 1846/47-1847/48 assessed in absence of return £100; exempt.

Pigot & Co's Directory, 1842: George Phillips, coal merchant, Wharf.
1842/43, 1846/47 boat owner & coal merchant; 1847/48 boat owner, etc.

820 PHIPP, Daniel, coal merchant, wharfinger, carter, corn merchant.

Year	Amount returned £	Commissioners' estimate £	Income proved £	Final assessment £
1842/43	95w 43c	150	–	150
1846/47	–	100	100	–
1847/48	–	100	100	–
1848/49	100	–	100	–
1849/50	100	150	–	150
1850/51	–	150	–	150
1851/52	–	150	–	150
1852/53	150	–	–	150
1853/54	–	150	–	150
1854/55	150	–	–	150
1855/56	150	200	–	200
1856/57	200	350	–	350
1857/58	350	400	–	400
1858/59	400	500	–	500
1859/60	–	500	–	500

Abbreviations: w, wharfinger; c, carter.
1842/43, 1846/47-1852/53 Phipps; 1853/54-1859/60 Phipp.
1842/43 wharfinger, carter; 1846/47-1849/50 wharfinger, etc.; 1850/51 wharfinger;
1851/52 coal merchant, etc.; 1852/53-1854/55 corn (sic) merchant;
1855/56-1859/60 coal merchant.
1842/43 returned £15 as farmer but deleted.
1856/57 marked "Devizes and Bath"; 1858/59 marked "Devizes"; 1859/60 marked "Devizes and Bristol".

Pigot & Co's Directory, 1842: Daniel Phipps (*sic*), wharfinger, Devizes Wharf.

821 PHIPP, James, innkeeper, Cross Keys.

1853/54 returned and assessed £65.15.0; exempt.
1855/56 assessed in absence of return £100.
1856/57 returned £100; assessed £200.
1857/58 assessed in absence of return £200.
1858/59 returned £150; assessed £200.
1859/60 assessed in absence of return £200.

1854/55 no assessment made. Marked "Ponting, George Butler, late Phipp, innkeeper; (assessments resume 1855/56)
1856/57 Cross Keys noted.
Cross reference: Phipp, John, farrier & innkeeper, St.Mary; Ponting, George Butler, innkeeper, St.Mary; Truman, Samuel, innkeeper, St.Mary.

822 PHIPP, John, farrier, innkeeper, beerhouse keeper. [by comparison, Cross Keys]

1851/52 returned and assessed £140; exempt.
1852/53 assessed in absence of return £150.
1853/54 assessed in absence of return £100.
1854/55 assessed in absence of return £50; exempt.

1851/52 farrier & beerhouse keeper; 1852/53-1853/54 farrier & innkeeper; 1854/55 farrier.
1855/56 "John" deleted, "James" substituted.
Pigot & Co's Directory, 1842: James Phipps, blacksmith, Monday Market Street.
Cross reference: Phipp, James, innkeeper, St.Mary; Ponting, George Butler, innkeeper, St.Mary; Truman, Samuel, innkeeper, St.Mary.

823 PHIPP, Samuel, corn porter.

1853/54 returned £50; exempt.
1854/55-1855/56 assessed in absence of return £50; exempt.
1856/57-1857/58 recorded; no assessments made; exempt.
1858/59 assessed in absence of return £80.
1859/60 returned £80; assessed £100.

1859/60 assessment increased possibly on objection by surveyor of taxes.

824 PHIPPS, David.

1842/43 name only entered.

825 PILE, Benjamin, tea dealer, grocer.

1842/43, 1846/47-1847/48 assessed in absence of return £80; exempt.
1848/49 assessed in absence of return £80; income proved at £81.16.0; exempt.
1849/50 assessed in absence of return £80; exempt.

1842/43 tea dealer & grocer; 1846/47-1849/50 tea dealer.
Pigot & Co's Directory, 1842: Benjamin Pile, shopkeeper & dealer in groceries & sundries.

826 PONTING, George Butler, innkeeper. [by comparison, Cross Keys]

1854/55 returned and assessed £125.

1854/55 marked "late Phipp, innkeeper".
Cross references: Phipp, James, innkeeper, St.Mary; Phipp, John, farrier & innkeeper, St.Mary;
    Truman, Samuel, innkeeper, St.Mary.

827 PRICE, Ezra, piano forte seller, music seller.

1859/60 assessed in absence of return £130.

1858/59 marked "see Market Lavington".
1859/60 marked [Market Lavington] "at Devizes, removed to St.Mary".
Cross reference: Price, Ezra, grocer & piano forte tuner, Market Lavington.

828 PRITCHARD, George, tailor.

1842/43, 1846/47-1849/50 assessed in absence of return £50; exempt.

Pigot & Co's Directory, 1842: George Pritchard, tailor, Sheep Street.

829 RANDELL, George, baker, grocer.

1842/43 returned and assessed £150.
1846/47 returned and assessed £160.
1847/48 returned £160; assessed £150 and £13 interest.
1848/49 assessed in absence of return £163; income proved at £125.6.0; exempt.
1849/50 returned £131.12.0; assessed £150.
1850/51-1854/55 returned and assessed £160.
1855/56-1857/58 returned £155; assessed 160.
1858/59-1859/60 returned and assessed £160.

1846/47-1849/50, 1853/54 Randle.
1842/43 baker & grocer; 1846/47-1849/50 baker, etc.; baker 1850/51-1859/60.

1846/47-1847/48 interest included in total figure.
1856/57 returned £160 but no assessment made.
Pigot & Co's Directory, 1842: George Randell, baker, New Park Street.

830 RANDELL, J.Ashley, cabinet maker, auctioneer.

1846/47-1852/53 assessed in absence of return £80; exempt.

1846/47-1849/50 cabinet maker; 1850/51-1852/53 auctioneer & cabinet maker.
1853/54 marked "late, now -," "gone".

831 RANDELL, James T., tallow chandler, brickmaker, coal merchant.

1842/43 returned £200; assessed £400.
1846/47-1847/48 returned £250; assessed £350.
1848/49 returned and assessed £350.

1842/43 tallow chandler & brickmaker; 1846/47-1848/49 tallow chandler, brickmaker & coal
    merchant; 1849/50 brickmaker & coal merchant.
1842/43 James, otherwise J.T.
1849/59 marked "see Rowde" (no assessment made in Rowde).
Pigot & Co's Directory, 1842: James Randell, coal merchant, Maryport Wharf; tallow chandler,
    Maryport Street.

832 REYNOLDS, Charles, butcher.

1842/43 assessed in absence of return £54.6.8; exempt.

Pigot & Co's Directory, 1842: Charles Reynolds, butcher, Sidmouth Street.

833 REYNOLDS, William & Stephen, curriers. [also REYNOLDS, Robert]

1842/43 returned and assessed £150.
1846/47-1847/48 assessed in absence of return £300.
1848/49 returned and assessed £190; exempt.
1849/50 returned and assessed £168; exempt.
1850/51 assessed in absence of return £168; exempt.
1851/52 returned and assessed £220; exempt.
1852/53 returned and assessed £220; income proved at £262; exempt.
1853/54 returned and assessed £225.
1854/55 returned and assessed £240.
1855/56 returned £220; assessed £240.
1856/57 assessed in absence of return £260.
1857/58-1859/60 returned and assessed £260.

1842/43 Robert Reynolds.
1848/49-1852/53 entitled to exemption as partnership income.
Pigot & Co's Directory, 1842: Robert Reynolds, currier & leather cutter, Maryport Street.

834 ROBBINS, Samuel, timber merchant.

1848/49 returned and assessed £100.
1851/52-1852/53 returned £80; assessed £100.

1849/50-1850/51 marked "return at Woodborough".
Pigot & Co's Directory, 1842: Samuel Robbins, timber merchant, Wharf.
Cross reference: Robbins, Samuel, timber merchant, Woodborough.

835 ROMAIN, William, builder. [also ROMAIN, John]

1842/43 returned £40; assessed £130.
1846/47-1849/50 returned £130; assessed £150.
1850/51 returned and assessed £150.
1851/52 returned and assessed £130.
1852/53-1855/56 returned £130; assessed £150.
1856/57-1857/58 returned £120; assessed £150.
1858/59 returned and assessed £100.
1859/60 assessed in absence of return £100; exempt.

1842/43, 1846/47-1858/59 William Romain; 1859/60 William & John Romain.
1859/60 entitled to exemption as partnership income.
Pigot & Co's Directory, 1842: William Romain, builder, carpenter & wheelwright, timber mer-
    chant, New Park Street.

836 RUTTER, John.

1842/43 name only entered.

837 SAINSBURY, George Taylor, slate merchant, brickmaker, druggist, chemist.

Year	Amount returned £	Commissioners' estimate £	Income proved £	Final assessment £
1842/43	150b	320	–	320
	170d			
1846/47	120b	120	–	120
1847/48	150b	–	–	150
	50c	–	50	–
1848/49	130b	–	–	130
1851/52	150	200	–	200
1853/54	200s	–	–	200

	200b	–	–	200
1854/55	500	–	–	500
1855/56	500	600	–	600

Abbreviations: b, brickmaker; c, chemist; d, druggist; s, slate merchant.
1842/43, 1846/47-1852/53 brickmaker; 1842/43 druggist; 1847/48 chemist; 1853/54-1855/56 slate merchant & brickmaker.
1847/48-1849/50 marked "G.B.Bunter chemist, late Sainsbury"
1849/50-1850/51, 1852/53, 1856/57-1859/60 assessed in Rowde.
1855/56 marked "at Seend & Rowde".
The exemption claimed in 1847/48 is anomalous but entry is made against George Taylor Sainsbury.
Pigot & Co's Directory, 1842: George Taylor Sainsbury, chemist & druggist, Market; agent to Economic Life Office, Market Place.
Cross references: Bunter, G.B., chemist, St.Mary; Madge, James Cornelius, chemist, St.Mary; Sainsbury, George Taylor, brickmaker, Rowde.

838 SAINSBURY & SAUNDERS, coal merchants. [also SAUNDERS, Henry]

1846/47 returned and assessed £600.
1847/48-1849/50 returned £500; assessed £600.
1850/51-1852/53 returned and assessed £500.
1853/54-1854/55 returned and assessed £250.
1855/56-1856/57 returned £250; assessed £300.
1857/58 returned and assessed £250.

1846/47-1852/53 Sainsbury & Saunders; 1853/54-1857/58 Henry Saunders.
1858/59-1859/60 marked "Nursteed". (no assessments made in Nursteed).

839 SAPP, Elias.

1846/47-1848/49 assessed in absence of return £90; exempt.

No occupation noted.

840 SAYER, John, shoemaker.

1842/43, 1846/47-1849/50 assessed in absence of return £60; exempt.

Pigot & Co's Directory, 1842: John Sayer, boot & shoe maker, New Park Street.

841 SEDGEFIELD, Edward, grocer, Fire Office agent. [also SEDGEFIELD, Mrs Sarah, SEDGFIELD, (sic) John]

1842/43, 1846/47 returned and assessed £200g, £15f.
1847/48 assessed in absence of return £215.

1848/49 returned and assessed £215.
1849/50-1851/52 returned and assessed £190.
1852/53 assessed in absence of return £190.
1853/54 returned £5; no assessment made.
1854/55 returned £30; assessed £100.
1855/56-1856/57 returned and assessed £110.
1857/58 assessed in absence of return £120.
1858/59-1859/60 returned and assessed £120.

Abbreviations: g, grocer; f, Fire Office agent.
1842/43, 1846/47-1849/50 Edward Sedgefield; 1850/51-1852/53 Mrs Sedgefield;
1853/54-1855/56 Sarah Sedgefield; 1856/57-1859/60 John Sedgfield (*sic*).
1842/43, 1846/47-1854/55 grocer & Fire Office agent; 1855/56-1859/60 grocer & agent.
1852/53 marked "now Jarman". (no reference elsewhere to Jarman)
1857/58 [Potterne] "Marshman, Samuel now Sedgefield, John, baker & grocer".
1858/59 [Potterne] "Marshman, Samuel - see Sedgefield, St.Mary"
Pigot & Co's Directory, 1842: Edward Sedgefield, grocer, wine merchant (British wines & spir-
    its), agent to County (Fire) & Provident (Life) Office, Maryport Street.
Cross references: Marshman, Samuel, baker & grocer, Potterne; Sedgefield, John, baker & grocer,
    Potterne.

842 SELBY, Thomas, bacon factor. [also SELBY, Harriet]

1842/43, 1846/47-1850/51 assessed in absence of return £100; exempt.
1852/53 returned £88.4.0; assessed £100; income proved at £88.4.0; exempt.
1853/54-1854/55 returned and assessed £120.
1855/56-1856/57 assessed in absence of return £150.
1858/59-1859/60 returned and assessed £150.

1842/43, 1846/47-1857/58 Thomas Selby; 1858/59-1859/60 Harriet Selby.
1851/52 no assessment made.
1857/58 marked "dead"; no assessment made.
Pigot & Co's Directory, 1842: Thomas Selby, cheese & bacon factor, Northgate Street.

843 SHEPHERD, James, carpenter.

1846/47-1848/49 assessed in absence of return £20; exempt.
1849/50 assessed in absence of return £50; exempt.

844 SHEPPARD, William, coachman, coachmaster, innkeeper. [by comparison, Nags Head]

1842/43 returned and assessed £70; exempt.
1846/47-1848/49 assessed in absence of return £70; exempt.
1849/50 assessed in absence of return £150; reduced to £120 on appeal; exempt.
1850/51 returned and assessed £120; exempt.

1851/52 assessed in absence of return £120; income proved at £95; exempt.
1852/53 assessed in absence of return £120; income proved and assessment discharged but no sum recorded.
1853/54 returned and assessed £100.

1842/43 coachman, 1846/47-1849/50 coachmaster, 1850/51-1852/53 coachmaster & innkeeper, 1853/54 innkeeper.
1854/55 Sheppard deleted, Joseph Willis substituted.
Cross reference: White, William, innkeeper & cheese factor, St.Mary; Willis, Samuel & Son, coachmaker & innkeeper, St.Mary.

845 SHILSTONE, John, broker.

1853/54 returned £94; assessed £100; income proved at £94.
1854/55-1856/57 assessed in absence of return £100.
1857/58-1858/59 returned and assessed £100.
1859/60 returned £100; assessed £150.

1854/55 Shilston.

846 SIVELL, Henry, grocer.

1842/43 returned and assessed £250.
1846/47-1847/48 assessed in absence of return £250.
1848/49 returned £250; assessed £300.
1849/50 returned £127.8.0; assessed £250.
1850/51-1855/56 returned £200; assessed £250.
1856/57-1859/60 returned £250; assessed £300.

1842/43, 1846/47-1851/52 Sivill.
Pigot & Co's Directory, 1842: Henry Sivell, grocer & tea dealer, New Park Street

847 SKINNER, Joseph, tinman, agent.

1842/43 assessed in absence of return £100; income proved at £133.6.2.
1846/47 assessed in absence of return £90; exempt.

1842/43 tinman & agent; 1846/47 tinman.
1847/48 marked "St.John".
Pigot & Co's Directory, 1842: Joseph Skinner, brazier & tinman, Brittox.
Cross reference: Skinner, Joseph, tinman, St.John.

848 SLADE, John, solicitor.

1842/43 returned £250; assessed £300.
1846/47 returned and assessed £300.

Pigot & Co's Directory, 1842: John Slade, attorney, New Park Street.

849 SLOPER, Joseph, linen draper.

1850/51 assessed in absence of return £150.
1851/52 assessed in absence of return £100; income proved at £132.10.0; exempt.
1852/53 assessed in absence of return £120; assessment discharged on appeal but no sum recorded.
1853/54 returned £70 and £24 interest; assessed £120.
1854/55 returned and assessed £100.
1855/56 assessed in absence of return £100.
1856/57-1859/60 returned £70; assessed £120.

1850/51 marked "late Wolfe linen draper".
Cross reference: Sloper, Joseph, linen draper, St.John; Wolfe, John, draper, St.Mary.

850 SLY, William, saddler, trumpeter in yeomanry.

Year	Amount returned £	Commissioners' estimate £	Final assessment £
1842/43	160	–	160
1846/47	150	–	150
1847/48	150	–	150
1848/49	140	150	150
1849/50	150	–	150
1850/51	140	150	150
1851/52	138.10.0	150	150
1852/53	139.15.0	150	150
1853/54	114.3.8 10t	150	150
1854/55	123	150	150
1855/56	124	150	150
1856/57	120	160	160

Abbreviation: t, trumpeter in yeomanry.
1842/43, 1846/47-1856/57 saddler; 1853/54-1854/55 trumpeter in yeomanry.
1857/58 marked "Charged Sly & Son see St.John".
Pigot & Co's Directory, 1842: William Sly, saddler & harness maker, Brittox.
Cross reference: Sly, William, harness maker, St.John.

851 SMALLBONES, James, linen draper.

Year	Amount returned £	Commissioners' estimate £	Final assessment £
1842/43	300	–	300

1846/47	270	350	350
1847/48	300	350	350
1848/49	250	350	350
1849/50	250	300a	250
1850/51	300	–	300
1851/52	300	–	300
1852/53	250	300	300
1853/54	300	–	300
1854/55	200	250	250
1855/56	300	–	300
1856/57	200	300	300
1857/58	250	–	250
1858/59	150	200	200
1859/60	200	250	250

Pigot & Co's Directory, 1842: James Smallbones, linen & woollen draper, Sidmouth Street.

852 SMITH, George, William & Mary, linen drapers.

1842/43 returned and assessed £300.
1846/47 assessed in absence of return £300.
1847/48 returned and assessed £300.
1848/49-1850/51 assessed in absence of return £200; exempt.
1851/52-1852/53 assessed in absence of return £315; £210 exempt.
1853/54 assessed in absence of return £115.
1854/55-1859/60 assessed in absence of return £300.

1842/43, 1846/47-1847/48 George Smith; 1848/49-1850/51 George & William Smith;
1851/52-1859/60 George, William & Mary Smith (sometimes Mrs Smith)
1851/52-1852/53 £105 left in charge, 1852/53 marked "Mrs Smith liable".
1853/54 assessment on Mrs Smith only, G & W Smith being exempt.
Pigot & Co's Directory, 1842: George Smith, linen & woollen draper, Brittox.

853 STAPLES, William, grocer.

1849/50 assessed in absence of return £80; exempt.
1850/51 assessed in absence of return £100; exempt.
1853/54 returned and assessed £84; exempt.
1854/55 assessed in absence of return £84; exempt.

1849/50 marked "Day, Ozias late now Staples, grocer";Vines, Uriah now Staples".
1851/52-1852/53 no assessments made.
1855/56 marked "gone".
1856/57 marked "now Holder".
1857/58 marked "late Holder now Humphrey & Carter".
Cross references: Day, Ozias, grocer, St.Mary; Holder, Charles, grocer, St.Mary; Humphrey,Tho-
    mas & Carter, John, grocers, St.Mary;Vines, Uriah, grocer, St. Mary.

854 STEVENS, Jonathan, fruiterer.

1846/47–1849/50 assessed in absence of return £50; exempt.

855 STOCKWELL, John, plumber, glazier. [also STOCKWELL, ADLAM & GREGORY]

1842/43 assessed in absence of return £232.10.0; exempt.
1846/47–1848/49 assessed in absence of return £100; exempt.
1849/50 assessed in absence of return £60; exempt.
1853/54 returned and assessed £120.
1854/55 assessed in absence of return £120; reduced to £100 but no appeal noted.
1855/56 returned and assessed £100.
1856/57 recorded but no assessment made.
1857/58 assessed in absence of return £100.
1858/59 returned and assessed £100.
1859/60 assessed in absence of return £130.

1842/43 Stockwell, Adlam & Gregory; 1846/47–1854/55 John Stockwell;
1855/56–1859/60 John Stockwell & Son.
1842/43 plumbers & glaziers; 1846/47 glazier; 1847/48–1849/50, 1853/54–1859/60
   plumber.
1842/43 entitled to exemption as partnership income.
1850/51–1852/53 no assessments made.
Cross reference: Adlam, Samuel, plumber, glazier, painter, St.Mary; Gregory, George, painter,
   St.Mary.

856 STRANGE, Robert, attorney, solicitor.

1842/43 returned £80; assessed £120.
1846/47 returned £50; assessed £120; reduced to £80 on appeal.
1847/48–1849/50 returned and assessed £80; exempt 1848/49.
1850/51 assessed in absence of return £80; exempt.

1842/43 solicitor; 1846/47–1850/51 attorney.
Pigot & Co's Directory, 1842: Robert Strange, attorney, agent to Globe Fire Office, New Park
   Street.

857 TABOIS, F[rederick] W[illiam], cutler, etc.

1842/43, 1846/47–1847/48 assessed in absence of return £100; exempt.

Pigot & Co's Directory, 1842: Frederick William Tabois, ironmonger & cutler, Brittox.

858 THOMAS, George, innkeeper. [by comparison, White Lion]

1842/43 assessed in absence of return £100; exempt.

Pigot & Co's Directory, 1842: George Thomas, White Lion, Northgate Street.
Cross references: Biggs, George, innkeeper, St. Mary; Trueman, Richard, innkeeper, St. Mary.

859 THOMPSON, Peter, baker, pork butcher.

1842/43 returned and assessed £150.
1846/47 assessed in absence of return £120; assessment discharged on appeal but no sum recorded.
1847/48 assessed in absence of return £160; income proved at £120; exempt.
1848/49 assessed in absence of return £120; income proved at £94.7.0; exempt.
1849/50-1851/52 assessed in absence of return £120; exempt.

1842/43, 1846/47-1847/48 baker; 1848/49 baker, etc.; 1849/50-1851/52 baker & pork butcher.
Pigot & Co's Directory, 1842: Peter Thompson, baker, cheese & bacon factor, New Park Street.

860 THOMPSON, Stephen, tailor.

1842/43 assessed in absence of return £120; exempt.
1846/47 returned and assessed £150.
1847/48 assessed in absence of return £150.
1848/49-1849/50 returned and assessed £150.
1850/51 assessed in absence of return £150.
1851/52-1858/59 returned and assessed £150.
1859/60 assessed in absence of return £150.

Pigot & Co's Directory, 1842: Stephen Thompson, tailor, Northgate Street.

861 TRINDER, Charles, surgeon, medicine.

1842/43 returned and assessed £350m, £25 bond security.
1846/47 returned and assessed £321.13.4.
1847/48 returned and assessed £350s, £21.13.4 interest.
1848/49 assessed in absence of return £271.6.8.
1849/50 returned and assessed £250s, £21.13.4 interest.
1850/51 returned and assessed £200.

Abbreviations: m, medicine; s, surgeon.
1842/43 medicine; 1846/47-1850/51 surgeon.
1846/47 includes "interest on money".
Pigot & Co's Directory, 1842: Charles Trinder, surgeon, New Park Street.

862 TRUEMAN, Richard, innkeeper, White Lion.

1853/54 assessed in absence of return £100; income proved at £65.
1854/55–1856/57 assessed in absence of return £100.
1857/58 returned £80; assessed £100.
1858/59 returned and assessed £100.
1859/60 assessed in absence of return £100.

1856/57 White Lion noted.
Cross references: Biggs, George, innkeeper, St. Mary; Thomas, George, innkeeper, St.Mary.

863 TRUMAN, Samuel, innkeeper [by comparison, Cross Keys].

1842/43, 1846/47–1849/50 assessed in absence of return £80; exempt.

Pigot & Co's Directory, 1842: Samuel Truman, Cross Keys, Market Street.
Cross reference: Phipp, James, innkeeper, St.Mary; Phipp, John, farrier & innkeeper, St.Mary;
    Ponting, George Butler, innkeeper, St.Mary.

864 VINCENT, J[ohn] P[hillips], veterinary surgeon.

1842/43 returned and assessed £158.15.4.

Pigot & Co's Directory, 1842: John Phillips Vincent, veterinary surgeon, Northgate Street.
Cross reference: Vincent, J.P., veterinary surgeon, St.John.

865 VINES, Uriah, grocer.

1842/43, 1846/47–1849/50 assessed in absence of return £100; exempt.

1849/50 marked "now Staples".
Pigot & Co's Directory, 1842: Uriah Vines, baker, grocer, Northgate Street.
Cross references: Day, Ozias, bacon & cheese factor, St. Mary; Holder, Charles, grocer, St.Mary;
    Humphrey, Thomas & Carter, John, grocers, St.Mary; Staples, William, grocer, St.Mary.

866 WADWORTH, William John, baker, pig killer.

1842/43 assessed in absence of return £150; income proved at £146; exempt.
1846/47 assessed in absence of return £160.
1847/48 assessed in absence of return £160; income proved at £120; exempt.

William Wadworth Junior 1848/49.
1842/43 baker & pig killer; 1846/47–1847/48 baker, etc.
1848/49 marked "now in Week".
Pigot & Co's Directory, 1842: William Wadworth, baker, cheese & bacon factor, New Park Street.
Cross reference: Wadworth, William, cheese factor, Week.

867 WAITE, Ann, blacksmith.

1842/43, 1846/47-1849/50 assessed in absence of return £80; exempt.

Pigot & Co's Directory, 1842: Ann Waite, blacksmith, Sheep Street.

868 WALKER, John, draper.

1851/52-1854/55 returned and assessed £160.
1855/56 assessed in absence of return £160.
1856/57 returned and assessed £160.
1857/58-1859/60 returned £160; assessed £200.

1850/51 marked "Marten late now Walker, linen draper".
1855/56 figures indistinct, seemingly £100 but likely to be £160.
Cross references: Marten, -, linen draper, St.Mary; Overy, Alfred, linen draper, St.Mary.

869 WARD, Thomas Ponson, cabinet maker.

1842/43 assessed in absence of return £50; exempt.

870 WATTS, William, bricklayer.

1854/55 assessed in absence of return £100.
1855/56-1856/57 returned and assessed £100.
1857/58 returned £80; assessed £100.
1858/59-1859/60 returned and assessed £100.

871 WAYLEN, George, surgeon

Year	Amount returned £	Commissioners' estimate £	Final assessment £
1846/47	–	125	125
1847/48	125	210	210
1848/49	200	–	200
1849/50	200	–	200
1850/51	–	250	250
1851/52	190	250	250
1852/53	–	250	250
1853/54	200	250	250
1854/55	200	250	250
1855/56	–	250	250
1856/57	–	142	142

1857/58	–	150	150
1858/59	200	–	200
1859/60	250	–	250

1846/47 assessed in partnership with William Waylen.
Cross reference: Waylen, William, surgeon, St.Mary.

872 WAYLEN, Robert, schoolmaster, education, wine manufacturer.

Year	Amount returned $£$	Commissioners' estimate $£$	Final assessment $£$
1852/53	160s	–	210
	50w		
1853/54	140s	–	190
	50w		
1854/55	150	–	150
1855/56	128	–	128
1856/57	117	–	117
1857/58	150	–	150
1858/59	193	–	193
1859/60	241	–	241

Abbreviations: s, schoolmaster or education; w, wine manufacturer.
1852/52-1853/54 education; 1854/55-1859/60 schoolmaster; 1852/53-1855/56 wine manufacturer.

873 WAYLEN, William, innkeeper. [by comparison, Old Crown]

1846/47 assessed in absence of return £100; exempt.

1847/48 marked "William Waylen, innkeeper, now Dyke".
Cross reference: Chandler, James, innkeeper, St. Mary; Dyke, George, innkeeper, St.Mary.

874 WAYLEN, William, surgeon.

1842/43 returned and assessed£200.
1846/47 assessed in absence of return £125.
1847/48 returned and assessed £40.
1848/49 returned and assessed £90.
1849/50 Schedule E £50; exempt.

1846/47 assessed in partnership with George Waylen.
Pigot & Co's Directory, 1842: William Waylen, surgeon, Brittox.
Cross reference: Waylen, George, surgeon, St.Mary.

875 WESTON, Henry, hair dresser, grocer.

1842/43, 1846/47-1848/49 assessed in absence of return £100; exempt.
1849/50 assessed in absence of return £50; exempt.
1852/53 returned and assessed £95; income proved at £110; exempt.
1853/54 returned £72.14.0; assessed £100; income proved at £72.14.0; exempt.
1854/55 assessed in absence of return £80; exempt.
1855/56 assessed in absence of return £80.
1856/57 assessed in absence of return £80; confirmed on appeal.
1857/58 returned £62; assessed £80; exempt.
1858/59 recorded; no assessment made; exempt.
1859/60 returned £82; no assessment made; exempt.

1842/43, 1846/47 hair dresser, etc; 1847/48-1849/50 hair dresser; 1852/53-1859/60 grocer, hair dresser (etc., 1852/53-1853/54).
1850/51-1851/52 no assessments made.
Pigot & Co's Directory, 1842: Henry Weston, perfumer & hair dresser & toy dealer, shopkeeper & dealer in groceries & sundries, Chapel Corner.

876 WESTON, John, baker, grocer.

1848/49 assessed in absence of return £120; income proved at £90; exempt.
1849/50-1850/51 assessed in absence of return £120; exempt.
1851/52 returned £80; assessed £120; exempt.
1852/53-1853/54 assessed in absence of return £100; exempt.
1854/55 returned £100; assessed £150; reduced to £125 but no appeal noted.
1855/56 returned £80; assessed £125.
1856/57 returned £100; assessed £125.

1848/49-1850/51, 1856/57 baker; 1851/52-1855/56 baker & grocer.
1857/58 marked "now Higgs, baker, etc."
Cross reference: Higgs, Elijah Andrew, grocer, St.Mary.

877 WHEELER, Mary Ann Elizabeth, schoolmistress, shopkeeper.

1842/43, 1846/47-1849/50 assessed in absence of return £65; exempt.

1842/43 schoolmistress & shopkeeper; 1846/47-1849/50 schoolmistress.
Pigot & Co's Directory, 1842: Mary & Elizabeth Wheeler, grocers & tea dealers, Sidmouth Street.

878 WHEELER, Richard, pork butcher, dairyman.

1842/43, 1846/47-1850/51 assessed in absence of return £60; exempt.
1851/52 assessed in absence of return £60; income proved at £57; exempt.

1852/53-1855/56 assessed in absence of return £60; exempt.
1856/57 recorded; no assessment made; exempt.
1857/58 returned £41.12.0; no assessment made; exempt.
1858/59 recorded; no assessment made; exempt.
1859/60 returned £52; assessed £100.

1842/43, 1846/47-1856/57 pork butcher; 1857/58-1859/60 pork butcher & dairyman.
Pigot & Co's Directory, 1842: Richard Wheeler, pork butcher, Sidmouth Street.

879 WHEELER, Robert, tailor.

1842/43, 1846/47-1855/56 assessed in absence of return £60; exempt.
1856/57-1859/60 recorded; no assessments made; exempt.

Pigot & Co's Directory, 1842: R.Wheeler, tailor, New Park Street.

880 WHEELER, Thomas, gunsmith.

1842/43, 1846/47-1855/56 assessed in absence of return £75; exempt.
1856/57-1859/60 recorded; no assessments made; exempt.

Pigot & Co's Directory, 1842: William Wheeler, gun maker, Little Brittox.

881 WHITE, George, ironmonger.

1842/43, 1846/47-1847/48 assessed in absence of return £95; exempt.
1848/49 assessed in absence of return £95; income proved at £113; exempt.
1849/50 assessed in absence of return £95; exempt.
1850/51 assessed in absence of return £95 and £32 interest; income proved at £110;
   exempt.
1851/52 assessed in absence of return £120 and £32 interest; income proved at £120;
   exempt.
1852/53 returned £115; assessed £120; income proved at £117; exempt.
1853/54 returned £115; assessed £150; reduced to £125 but no appeal noted.
1854/55 returned £110; assessed £125.
1855/56 returned £112; assessed £125.
1856/57 returned £110; assessed £125.
1857/58 returned £120 and £41.12.0 interest; assessed £130.
1858/59-1859/60 returned £115; assessed £130.

1851/52 interest charged under Schedule C.
Pigot & Co's Directory, 1842: George White, ironmonger, Sidmouth Street.

882 WHITE, William, innkeeper, cheese factor. [by comparison, Nags Head]

1842/43 returned £70; assessed £125; exempt.

Pigot & Co's Directory, 1842: White, -, Nags Head, New Park Street.
Cross references: Sheppard, William, innkeeper, St.Mary; Willis, Samuel & Son, innkeeper, St.Mary.

883 WILD, Decimus, innkeeper, White Bear.

1853/54 returned £140; assessed £150.
1854/55 returned £110; assessed £150.
1855/56 returned £120; assessed £150.
1856/57 returned £130; assessed £300.
1857/58 returned £205; assessed £300.
1858/59 returned £180; assessed £300.

1852/53 marked "Macklin now Decimus Wild innkeeper".
1853/54 marked "late Macklin innkeeper".
1859/60 marked "Macklin, Thomas, innkeeper, White Bear".
1859/60 [Bedborough] marked "late Cole, innkeeper, Bell".
Cross reference: Macklin, James, innkeeper, St.Mary; Macklin, Thomas, innkeeper, St.Mary; Wild, Decimus, innkeeper, Bedborough.

884 WILD, George, innkeeper, Three Crowns.

1856/57 assessed in absence of return £100.
1857/58-1859/60 returned and assessed £100.

1856/57 [St.John] entered but deleted.
1857/57-1859/60 marked "late Chandler, Three Crowns".
Cross reference: Chandler, James, innkeeper, St.Mary.

885 WILLIS, Samuel.

1850/51-1851/52 assessed in absence of return £57.2.6; exempt.

No occupation noted.

886 WILLIS, Samuel & Son, coachmakers, innkeeper, Nags Head. [also WILLIS, Joseph]

1842/43 assessed in absence of return £130; exempt.
1846/47-1847/48 assessed in absence of return £120; exempt.
1848/49 assessed in absence of return £120; income proved at £110; exempt.
1849/50 returned and assessed £110; exempt.
1850/51-1851/52 assessed in absence of return £110; exempt.
1852/53 returned and assessed £110; income proved at £142; exempt.
1853/54 returned £100; assessed £130.

1854/55 returned £100; assessed £150.
1855/56 returned and assessed £150.
1856/57 returned £150; assessed 80c, 160i.
1857/58 returned £200; assessed £240.
1858/59 returned £200; assessed £250.
1859/60 returned £210; assessed £300.

Abbreviations: c, coachmaker; i, innkeeper.
1842/43 Samuel Willis & Son; 1846/47-1849/50 Samuel & Joseph Willis;
1850/51-1859/60 Joseph Willis.
1842/43, 1846/47-1855/56 coachmaker(s); 1855/56-1859/60 coachmaker & innkeeper.
1854/55 marked "Return to make for innkeeper".
1857/58 Nags Head noted.
Pigot & Co's Directory, 1842: Samuel Willis & Son, brightsmiths, coachmakers, Maryport
    Street.
Cross references: Sheppard, William, innkeeper, St.Mary; White, William, innkeeper, St.Mary.

887 WISE, Joseph, coachmaker.

1842/43 assessed in absence of return £60; exempt.

Pigot & Co's Directory, 1842: Joseph Wise, coachmaker, Maryport Street.

888 WITHINGTON, W., watchmaker.

1856/57-1857/58 recorded but no assessments made.

1855/56 marked "Wood, John now Waddington (sic) watchmaker".
1858/59 marked "removed into St.John".
Cross references: Withington, William Bamforth, watchmaker, St.John; Wood, John, watch-
    maker, St.Mary.

889 WOLFE, John, draper.

1842/43, 1846/47-1848/49 assessed in absence of return £100; exempt.
1849/50 returned and assessed £100; exempt.

1850/51 marked "Sloper, Joseph late Wolfe, linen draper".
Pigot & Co's Directory, 1842: John Wolfe, linen & woollen draper, Brittox.
Cross reference: Sloper, Joseph, linen draper, St.Mary.

890 WOOD, John, watchmaker.

1842/43, 1846/47-1853/54 assessed in absence of return £80; exempt.
1854/55 assessed in absence of return £60; exempt.

1855/56 marked "now Waddington (*sic*), watchmaker".
Pigot & Co's Directory, 1842: John Wood, watch & clock maker, Northgate Street.
Cross reference: Withington, W., watchmaker, St.Mary; Withington, William Bamforth, watchmaker, St.John.

891 WOODMAN, John, bricklayer.

1846/47-1847/48 assessed in absence of return £97; exempt.
1848/49 assessed in absence of return £97; income proved at £65.11.7; exempt.
1849/50-1850/51 assessed in absence of return £97; exempt.
1851/52 assessed in absence of return £100; exempt.
1852/53 assessed in absence of return £50; exempt.
1853/54 returned £33; assessed £60; exempt.
1854/55-1855/56 assessed in absence of return £60; exempt.
1856/57-1859/60 recorded; no assessments made; exempt.

Pigot & Co's Directory, 1842: John Woodman, bricklayer, Green.

892 YOUNG, Joseph, carrier.

1853/54 returned £75.8.0; assessed £80; exempt.
1854/55 assessed in absence of return £80; exempt.
1855/56-1856/57 assessed in absence of return £100.

Cross reference: Young, Joseph, carrier, St.John.

893 YOUNG, Joseph Eden, innkeeper, White Hart.

1857/58 returned £60; assessed £100.
1858/59-1859/60 returned and assessed £100.

1857/58 marked "Dangerfield, Isaiah now Joseph Young". White Hart noted.
Cross reference: Dangerfield, Isaiah, innkeeper, St.Mary.

ALLCANNINGS

894 AKERMAN, Stephen, baker, brewer.

1851/52 returned and assessed £100; exempt.
1852/53-1854/55 returned £50; assessed £100; exempt 1852/53.
1855/56 assessed in absence of return £100.

1856/57 marked "now Bailey".
Cross reference: Bailey, John, grocer, baker & brewer, Allcannings.

895 BAILEY, John, baker, grocer, brewer. [also BAILEY, Joseph]

1848/49 returned £50; assessed £75; exempt.
1849/50-1850/51 assessed in absence of return £70; exempt.
1851/52 returned £50; assessed £70; income proved at £50; exempt.
1852/53 assessed in absence of return £70; exempt.
1853/54 returned and assessed £60; exempt.
1854/55 returned £50; assessed £100.
1855/56-1856/57 assessed in absence of return £100.
1857/58 returned £50; assessed £100.
1858/59 returned £20b&g, £30br; assessed £100.
1859/60 assessed in absence of return £100.

Abbreviations: b&g, baker & grocer; br, brewer.
1848/49-1853/54 Joseph Bailey; 1854/55-1859/60 John Bailey.
1848/49-1855/56 baker & grocer; 1856/57-1859/60 baker, grocer & brewer.
1856/57 marked "Akerman, Stephen now Bailey".
Cross reference: Akerman, Stephen, baker, brewer, Allcannings.

896 CANNING, Jane, interest on money.

1853/54 returned and assessed £90; exempt.

897 CHANDLER, Thomas, baker, brewer, maltster.

1842/43 returned £200; assessed £150.

1842/43 baker, brewer & maltster; 1846/47 baker & brewer.
1846/47 marked "q.left".

898 HISCOCK, John.

1842/43 name only entered.

899 M [illeg] Revd. A.

1850/51 returned £451.3.0 or £1151.3.0 but no assessment made.
By comparison with *Clergy List*, this entry relates to Revd. T.A. Methuen.

Figures illegible.

900 MASLEN, Daniel, maltster, baker, butcher.

1842/43 returned and assessed £100.
1846/47 returned £20; assessed £85; income proved at £70 but assessment stood.
1847/48 returned £20; assessed £85; income proved at £70; exempt.
1848/49 returned £40; assessed £70.
1849/50-1850/51 assessed in absence of return £70.
1851/52 returned £20; assessed £40.
1852/53 returned £30; assessed £70; income proved at £109; exempt.
1853/54 returned £20; assessed £100; reduced to £65 but no appeal noted.
1854/55 returned £20; assessed £65.
1855/56-1856/57 assessed in absence of return £65.
1857/58-1858/59 returned £20; assessed £65.
1859/60 assessed in absence of return £65.

1842/43 maltster; 1846/47-1852/53 baker & butcher; 1853/54-1855/56 baker & farmer;
1856/57-1859/60 baker.

901 MASLEN, James, butcher, innkeeper, miller, grocer, baker. [possibly Kings Arms]

Year	Amount returned £	Commissioners' estimate £	Income proved £	Final assessment £
1842/43	–	30	30	–
1846/47	30	100	100	–
1847/48	20	100	100	–
1848/49	80	100	100	–
1849/50	–	100	100	–
1850/51	–	100	100	–
1851/52	60	100	80	–
1852/53	40	–	–	40
1853/54	20	50	–	50

1854/55	10	50	50	–
1855/56	–	150	–	150
1856/57	–	150	–	150
1857/58	65	150	–	150
1858/59	5b	150	–	150
	10g		
	5ba		
1859/60	–	150	–	150

Abbreviations; b, butcher, ba, baker, g, grocer.
1842/43 innkeeper; 1846/47-1848/49 innkeeper & butcher; 1849/50-1854/55 butcher;
    1855/56-1857/58 butcher & miller at Stanton; 1858/59 butcher, grocer, & baker at
    Stanton; 1859/60 butcher, grocer & baker.
1855/56 marked "Mill at Stanton".
Cross reference: Maslen, James, miller, Stanton St. Bernard.

902 MASLEN, Joseph, shoemaker.

1846/47-1849/50 assessed in absence of return £40; exempt.

903 MASLEN, Michael, baker, shopkeeper, property out of Great Britain, interest. [also MASLEN, Richard]

1842/43 returned and assessed £40; exempt.
1846/47-1847/48 assessed in absence of return £40; exempt.
1848/49 returned £50; assessed £40; exempt.
1849/50-1850/51 assessed in absence of return £40; exempt.
1851/52 returned and assessed £45; income proved at £49; exempt.
1852/53 returned £14 and £37 interest; assessed £51; exempt.
1853/54-1855/56 assessed in absence of return £50; exempt.
1856/57 recorded; no assessment made; exempt.

1842/43, 1846/47 Richard Maslen; 1847/48-1856/57 Michael Maslen.
1842/43 baker; 1846/47-1856/57 baker & shopkeeper; 1846/47 property out of Great Britain;
    1853/54-1856/57 interest.

904 MASLEN, Thomas, butcher, maltster.

1851/52 returned £45; assessed £90; income proved at £45; exempt.
1852/53 returned and assessed £60; exempt.
1853/54 returned £45; assessed £60; exempt.
1854/55-1855/56 assessed in absence of return £60; exempt.
1856/57-1859/60 recorded; no assessments made; exempt.

905 TASKER, Robert, blacksmith, innkeeper, Kings Arms.

1850/51 assessed in absence of return £100; exempt.
1851/52 returned £45; assessed £100; income proved at £50; exempt.
1852/53 returned and assessed £60; exempt.
1853/54 returned £40; assessed £50; exempt.
1854/55 returned and assessed £40; exempt.
1855/56 assessed in absence of return £20; exempt.
1856/57 recorded; no assessment made; exempt.
1857/58 returned £20i, 20b; assessed £90.
1858/59 returned £20o, 20b; assessed £90.
1859/60 assessed in absence of return £90.

1850/51-1852/53 innkeeper; 1853/54-1859/60 innkeeper & blacksmith.
1856/57 Kings Arms noted.

906 WALTER, Thomas, coal merchant.

1842/43 returned and assessed £20; exempt.
1846/47-1850/51 assessed in absence of return £20; exempt.

907 WHITE, Jane, shopkeeper & baker.

1846/47 returned £40; assessed £100; income proved at £126; exempt.
1847/48-1848/49 returned £40; assessed £100; exempt.
1849/50-1850/51 assessed in absence of return £100; exempt.

ALLINGTON

908 GODWIN, James, maltster, profits arising from a horse called Hotspur.

1842/43 returned and assessed £25.
1855/56 returned and assessed £84.5.0.
1856/57 assessed in absence of return £100.
1857/58 returned £47; assessed £100; reduced to £62 but no appeal noted.
1858/59 assessed in absence of return £80; reduced to £60 but no appeal noted.
1859/60 returned £35; assessed £50.

1842/43 maltster; 1855/56 profits arising from a horse called Hotspur;
1856/57-1859/60 profits from stallion Hotspur.
1856/57 marked "property in A & B...to be charged".

ALTON BARNES

909 SMITH, W. Anderton, clerk in holy orders.

1848/49 returned and assessed £70.

CHARLTON

910 BAYNHAM, Arthur, private tutor.

1853/54-1854/55 assessed in absence of return £80.
1855/56-1856/57 assessed in absence of return £50.
1857/58-1858/59 assessed in absence of return £25.

1859/60 marked "ceased for 18 months".

911 COBDEN, Revd. H.E., private tuition.

1846/47 recorded but no assessment made.
1847/48 marked "Returns in London".

912 HEAD, William, innkeeper. [by comparison, Poores Arms]

1842/43 returned and assessed £120.

1846/47 marked "Witchell, John late Head, innkeeper".
Cross reference: Witchell, John, innkeeper, Charlton.

913 SKRINE, Revd. Wadham Huntley.

1848/49 entry only, deleted.

914 WITCHELL, John, innkeeper, Poores Arms.

1846/47 assessed in absence of return £120; reduced to £74 on appeal; exempt.
1847/48-1850/51 assessed in absence of return £100; exempt.
1851/52 returned £85; assessed £100; exempt.
1852/53 returned £60; assessed £100; reduced to £75; exempt.
1853/54-1854/55 returned and assessed £120.
1855/56-1856/57 returned £100; assessed £120.
1857/58-1859/60 returned and assessed £120.

1846/47 marked "Witchell, John late Head, innkeeper".
1852/53 no appeal noted.
1856/57 Poores Arms noted.
Cross reference: Head, William, innkeeper, Charlton.

CHIRTON

915 CHANDLER, Charles, miller, maltster. [by comparison, Church Mill]

Year	Amount returned	Commissioners' estimate	Final assessment
	£	£	£
1842/43	60	100	80
1846/47	–	80	80
1847/48	–	80	80
1848/49	80	–	80
1849/50	80	–	80
1850/51	80	120	120
1851/52	60	100	100
1852/53	80	100	100
1853/54	120m	140	140
	80mr	–	80
1854/55	–	300	300
1855/56	237	300	300
1856/57	300	500	500
1857/58	250	600	600
1858/59	–	200	200

Abbreviations: m, miller; mr, maltster.
1842/43, 1846/47-1852/53 miller; 1853/54-1858/59 miller & maltster.
1851/52 £70 maltster returned but deleted.
1857/58 marked "see explanation in return".
1858/59 marked "Chandler, Charles now Thomas Tanner, maltster. No malthouse in Chirton but both malthouses are in Marden".
Cross references: Chandler, Charles, maltster, Marden; Charlton, Thomas & John, maltsters, Marden & Week; Tanner, Thomas, miller, Chirton.

916 CLEATHER, Revd. G[eorge] E[llis], private tuition.

1855/56 returned and assessed £180.
1856/57-1857/58 returned and assessed £100.
1858/59 returned and assessed £96.
1859/60 returned and assessed £95.

Cross reference: Cleather, Revd. G.P., tutor, Chirton.

917 CLEATHER, Revd. G[eorge] P[arker], tutor, pupils, private tuition, curate.

1842/43 returned and assessed £321.
1846/47 returned and assessed £350.
1847/48 returned and assessed £280.
1848/49 returned and assessed £370.
1849/50 returned and assessed £360.
1850/51 returned and assessed £370.
1851/52 returned and assessed £345.
1852/53 returned and assessed £300.
1853/54 returned and assessed £100t, £100c.
1854/55 returned and assessed £200.

Abbreviations: t, tuition, c, curate.
1842/43 (curate entered but deleted) tutor; 1846/47-1847/48 pupils;
1848/49-1853/54 private tuition; 1853/54-1854/55 curate.
1842/43 £80 curate entered but deleted.
1846/47 figures entered on 1847/48 certificate of assessment.
1853/54 marked "gone".
Cross reference: Cleather, Revd. G.E., private tuition, Chirton.

918 HOWELL, John, shopkeeper.

1842/43, 1846/47-1849/50 assessed in absence of return £50; exempt.

919 SHEPPARD, William, harness maker.

1842/43, 1846/47-1849/50 assessed in absence of return £50; exempt.

920 TANNER, Thomas, miller, Church Mill.

1858/59 returned £310; assessed £500.
1859/60 returned and assessed £500.

1858/59 marked "Chandler, Charles now Thomas Tanner".
1859/60 "maltster" entered but deleted, marked "Query this".
Cross reference: Chandler, Charles, miller, maltster, Chirton.

921 WITCHELL, John, blacksmith, beerseller. [also WITCHELL, George]

1846/47-1849/50 assessed in absence of return £50; exempt.
1857/58-1859/60 recorded; no assessments made; exempt.

1846/47-1849/50 John Witchell, blacksmith; 1857/58-1859/60 George Witchell, blacksmith
   & beerseller.
1857/58 £40 returned but no assessment made.

CHEVERELL MAGNA

922 BUTCHER, James, mealman.

1848/49 returned and assessed £40; exempt.
1849/50 assessed in absence of return £30; exempt.

923 BUTCHER, John, Junior.

1848/49 returned and assessed £30; exempt.
1849/50 assessed in absence of return £30; exempt.

No occupation noted.

924 CHAPMAN, Thomas, cordwainer.

1842/43 returned and assessed £50; exempt.
1846/47 assessed in absence of return £50; exempt.
1847/48 assessed in absence of return £60; exempt.
1848/49 returned and assessed £58; exempt.
1849/50 assessed in absence of return £40; exempt.

925 COOK, Revd. Thomas, annuity.

1846/47-1848/49 recorded; no assessments made.
1846/47 marked "Return".

926 COOMBE, W.W., shopkeeper.

1857/58 returned £65; no assessment made; exempt.
1858/59-1859/60 recorded; no assessments made; exempt.

927 DEANE, Robert, innkeeper, Bell, engine master.

1848/49-1850/51 assessed in absence of return £70; exempt.
1851/52 returned and assessed £90; exempt.
1852/53 returned and assessed £90; income proved at £94; exempt.
1853/54 returned £80; assessed £90; exempt.
1854/55 returned £70; assessed £100.
1855/56 returned £80; assessed £100.
1856/57 returned £40i, £30e; assessed £100.
1857/58 returned £60; assessed £100; income proved at £80; exempt.
1858/59-1859/60 recorded; no assessments made; exempt.

Abbreviations: i, innkeeper; e, engine master.
1848/49-1851/52 innkeeper; 1852/53 innkeeper, etc; 1853/54-1859/60 innkeeper & engine master.
1848/49 Hannah Edwards deleted, Robert Deane substituted.
1856/57 Bell noted.
Cross reference: Edwards, Hannah, innkeeper, Cheverell Magna.

928 DUNFORD, Giffard, millwright.

1857/58 returned £60; no assessment made; exempt.
1858/59-1859/60 recorded; no assessments made; exempt.

929 DUNFORD, William, brickmaker.

1848/49 returned and assessed £50; exempt.
1849/50 assessed in absence of return £50; exempt.

1847/48 Durnford, Thomas entered but deleted; 1848/49 William Dunford.
1842/43 marked "See West Lavington".
Cross reference: Dunford, Thomas, brickmaker, West Lavington.

930 DUTCH, James, carpenter, joiner.

Year	Amount returned	Commissioners' estimate	Income proved	Final assessment
	£	£	£	£
1842/43	80	–	80	–
1846/47	95	–	95	–
1847/48	–	95	90	–
1848/49	84	100	100	–
1849/50	–	50	50	–
1850/51	No assessment made			
1851/52	70	70	90	–
1852/53	76	–	98	–
1853/54	76	90	–	90
1854/55	30	100	–	100
1855/56	–	100	–	100
1856/57	No assessment made			
1857/58	40	No assessment made		

1842/43 carpenter; 1846/47-1849/50 carpenter & joiner; 1851/52-1856/57 carpenter.
1856/57-1857/58 marked "dead".

931 DUTCH, Joseph, shopkeeper, carpenter, grocer.

1848/49 returned and assessed £24; exempt.
1849/50 assessed in absence of return £24; exempt.

1857/58-1859/60 recorded; no assessments made; exempt.

932 EDWARDS, Hannah, innkeeper. [by comparison, Bell]

1842/43 returned and assessed £70; exempt.
1846/47-1847/48 assessed in absence of return £70; exempt.

1848/49 Hannah Edwards deleted, Robert Deane substituted.
Pigot & Co's Directory, 1842: Hannah Edwards, Bell, Great Cheverell.
Cross reference: Deane, Robert, innkeeper, Cheverell Magna.

933 GALE, Thomas, blacksmith.

1846/47-1847/48 assessed in absence of return £40; exempt.
1848/49 returned £50; exempt.
1849/50 assessed in absence of return £50; exempt.

934 HAYDEN, Thomas, mason.

1846/47-1847/48 assessed in absence of return £50; exempt.
1848/49 returned £40; exempt.
1849/50 assessed in absence of return £40; exempt.

935 LIGHT, William, baker, grocer.

1842/43 returned and assessed £90; exempt.
1846/47-1849/50 assessed in absence of return £90; exempt.
1851/52 returned and assessed £60; exempt.
1852/53 assessed in absence of return £60; exempt.
1853/54 returned £20; assessed £60; income proved at £40; exempt.
1854/55-1855/56 assessed in absence of return £40; exempt.
1856/57-1859/60 recorded; no assessments made; exempt.

1842/43, 1846/47-1849/50 baker; 1851/52-1859/60 baker & grocer.
1850/51 no assessment made.

936 MATTHEWS, William.

1846/47-1849/50 marked "Return in Potterne". (No occupation noted).
Cross reference: Matthews, William, brickmaker, Potterne.

937 POTTER, James, bellman, bellmaker, baker.

1842/43 returned and assessed £40; exempt.
1846/47 assessed in absence of return £30; exempt.

1847/48 assessed in absence of return £50; exempt.
1848/49-1849/50 assessed in absence of return £30; exempt.
1851/52 returned £12; assessed £50; income proved at £44; exempt.
1852/53-1855/56 assessed in absence of return £60; exempt.
1856/57-1859/60 recorded; no assessments made; exempt.

1842/43, 1848/49 bellmaker; 1846/47, 1847/48, 1849/50 bellman; 1851/52-1859/60 baker.
1850/51 no assessment made.
1857/58 returned £20 but no assessment made.

938 PRICE, William, pork butcher.

1846/47-1849/50 assessed in absence of return £20; exempt.

939 PRICE, William, Junior, miller.

1842/43 returned £40; assessed £50; exempt.
1846/47-1849/50 assessed in absence of return £50; exempt.

940 PURNELL, Ann, baker. [also PURNELL, Samuel]

1842/43 returned and assessed £20; exempt.
1846/47-1847/48 assessed in absence of return £20; exempt.
1848/49 returned and assessed £10; exempt.
1849/50 assessed in absence of return £10; exempt.

1842/43 Samuel Purnell; 1846/47-1849/50 Ann Purnell.
1846/47-1849/50 baker, etc.

941 SAWYER, Mark & Son, millwrights. [also SAWYER, Joseph & Nathaniel]

Year	Amount returned	Commissioners' estimate	Income proved	Final assessment
	£	£	£	£
1842/43	100	–	100	–
1846/47	–	120	120	–
1847/48	–	120	120	–
1848/49	–	150	110	–
1849/50	–	110	110	–
1850/51	–	110	110	–
1851/52	60 20interest	110	104.10.0	20
1852/53	130	150a	119.6.8	–

	20interest			
1853/54	100	120	–	130
1854/55	50	150	–	150
1855/56	–	150	–	150
1856/57	–	150a	–	112.10.0
1857/58	70	112	52	–
1858/59	75	–	–	75
1859/60	–	75	–	75

1842/43, 1848/49-1852/53 Mark Sawyer; 1846/47-1847/48 Mark Sawyer & Son; 1853/54-1854/55 Joseph Sawyer; 1855/56 Joseph & Nathaniel Sawyer; 1856/57-1857/58 Nathaniel Sawyer; 1858/59-1859/60 Joseph Sawyer.
1853/54 assessment increased by General Commissioners to £130.

942 WEBB, John, miller, Cheverell Mill. [also WEBB, James & Joseph]

Year	Amount returned £	Commissioners' estimate £	Income proved £	Final assessment £
1846/47	–	30	30	–
1847/48	–	30	30	–
1848/49	180	–	180	–
1849/50	–	180	180	–
1850/51	–	180	180	–
1851/52	80	120	80	–
1852/53	100	–	107.3.4	–
1853/54	50	100	–	100
1854/55	80	100	–	100
1855/56	80	100	–	100
1856/57	–	100	–	100
1857/58	80	100	–	100
1858/59	–	100	–	100
1859/60	–	100	–	100

1846/47-1847/48, 1851/52-1859/60 John Webb; 1848/49-1850/51 John James & Joseph Webb.
1848/49-1850/51 exemption claimed as partnership.
1856/57 Cheverell Mill noted.

943 WILLIAMS, Thomas, cutler.

1842/43 returned and assessed £40; exempt.

1842/43 marked "charged in . . ." (illegible).
1846/47 marked "q. Return in London".
1847/48 marked "gone. q. in London" or "given up" (illegible).

CHEVERELL PARVA

944 BOLTER, Isaac, brickmaker.

Year	Amount returned £	Commissioners' estimate £	Income proved £	Final assessment £
1842/43	30	–	30	–
1846/47	–	50	50	–
1847/48	–	70	70	–
1848/49	–	70	70	–
1849/50	–	70	70	–
1852/53	50	–	70.10.0	–
1853/54	50	–	50	–
1854/55	–	50	50	–
1855/56	30	50	50	–
1856/57	40	–	–	–
1857/58	–	50	50	–
1858/59	15	50	–	–
1859/60	40	60	–	60

1850/51–1851/52 no assessments made.
1856/57, 1858/59 no assessments made.
1858/59 marked "Has 2 brickyards".

945 BOLTER, Samuel, grocer.

1858/59 returned £15; no assessment made; exempt.
1859/60 returned £10 but deleted.

946 BOX, Richard.

1846/47–1847/48 marked "returned at Devizes".
No occupation noted.
Cross reference: Box, Richard, corn dealer, St. Mary.

947 INGRAM, James, shopkeeper, etc.

1853/54–1855/56 assessed in absence of return £50; exempt.
1856/57–1859/60 recorded; no assessments made; exempt.

1853/54 shopkeeper, etc; 1854/55–1859/60 shopkeeper.
1858/59 returned £15.
Pigot & Co's Directory, 1842: James Ingram, grocer & dealer in sundries, West Lavington.

948 JAMES, Alfred, maltster.

1842/43 returned and assessed £30; exempt.

949 SELF, Harry, mealman.

1842/43 assessed in absence of return £50; exempt.
1846/47-1849/50 assessed in absence of return £70; exempt.

Pigot & Co's Directory, 1842: Henry Self, miller, Great Cheverell.

950 WARD, Benjamin, baker.

1842/43 returned and assessed £20; exempt.
1846/47-1847/48 assessed in absence of return £20; exempt.
1848/49-1849/50 assessed in absence of return £50; exempt.

EASTERTON

951 COLLINGBORN, John M., baker & shopkeeper.

1842/43 assessed in absence of return £20; exempt.

1846/47 marked "given up business".

952 DAVIS, Thomas, innkeeper. [by comparison, Royal Oak]

1842/43 returned £5; assessed £75; exempt.
1846/47-1848/49 assessed in absence of return £75; exempt.
1849/50-1852/53 assessed in absence of return £100; exempt.
1853/54 assessed in absence of return £80; income proved £85; exempt.

1854/55 entry deleted Philpott, John, innkeeper, Royal Oak substituted.
Pigot & Co's Directory, 1842: Thomas Davies (sic), Royal Oak, Easterton.
Cross reference: Philpott, John, innkeeper, Easterton.

953 DRAPER, James, dealer & baker.

1854/55-1855/56 assessed in absence of return £40; exempt.
1856/57-1859/60 recorded; no assessments made; exempt.

1855/56 marked "Draper, Philip given up to James Draper".
Cross reference: Draper, Philip, dealer, baker, Easterton.

954 DRAPER, Philip, dealer, baker.

Year	Amount returned £	Commissioners' estimate £	Income proved £	Final assessment £
1846/47	–	50	50	–
1847/48	–	120	96.14.0	–
1848/49	70	96.14.0	96.14.0	–
1849/50	–	50	50	–
1850/51	–	50	50	–
1851/52	–	50	104	–
1852/53	–	104	–	152
1853/54	30	–	–	30
1854/55	–	30	–	30

1846/47-1852/53 dealer; 1853/54-1854/55 dealer & baker.
1854/55 marked "£120 in Market Lavington"; (no assessment in Market Lavington).
1855/56 marked "given up to James Draper".
Pigot & Co's Directory, 1842: Philip Draper, baker, grocer & dealer in sundries, Easterton.
Cross reference: Draper, James, dealer, baker, Easterton.

955 GRANT, John, maltster. [also GRANT, William]

1842/43 returned £20; assessed £40 but reduced to £20.
1846/47 assessed in absence of return £20; exempt.
1847/48 assessed in absence of return £20; income proved at £50; exempt.
1848/49-1850/51 assessed in absence of return £50; exempt.
1851/52 assessed in absence of return £20; income proved at £35; exempt.
1852/53 assessed in absence of return £50; exempt.
1853/54 returned £3; assessed £40; exempt.
1854/55 assessed in absence of return £40.

1842/43 John Grant; 1846/47-1847/48 John Grant & Brother; 1848/49-1854/55 John & William Grant.
1842/43 assessment reduced but no appeal noted.
1855/56 marked "left Easterton business ceased".
1856/57 marked "removed from Easterton".
1857/58 marked "removed from Easterton to Wilcot".
Pigot & Co's Directory, 1842: John Grant, maltster, Easterton.
Cross reference: Grant, John & James, maltsters, Wilcot.

956 HOBBS, Charles P., minister.

1842/43 returned and assessed £100; exempt.
1846/47-1847/48 assessed in absence of return £100; exempt.
1848/49-1849/50 assessed in absence of return £110; exempt.

957 MAYNARD, William, blacksmith.

1842/43, 1846/47–1849/50 assessed in absence of return £30; exempt.

Pigot & Co's Directory, 1842: William Maynard, blacksmith, Easterton.

958 MEREDITH, Samuel, Chief Constable.

1842/43 entry only, marked "Schedule E".

959 NEVILLE, John.

1846/47–1848/48 name only entered, no assessments made.
1846/47 marked "q. who or what".
Pigot & Co's Directory, 1842: John Neville, draper, grocer & dealer in sundries, Littleton.

960 PHILPOTT, John, innkeeper, Royal Oak. [also PHILPOTT, Caroline]

1853/54 assessed in absence of return £70; reduced to £60.
1854/55 assessed in absence of return £100.
1855/56 returned £60; assessed £100.
1856/57 assessed in absence of return £100; reduced to £90 on appeal; exempt.
1857/58–1859/60 recorded; no assessments made; exempt.

1853/54–1855/56 John Philpott; 1856/57–1859/60 Caroline Philpott.
1854/55 Davis, Thomas deleted, Philpott, John substituted.
1854/55 marked Royal Oak.
1856/57 marked "now Caroline".
Cross reference: Davis, Thomas, innkeeper, Easterton.

961 STILL, James.

1854/55–1855/56 assessed in absence of return £50; exempt.
1856/57–1859/60 recorded; no assessments made; exempt.

No occupation noted.

962 WILSON, David, yeoman.

1851/52 entry only, no assessment made.

ETCHILHAMPTON

963 BLEE[C]K, Revd. William.

1848/49 returned £30.19.4 but deleted.

964 COCKELL, Revd. H., stipend.

1842/43 returned £105 but deleted.

965 PLANK, George, pig dealer.

1858/59 assessed in absence of return £110; income proved at £75; exempt.
1859/60 returned £39 and £6.5.0 interest; assessed £75 and £6.5.0.

966 RUDMAN, Noah, carpenter.

1857/58 returned £45; no assessment made; exempt.
1858/59-1859/60 recorded; no assessments made; exempt.

967 WESTON, John, auctioneer.

1858/59-1859/60 recorded; no assessments made; exempt.

968 WAYLEN, James, artist.

1851/52 returned and assessed £50.
1852/53 returned and assessed £50; exempt.
1853/54-1854/55 assessed in absence of return £50.
1855/56 returned and assessed £50.
1856/57 returned and assessed £57 and £25 interest.
1857/58 returned and assessed £42.6.0 and £25 interest.
1858/59 returned and assessed £37.14.11 and £24.11.8 interest.
1859/60 returned and assessed £33.12.0 and £24.6.0 interest.

Pigot & Co's Directory, 1842: James Waylen, teacher of painting, Bellevue, Devizes.

LITTLETON PANNELL

969 BAKER, James, innkeeper, Wheat Sheaf.

1854/55 assessed in absence of return £100; reduced to £95.
1855/56 assessed in absence of return £100.
1856/57 assessed in absence of return £130.
1857/58 assessed in absence of return £175.
1858/59 returned £125; assessed £175.
1859/60 assessed in absence of return £175.

1856/57 Wheat Sheaf noted.

970 BAKER, William, baker, mealman.

1848/49-1849/50 assessed in absence of return £90; exempt.
1850/51 assessed in absence of return £250; reduced to £100 on appeal; exempt.
1851/52 assessed in absence of return £100; income proved at £80.

1848/49-1849/50 baker; 1850/51-1851/52 baker & mealman.
Pigot & Co's Directory, 1842: William Baker, miller, Littleton.

971 BUTCHER, Thomas, miller.

1852/53 returned £90; assessed £150; reduced to £115 on appeal; exempt.
1853/54-1856/57 assessed in absence of return £150.
1857/58 assessed in absence of return £160.
1858/59 returned £105; assessed £160.
1859/60 assessed in absence of return £160.

972 FARMER, John Seymour, miller.

1852/53 returned and assessed £65; exempt.
1854/55-1855/56 assessed in absence of return £100.
1856/57 assessed in absence of return £125.
1857/58-1859/60 assessed in absence of return £130.

1853/54 recorded but no assessment made.

973 MEAD, Henry, grocer, maltster.

1852/53 returned £20; assessed £50; income proved at £20; exempt.

1853/54-1855/56 assessed in absence of return £50; exempt.
1856/57-1859/60 recorded; no assessments made; exempt.

1852/53 grocer; 1853/54-1859/60 grocer & maltster.
1852/53 bears illegible note.

974 NEWMAN, Thomas, mealman.

1846/47-1847/48 assessed in absence of return £200.
1848/49 returned £200.
1849/50 returned £150; assessed £200.

Pigot & Co's Directory, 1842: Thomas Newman, grocer & dealer in sundries, chymist (sic), East
Lavington; miller, Littleton.

975 PEPLER, -.

Surname only entered 1858/59.

976 WILKINS, John, carpenter. [also WILKINS, Christopher]

1857/58 assessed in absence of return £30.
1858/59 returned and assessed £30.
1859/60 assessed in absence of return £30.

1857/58 Christopher Wilkins; 1858/59-1859/60 John Wilkins.
1857/58 "agency" entered but deleted.

977 WILTON, Revd. E[dward], clergyman & schoolmaster.

1853/54 returned £250 but entry deleted.

Pigot & Co's Directory, 1842: Revd. Edward Wilton, clergy, West Lavington.
Cross reference: Wilton, Revd. Edward, officiating minister & schoolmaster, West Lavington.

MANNINGFORD ABBOTTS

978 HAINES, John, miller, mealman.

1854/55-1856/57 assessed in absence of return £100.
1857/58 returned and assessed £100.
1858/59-1859/60 assessed in absence of return £100.

1854/55-1855/56 miller; 1856/57-1859/60 mealman.
1854/55 marked "late Sherry, miller".
Cross reference: Sherry, James, miller, Manningford Abbotts.

979 SHERRY, James, miller.

1842/43 returned and assessed £50.
1846/47-1847/48 assessed in absence of return £150.
1848/49 returned and assessed £150.
1849/50 returned £100; assessed £150.
1850/51 assessed in absence of return £150; reduced to £59.12.0 on appeal; exempt.
1851/52 assessed in absence of return £60; exempt.
1852/53 assessed in absence of return £100.
1853/54 returned and assessed £100.

1853/54 marked "now Haines miller".
Cross reference: Haines, John, miller, Manningford Abbotts.

MANNINGFORD BOHUN

980 COX, William, victualler.

1842/43 returned and assessed £25; exempt.
1846/47-1849/50 assessed in absence of return £15; exempt.

981 GALE, Henry, victualler, brewer Bottlesford.

1848/49 returned and assessed £30; exempt.
1849/50 assessed in absence of return £30; exempt.
1859/60 returned £60; assessed £100.

1848/49-1849/50 victualler; 1859/60 brewer Bottlesford.

982 WRIGHT, Joseph, carpenter.

1848/49 returned and assessed £50; exempt.
1849/50 assessed in absence of return £50; exempt.

MANNINGFORD BRUCE

983 GRANT, Alexander, parish priest.

1848/49 returned £318.5.0 but deleted.

984 ROBERTS, William, shopkeeper, grocer.

1842/43 returned and assessed £5; exempt.
1846/47-1850/51 assessed in absence of return £50; exempt.
1851/52-1855/56 assessed in absence of return £60; exempt.
1856/57-1859/60 recorded; no assessments made; exempt.

1842/43 shopkeeper; 1846/47-1859/60 grocer.

985 WAITE, Nathaniel, carpenter.

1857/58 returned and assessed £100.
1858/59-1859/60 assessed in absence of return £100.

MARDEN

986 CHANDLER, Charles, maltster. [also CHANDLER, John and Thomas]

1842/43 returned and assessed £50.
1846/47 returned and assessed £70.
1847/48 returned £70; assessed £100.
1848/49-1849/50 returned and assessed £70.
1850/51 assessed in absence of return £80.
1851/52 assessed in absence of return £100.
1852/53 returned £70; assessed £120.
1858/59 assessed in absence of return £150.

1842/43, 1850/51-1852/53 Charles Chandler; 1846/47-1849/50 Thomas Chandler;
1858/59 John & Thomas Chandler.
1853/54-1857/58 marked "charged in Chirton".
1858/59 marked "see Chirton".
1859/60 marked "maltsters, charged in Week".
Pigot & Co's Directory, 1842: Charles Chandler, maltster, Nursery, Devizes.
Cross references: Chandler, Charles, miller & maltster, Chirton; Chandler, Thomas & John, retail
    maltsters, Week.
Note: [Chirton] "both malthouses are in Marden".

987 GERRISH, James, miller.

1848/49 returned and assessed £70; exempt.
1849/50-1851/52 assessed in absence of return £70; exempt.

1852/53 marked "see Wells below".
Cross reference: Wells, Jasper, miller & shopkeeper, Marden.

988 MASTERS, Beatrice, schoolmistress.

1846/47-1849/50 assessed in absence of return £50; exempt.

989 NEATE, Stephen R., maltster.

1842/43 returned and assessed £20;
1846/47 returned £5; assessed £20.
1847/48 returned £12; assessed £20.
1848/49 assessed in absence of return £20; exempt.
1849/50 returned and assessed £10.
1850/51 assessed in absence of return £10.
1851/52-1854/55 returned and assessed £10.
1855/56 assessed in absence of return £10.

1856/57 marked "discontinued malting last year".

990 SKIPPER, Revd. J.B.

1848/49 name only entered.

991 STRATTON, Jacob, miller. [also STRATTON, Frederick]

1842/43 returned and assessed £160.
1846/47 returned and assessed £80.
1847/48 returned £50; assessed £80.
1848/49 returned and assessed £90; exempt.

1848/49 Stratton, Jacob Exors deleted, Frederick Stratton inserted.
Cross reference: Stratton, Jacob, maltster, Wilsford.

992 WELLS, Jasper, miller & shopkeeper.

1851/52 returned and assessed £70; exempt.
1852/53 assessed in absence of return £70; exempt.
1853/54 returned £55; assessed £60; exempt.
1854/55-1855/56 assessed in absence of return £60; exempt.
1856/57 recorded but no assessment made.
1857/58-1859/60 assessed in absence of return £60.

1852/53 Gerrish, James, miller, deleted marked "see Wells below".
1858/59 marked "has £48.15.0 real property".
Cross reference: Gerrish, James, miller, Marden.

MARKET LAVINGTON

993 ASHLEY, George.

1859/60 name only entered.

994 BOWLES, John Thomas, seedsman, corndealer.

1842/43, 1846/47–1849/50 assessed in absence of return £50; exempt.
1853/54 returned and assessed £60; exempt.
1854/55–1855/56 assessed in absence of return £100.
1856/57 returned £40; assessed £100.
1857/58 returned £50; assessed £105.
1858/59 returned £40; assessed £105.
1859/60 assessed in absence of return £105.

1842/43, 1846/47–1849/50 Bowle; 1853/54–1859/60 Bowles.
1842/43, 1846/47–1849/50 seedsman; 1853/54–1859/60 corndealer.
1846/47, 1847/48 [Newman] marked "now John Bowle druggist".
1850/51–1852/53 no assessments made.
Pigot & Co's Directory, 1842: John Thomas Bowle, corn dealer, East Lavington.
Cross reference: Newman, Thomas, druggist.

995 BOX, John, maltster.

1851/52–1852/53 assessed in absence of return £50; exempt.
1853/54 returned and assessed £53.10.0; exempt.
1854/55 returned £25; assessed £70; income proved at £50; exempt.
1855/56 assessed in absence of return £50; exempt.
1856/57–1859/60 recorded; no assessments made; exempt.

1854/55 [Box, Thomas] marked "not in business, his son Jno has business".
Cross reference: Box, Thomas, maltster, Market Lavington.

996 BOX, Richard, cornfactor.

1842/43 marked "returned at St.John".
Note: Assessed in St.Mary.
Cross reference: Box, Richard, corndealer, St.Mary.

997 BOX, Thomas, maltster.

1842/43, 1846/47–1852/53 assessed in absence of return £80; exempt.

1853/54 assessed in absence of return £50; exempt.

1854/55 marked "not in business, his son Jno has the business".
Pigot & Co's Directory, 1842: Thomas Box, maltster, East Lavington.
Cross reference: Box, John, maltster, Market Lavington.

998 BOX, William, contractor.

1855/56 assessed in absence of return £100.
1856/57 returned and assessed £100.
1857/58 returned £50; assessed £105.
1858/59 returned £100; assessed £105.
1859/60 returned £100; assessed £150.

1856/57 marked "q. brick yard".

999 CAMBRIDGE, William, machine maker.

1842/43, 1846/47 returned and assessed £210.
1847/48 returned £200; assessed £210.
1848/49 returned and assessed £210.

Pigot & Co's Directory, 1842: William Cambridge, engineer, ironfounder & manufacturer of
agricultural implements, East Lavington.

1000 CANNINGS, Henry, plumber, glazier.

1842/43, 1846/47-1848/49 returned and assessed £160.
1849/50 assessed in absence of return £160.
1850/51 returned and assessed £90; exempt.
1851/52-1852/53 assessed in absence of return £90; exempt.
1853/54-1855/56 assessed in absence of return £40; exempt.
1856/57-1859/60 recorded; no assessments made; exempt.

1842/43 plumber & glazier; 1846/47-1851/52 plumber, etc; 1852/53-1859/60 plumber.
Pigot & Co's Directory, 1842: Henry Cannings, painter, etc., East Lavington.

1001 CLEAVER, Henry, draper & grocer.

1842/43 returned and assessed £100; exempt.
1846/47-1848/49 assessed in absence of return £100; exempt.
1849/50 assessed in absence of return £100; income proved at £120; exempt.
1850/51-1852/53 assessed in absence of return £100; exempt.
1853/54-1855/56 assessed in absence of return £40; exempt.

1856/57–1859/60 recorded; no assessments made; exempt.

Pigot & Co's Directory, 1842: Henry Cleaver, grocer & dealer in sundries, draper, East Lavington.

1002 DRAPER, Samuel, carpenter. [also DRAPER, Thomas]

1842/43 assessed in absence of return £100; exempt.
1846/47–1849/50 assessed in absence of return £88; exempt.
1850/51 assessed in absence of return £88; income proved at £80; exempt.
1851/52 assessed in absence of return £88; income proved at £135.5.0; exempt.
1852/53 assessed in absence of return £130; exempt.
1853/54 returned £46; assessed £100; income proved at £50; exempt.
1854/55 returned £40; assessed £50; exempt.
1855/56 returned £30; assessed £50; exempt.
1856/57 returned and assessed £100.
1857/58 returned £50; assessed £100.
1858/59–1859/60 returned and assessed £100.

1842/43, 1846/47–1855/56, 1857/58 Samuel Draper; 1856/57, 1858/59–1859/60 Samuel & Thomas Draper.
Pigot & Co's Directory, 1842: Samuel Draper, carpenter & wheelwright, East Lavington.

1003 DRAPER, Stephen, innkeeper. [by comparison, Kings Arms]

1850/51–1852/53 assessed in absence of return £80; exempt.
1853/54 assessed in absence of return £100; income proved at £75; exempt.

1850/51 marked "late Lawes, innkeeper".
Cross reference: Lawes, Joseph, innkeeper, Market Lavington; Reed, John, innkeeper, Market Lavington.

1004 ELLIS, John, tailor. See SMITH, Frederick & ELLIS, John, tailors.

1005 FARMER, James, butcher.

1851/52 returned and assessed £50; income proved at £62; exempt.
1853/54 returned £50; estimated at £60 but no assessment made.
1854/55 returned £50; assessed £150; reduced to £135.
1855/56 returned £100; assessed £135.
1856/57–1859/60 returned £100; assessed £150.

1852/53 no assessment made.
1854/55 Assessment reduced but no appeal noted.

1006 GAUNTLETT, Caroline, butcher. [also GAUNTLETT, George]

1842/43 assessed in absence of return £100; exempt.
1846/47 assessed in absence of return £67; exempt.
1847/48-1849/50 assessed in absence of return £90; exempt.

1842/43 George Gauntlett; 1846/47-1849/50 Caroline Gauntlett.
Pigot & Co's Directory, 1842: George Gauntlett, butcher, East Lavington.

1007 GAUNTLETT, Henry, baker, confectioner.

1842/43 assessed in absence of return £100; exempt.
1846/47 assessed in absence of return £90; exempt.
1847/48-1852/53 assessed in absence of return £100; exempt.
1853/54 returned £91.6.0; assessed £100; income proved at £91.6.0; exempt.
1854/55 assessed in absence of return £100.
1855/56-1856/57 returned £75; assessed £100.
1857/58-1858/59 assessed in absence of return £100.
1859/60 returned £80; assessed £100.

1842/43, 1846/47-1849/50 baker; 1850/51-1859/60 baker & confectioner.
Pigot & Co's Directory, 1842: Henry Gauntlett, baker & confectioner, East Lavington.

1008 GRAY, John, gardener.

1842/43, 1846/47-1849/50 assessed in absence of return £40; exempt.

1842/43, 1846/47-1847/48 Gray; 1848/49 Grey.

1009 HAWKINS, Bryant Tinkes, baker, innkeeper, Bell.

1853/54-1855/56 assessed in absence of return £70; exempt.
1856/57-1859/60 recorded; no assessments made; exempt.

1856/57 Bell noted; "now J. Reed" deleted.
Cross reference: Reed, John, innkeeper [Kings Arms], Market Lavington.

1010 HAYWARD, John, surgeon

See composite entry for partnership under HITCHCOCK, Charles et alii.

1011 HAZELL, John, brewer, maltster.

1853/54 returned £80; assessed £120.

1854/55–1855/56 returned and assessed £120.
1856/57 returned and assessed £125.
1857/58–1858/59 returned £120; assessed £200.
1859/60 returned £80.10.0; assessed £100; income proved at £73; exempt.

1853/54–1855/56 brewer; 1856/57–1858/59 brewer & maltster; 1859/60 maltster.

1012 HERRIOTT, James, surgeon.

1848/49 returned £200; assessed £250.
1849/50 returned and assessed £250.
1850/51 assessed in absence of return £250.
1851/52–1854/55 returned and assessed £200.

1013 HINTON, James, bailiff.

1858/59–1859/60 returned and assessed £120.

1014 HITCHCOCK, Charles, surgeon. [also IVES, John; HAYWARD, John; WHITE, Frederick George; PEPLER, William Brown]

	Year	Amount returned £	Commissioners' estimate £	Income proved £	Final assessment £
CH	1842/43	239.17.6	–	–	239.17.6
JI		119.18.8	–	119.18.8	–
CH	1846/47	230.2.8	–	–	230.2.8
JI		115.1.4	–	115.1.4	–
CH	1847/48	204.13.0	–	–	204.13.0
JI		102.6.6	–	102.6.6	–
CH	1848/49	282.3.0	–	–	282.3.0
JI		94.1.0	–	–	94.1.0
CH	1849/50	–	371.5.0	–	371.5.0
JI		123.15.0	–	123.15.0	–
CH	1850/51	350.8.0	–	–	350.8.0
JI		116.15.0	–	116.15.0	–
CH	1851/52	251.10.0	–	–	251.10.0
JH		251.10.0	–	–	251.10.0
CH	1852/53	244.16.0	–	–	244.16.0
JH		244.16.0	–	–	244.16.0
CH	1853/54	217.4.0	–	–	217.4.0
JH		217.4.3	–	–	217.4.3
CH	1854/55	254.19.0	–	–	254.19.0
JH		254.19.0	–	–	254.19.0

CH	1855/56	263.18.6	–	–	263.18.6
JH		263.18.6	–	–	263.18.6
CH	1856/57	277.1.9	350a	–	202
JH		277.1.9	304a	–	231
CH	1857/58	293.13.0	–	–	293.13.0
JH		293.13.0	–	–	293.13.0
CH	1858/59	222.5.7	250c	–	250
JH		147.5.7	250c	–	250
FGW		159.5.7	250c	–	250
WBP		–	120	–	120
CH	1859/60	214	–	–	214
JH		214	–	–	214
FGW		214	–	–	214
WBP		214	–	–	214

Abbreviations: CH, Charles Hitchcock; JI, John Ives; JH, John Hayward; FGW, Frederick George White; WBP, William Brown Pepler; a, appeal; c, composite assessment.

1842/43, 1846/47-1847/48 2/3 share of profits Hitchcock, 1/3 share of profits Ives;

1848/49-1850/51 3/4 share of profits Hitchcock, 1/4 share of profits Ives;

1851/52-1857/58 equal share of profits Hitchcock & Hayward; 1858/59 equal share of profits Hitchcock, Hayward & White, reduced share to Pepler; 1859/60 equal share of profits Hitchcock, Hayward, White & Pepler.

1858/59 surgeons & apothecaries, otherwise surgeons throughout.

1849/50 return for Hitchcock appears to have been submitted to the Additional Commissioners rather than the assessor.

Note: 1851/52-1859/60 Hitchcock also ran the lunatic asylum at Fiddington House, West Lavington where he seemingly resided; for 1853/54-1857/58 the assessments on his profits as a surgeon in Market Lavington were made in West Lavington, (statutorily the assessment had to be made in the place of residence) separate assessments being made in respect of the lunatic asylum and the surgery; during this period the partners continued to be assessed in Market Lavington. In order to retain the integrity of the partnership business entity Hitchcock's assessments as a surgeon have been recorded in Market Lavington.

For 1857/58 White was assessed as a surgeon in Urchfont. His 1858/59 assessment was made originally in Urchfont but deleted and restated in Market Lavington.

Cross references: Hitchcock, Charles, lunatic asylum, West Lavington; Hayward, John, surgeon, Rushall; White, Frederick George, surgeon, Urchfont.

Pigot & Co's Directory, 1842: Hitchcock & Ives, surgeons, East Lavington.

1015 HOUSE, James, foundry.

1853/54 returned £60 but no assessment made.
1854/55 returned £30; assessed £60; exempt.
1855/56 assessed in absence of return £60; exempt.
1856/57-1859/60 recorded; no assessments made; exempt.

1016 HOUSE, William P., post master, innkeeper, Green Dragon.

1853/54 returned £72.15.0; assessed £100.
1854/55 assessed in absence of return £100.

1855/56 returned £85; assessed £100.
1856/57 returned £73; assessed £90.
1857/58 returned £100; assessed £160.
1858/59 returned £125; assessed £160.
1859/60 returned £75; assessed £160.

1853/54-1856/57 innkeeper; 1857/58-1859/60 innkeeper & post master.
1853/54 marked "Henry Philpott now House (Miss deleted) Mr".
1854/55 Green Dragon noted; marked "late Philpott".
Cross reference: Philpott, Henry, innkeeper, Market Lavington.

1017 HULBERT, Robert.

1842/43 name only entered.

1018 HUSBAND, John, interest.

1853/54 returned £900 but deleted.

1019 HUSSEY, William Slade, grocer.

1853/54 returned £62 but no assessment made.
1854/55 returned £40; assessed £62; exempt.
1855/56 assessed in absence of return £62; exempt.
1856/57-1859/60 recorded; no assessments made; exempt.

1020 IVES, John, surgeon.

See composite entry for partnership under HITCHCOCK, Charles *et alii*.

1021 LAWES, Joseph, innkeeper, [by comparison Kings Arms]

1842/43, 1846/47-1849/50 assessed in absence of return £80; exempt.

1850/51 marked "Draper, Stephen late Lawes".
Pigot & Co's Directory, 1842: Joseph Lawes, Kings Arms, East Lavington.
Cross reference: Draper, Stephen, innkeeper, Market Lavington; Reed, John, innkeeper, Market Lavington.

1022 MAYOW, Revd. Wynell Mayow, foreign securities, interest, pupil, other profits.

1853/54 returned and assessed £13.10.0F, £115o.

1854/55 returned and assessed £16ii, £15i, £115o.
1855/56 returned and assessed £48, £30, £10.
1856/57 returned and assessed £78f, £40p.
1857/58 returned and assessed £48f, £30i.
1858/59 returned and assessed £48fb, £135f, £90s.
1859/60 returned and assessed £189fb, £54s, £36s.

Abbreviations: f, foreign securities; F, French — illegible; fb, securities in British Plantations; i, interest on money; ii, interest on money in land (illegible); o, other profits; p, pupil; s, foreign securities as agent to Revd. Alfred Smith and Miss Smith.
1853/54 marked "query to be assessed under number or letter".
1853/54 returned in addition to amounts assessed but deleted, £500i; £805f.
1854/55 marked "interest on which duty is not deducted" and "profits from a resident in family".
1855/56 income not described.
Pigot & Co's Directory, 1842: Revd. M.W.Mayow, vicar,Vicarage, East Lavington.

1023 MEAD, Henry, corndealer, grocer, cordwainer.

1842/43 returned £60; assessed £100; exempt.
1846/47-1850/51 assessed in absence of return £100; exempt.
1851/52 returned £30; assessed £100; income proved at £60; exempt.
1852/53 returned £20; assessed £70; exempt.
1853/54 returned £45; estimated £70; no assessment made.
1854/55 assessed in absence of return £150.
1855/56 returned £100; assessed 150; reduced to £125.
1856/57-1859/60 returned £100; assessed £125.

1842/43 corndealer & cordwainer; 1846/47-1850/51 corndealer; 1851/52-1859/60 grocer, etc.
1855/56 Mary Mead entered and deleted.
Pigot & Co's Directory, 1842: Henry Mead, corn & seed dealer, boot & shoe maker, East Lavington.

1024 NEATE, James, brewer.

1859/60 returned and assessed £100.

1025 NEWMAN, Thomas, druggist.

1842/43 assessed in absence of return £50; exempt.
1846/47 assessed in absence of return £70; exempt.

1846/47, 1847/48 marked "now John Bowle druggist.
Cross reference: Bowles, John, seedsman, corndealer, Market Lavington.

1026 ORAM, John.

Name only entered 1855/56.

1027 PEERLESS, Thomas, mealman.

1855/56 returned £100; assessed £150.
1856/57 returned and assessed £150.

1855/56 marked "late Saunders, mealman.
1856/57-1859/60 marked "late Saunders".
Cross reference: Saunders, A.E., mealman & baker, Market Lavington.

1028 PERRETT, Richard, innkeeper, New Inn.

1853/54 returned £20; estimated £40; no assessment made.
1854/55-1855/56 assessed in absence of return £40; exempt.
1856/57-1859/60 recorded; no assessments made; exempt.

1856/57 New Inn noted.
Cross reference: Philpott, William, innkeeper, Market Lavington.

1029 PHILPOTT, Henry, innkeeper, maltster, brickmaker [by comparison, Green Dragon]

1842/43, 1846/47-1848/49 returned and assessed £200.
1849/50 assessed in absence of return £200.
1850/51 returned £160; assessed £200.
1851/52-1852/53 returned and assessed £200.

1849/50 Estimate of £300 deleted, £200 substituted.
1852/53 marked "dead".
1853/54 marked "now House (Miss deleted) Mr".
Pigot & Co's Directory, 1842: Henry Philpott, Green Dragon Inn & Excise Office, maltster,
    agent to Norwich Union Fire Office, East Lavington.
Cross reference: House, William, P., innkeeper, Market Lavington.

1030 PHILPOTT, John, maltster.

1842/43 returned £20; assessed £100; exempt.
1846/47-1852/53 assessed in absence of return £100; exempt.
1853/54 assessed in absence of return £100.

1854/55 marked "does not carry on malting".
Pigot & Co's Directory, 1842: John Philpott, maltster, West Lavington (sic).

1031 PHILPOTT, William, innkeeper & butcher. [by comparison New Inn]

1842/43, 1846/47-1849/50 assessed in absence of return £80; exempt.

Pigot & Co's Directory, 1842: William Philpott, butcher, innkeeper, New Inn, East Lavington.
Cross reference: Perrett, Richard, innkeeper, Market Lavington.

1032 PIPER, Joseph, grocer, maltster. [also PIPER, John]

1842/43, 1846/47-1852/53 assessed in absence of return £100; exempt.
1853/54 assessed in absence of return £100; income proved at £90; exempt.

1842/43, 1846/47-1849/50 Joseph Piper; 1850/51-1853/54 John Piper.
1842/43, 1846/47-1850/51 grocer; 1851/52-1853/54 maltster.
1854/55 marked "does not carry on any business".
Pigot & Co's Directory, 1842: Joseph Piper, grocer & dealer in sundries, East Lavington.

1033 POMROY, Daniel, shopkeeper, draper.

1842/43, 1846/47-1852/53 assessed in absence of return £80; exempt.
1853/54-1854/55 returned and assessed £80; exempt.
1855/56 assessed in absence of return £80; income proved at £75; exempt.
1856/57 returned £75; assessed £100.
1857/58 recorded; no assessment made; exempt.
1858/59-1859/60 returned £70; assessed £100.

1842/43, 1846/47-1855/56 shopkeeper; 1856/57-1859/60 draper.
Pigot & Co's Directory, 1842: Daniel Pomroy, boot & shoe maker, draper, East Lavington.

1034 POTTER, Thomas, innkeeper, dealer, brewer, beerseller, butcher, Angel. [also POTTER, Jane]

1842/43, 1846/47-1849/50 assessed in absence of return £100; exempt.
1851/52 returned £50; assessed £100; exempt.
1852/53 assessed in absence of return £100; exempt.
1853/54 returned £44.10.0; assessed £160; income proved at £80; exempt.
1854/55 returned £30; assessed £100; income proved at £50; exempt.
1855/56 assessed in absence of return £50; exempt.
1856/57-1859/60 recorded; no assessments made; exempt.

1842/43, 1846/47-1853/54 Thomas Potter; 1854/55-1859/60 Jane Potter.
1842/43, 1846/47-1849/50 innkeeper & dealer; 1851/52-1852/53 brewer & dealer; 1853/54 beerseller & innkeeper; 1854/55-1855/56 butcher (Angel); 1856/57-1859/60 butcher & innkeeper (Angel).
1850/51 no assessment made.
1853/54 illegible entry after "beerseller & innkeeper".

1854/55 Thomas deleted Jane substituted.
Pigot & Co's Directory, 1842: Thomas Potter, butcher, innkeeper, Angel, East Lavington.

1035 PRICE, Ezra, grocer & piano forte tuner at Devizes.

1856/57 returned £20g, £56p; assessed £100; reduced to £90 on appeal; exempt.
1857/58-1858/59 assessed in absence of return £120.

Abbreviations: g, grocer; p, piano forte tuner.
1859/60 returned £82 but deleted; marked "removed to St.Mary".
Cross reference: Price, Ezra, piano forte seller, St.Mary.

1036 REED, John, innkeeper, Kings Arms.

1858/59-1859/60 recorded; no assessments made; exempt.

1856/57 marked "Hawkins, B.T., now J. Reed, innkeeper". (Hawkins recorded at Bell and
    assessments continue)
Cross reference; Hawkins, Bryant Tinkes, innkeeper, Market Lavington; Draper, Stephen, inn-
    keeper, Market Lavington; Lawes, Joseph, innkeeper, Market Lavington.

1037 SAINSBURY, Samuel, draper & grocer.

1842/43 returned and assessed £95; exempt.
1846/47-1850/51 assessed in absence of return £95; exempt.
1851/52 assessed in absence of return £20; exempt.
1852/53-1853/54 assessed in absence of return £80; exempt.
1857/58-1858/59 recorded; no assessment made; exempt.
1859/60 assessed in absence of return £100.

1854/55 estimate of £100 but no assessment made.
1855/56-1856/57 marked "insolvent".
Pigot & Co's Directory, 1842: Samuel Sainsbury, grocer & dealer in sundries, draper, East
    Lavington.

1038 SAUNDERS, A[braham] E[dward], mealman & baker. [also SAUNDERS, A.E. & Sons]

1842/43 returned and assessed £120. (illegible £620)
1846/47 returned and assessed £120.
1847/48 returned and assessed £150.
1848/49-1850/51 assessed in absence of return £150.
1851/52 returned and assessed £150.
1852/53-1854/55 returned £150; assessed £200.

1842/43, 1846/47-1848/49 A.E.Saunders & Sons; 1849/50-1854/55 A.E.Saunders.
1842/43, 1846/47-1848/49 mealmen & bakers; 1849/50-1854/55 mealman & baker.
1854/55 marked "now Thomas Peerless".
Pigot & Co's Directory, 1842: Abraham Edward Saunders, miller, East Lavington.
Cross reference: Peerless, Thomas, mealman, Market Lavington.

1039 SAXTY, James, draper, etc.

1848/49-1849/50 assessed in absence of return £90; exempt.

1848/49-1849/50 draper; 1855/56-1859/60 draper, etc.
1850/51-1854/55 No assessments made.
1855/56-1859/60 marked "returns made at Trowbridge".

1040 SMITH, Frederick & ELLIS, John, tailors. [also SMITH, Frederick]

1853/54 returned £40; no assessment made.
1854/55-1855/56 assessed in absence of return £40; exempt.
1856/57-1859/60 recorded; no assessments made; exempt.

1853/54 Frederick Smith; 1854/55-1859/60 Frederick Smith & John Ellis.

1041 STAGG, Thomas, wine merchant.

1853/54 returned and assessed £125.
1854/55 returned £120; assessed £125.
1855/56 returned and assessed £125.

1856/57 marked "dead", "query successor", "now Wm. Titt".
1857/58 marked "see William Wallace Titt".
Cross reference: Titt, William Wallace, spirit merchant, Market Lavington.

1042 TITT, William Wallace, spirit merchant.

1857/58-1859/60 returned and assessed £100.

1856/57 marked "Stagg, Thomas, wine merchant now Wm. Titt".
1857/58 marked "Stagg, Thomas, spirit merchant, see William Wallace Titt".
Cross reference: Stagg, Thomas, wine merchant, Market Lavington.

1043 TUCKER, William, surgeon.

1842/43 returned and assessed £205.
1846/47 returned £205; assessed £250.

Pigot & Co's Directory, 1842: William Tucker, surgeon, East Lavington.

1044 TUCKER, Walter, cabinet maker & auctioneer.

1842/43 returned £145; assessed £175.
1846/47 assessed in absence of return £175.
1847/48-1849/50 assessed in absence of return £200.
1850/51 returned £120; assessed £150.

1851/52, 1857/58, 1859/60 marked "return at Salisbury".
1858/59 recorded; no assessment made.
Pigot & Co's Directory, 1842: Walter Tucker, cabinet maker, agent to Farmers' & General Fire
   Office, auctioneer, East Lavington.

1045 WARD, Benjamin, grocer.

1842/43, 1846/47-1849/50 assessed in absence of return £60; exempt.

Pigot & Co's Directory, 1842: Benjamin Ward, grocer & dealer in sundries, East Lavington.

1046 WEBB, John, bricklayer.

1842/43 assessed in absence of return £10; exempt.
1846/47-1849/50 assessed in absence of return £20; exempt.

Pigot & Co's Directory, 1842: John Webb, bricklayer, East Lavington.

1047 WILLETT, John, Doctor of Medicine.

1846/47 returned and assessed £200.
1847/48 assessed in absence of return £200.

Pigot & Co's Directory, 1842: Dr.John Willett, M.D., gentry, surgeon, physician at Lunatic Asylum, Fiddington.

1048 WILLETT, Robert, Asylum keeper.

1846/47-1847/48 marked "return in West Lavington".

Pigot & Co's Directory, 1842: Robert Willett & Son, proprietor, Lunatic Asylum, Fiddington.
Cross reference: Willett, Robert, lunatic asylum, West Lavington.

1049 WILLETT, Robert Smith, spirit merchant.

1846/47-1847/48 assessed in absence of return £100; exempt.

NORTH NEWNTON & HILLCOTT

1050 DOWSE, James, baker & grocer.

1856/57 returned and assessed £35.
1857/58-1859/60 recorded; no assessments made; exempt.

1051 DUNFORD, George, butcher.

1842/43 returned and assessed £50; exempt.
1846/47-1848/49 assessed in absence of return £50; exempt.

1052 EDWARDS, William, tailor.

1852/53-1855/56 assessed in absence of return £50; exempt.
1856/57-1859/60 recorded; no assessments made; exempt.

1053 HUNTLEY, John Simster(?), mealman.

1859/60 returned £50; assessed £100; income proved at £50; exempt.

1054 KEEPENCE, George, builder.

1856/57 assessed in absence of return £100; reduced to £83 on appeal; exempt.
1857/58-1858/59 recorded; no assessments made; exempt.
1859/60 returned £70; assessed £80; exempt.

1055 KNEE, James, miller.

1842/43 returned and assessed £20; exempt.
1846/47-1847/48 assessed in absence of return £20; exempt.
1848/49 assessed in absence of return £60; exempt.

1056 MARTIN, George, brewer, grocer. [also MARTIN, Henry Alexander]

1842/43 returned and assessed £18; exempt.
1846/47-1849/50 assessed in absence of return £30; exempt.
1854/55 returned and assessed £60; exempt.
1855/56 assessed in absence of return £60; exempt.
1856/57 returned £60 but no assessment made.

1857/58-1858/59 recorded; no assessments made; exempt.
1859/60 returned £50 but no assessment made.

1842/43, 1846/47-1849/50, 1854/55-1855/56 George Martin; 1856/57-1859/60 Henry
Alexander Martin.
1842/43, 1846/47-1849/50 brewer; 1854/55-1859/60 grocer & brewer.
1850/51-1853/54 no assessments made.
1856/57 George deleted, Henry Alexander substituted.

1057 PAGE, Thomas, mealman.

1854/55 returned £105; assessed £150; reduced to £105.
1855/56 returned £65; assessed £105.

1854/55 no appeal noted; marked "q. deductions".
1856/57 marked "now Stratton & Skeate (sic), mealmen"; "Page, Thomas ceased business in
September 1855".
1857/58 marked "now Stratton & Keate (sic)"; "no trade carried on".
Cross reference: Stratton & Skeate, mealmen, North Newnton & Hillcott.

1058 ROGERS, Francis James H., barrister.

1842/43 entry only.

1059 SKEATE, -, (possibly KEATE, S.) mealman.

1857/58 assessed in absence of return £105.

1857/58 marked "late Stratton & Skeate"; Page, Thomas now Stratton & Keate (sic), mealmen".
1858/59-1859/60 marked "late S".
Cross reference: Page, Thomas, mealman; North Newnton & Hillcott; Stratton & Skeate,
mealmen, North Newnton & Hillcott.

1060 STRATTON, William, trustee for Strattons Estate, mealman.

1857/58-1859/60 recorded but no assessments made.

1857/58 trustee for Stratton Estate; 1858/59-1859/60 trustee for Strattons (sic) Estate,
mealman.
1858/59 marked "Query".
Cross reference: Page, Thomas, mealman, North Newnton & Hillcott; Stratton & Skeate,
mealmen, North Newnton & Hillcott.

1061 STRATTON & SKEATE, Mealmen - See Stratton, Frederick; Skeate, -.

1062 WELLS, Joseph, innkeeper.

1856/57-1857/58 recorded; no assessments made; exempt.
1858/59 assessed in absence of return £50.
1859/60 returned and assessed £50; exempt.

1063 WILD, Robert, land measurer.

1853/54 returned £95; assessed £100; income proved at £95; exempt.
1854/55 assessed in absence of return £95; exempt.
1855/56-1856/57 assessed in absence of return £100.
1857/58 returned and assessed £100.
1858/59 assessed in absence of return £100.
1859/60 returned and assessed £100.

PATNEY

1064 AKERMAN, Stephen

1842/43 name only entered and deleted.

1065 HAILSTONE, John, carpenter.

1842/43 returned and assessed £65; exempt.
1846/47-1849/50 assessed in absence of return £65; exempt.

1066 WELLS, John, cordwainer.

1842/43 returned and assessed £10; exempt.
1846/47-1849/50 assessed in absence of return £30; exempt.

RUSHALL

1067 BARTLETT, John, surgeon, etc.

1846/47 returned and assessed £230.
1847/48-1848/49 returned and assessed £255.
1849/50 returned and assessed £250.

1850/51 entry deleted, Cream, Robert Chevalier, surgeon substituted.

Cross references: Cream, Robert Chevalier, surgeon, Rushall; Febb, Thomas H., surgeon, Rushall; Hayward, John, surgeon, Rushall.

1068 CREAM, Robert Chevalier, surgeon.

1850/51 assessed in absence of return £250.
1851/52 returned £150; assessed £250.
1852/53 returned and assessed £200.
1853/54 assessed in absence of return £200.
1854/55 returned and assessed £200.
1855/56 returned £150; assessed £250.
1856/57 assessed in absence of return £250.

1854/55, 1858/59 Chevallier.
1857/58 faint illegible; no assessment made.
1858/59 marked "now Hayward, John".
Cross references: Bartlett, John, surgeon, etc., Rushall; Febb, Thomas H., surgeon, Rushall; Hayward, John, surgeon, Rushall.

1069 FEBB, Thomas H., surgeon.

1842/43 returned and assessed £230.

Cross references: Bartlett, John, surgeon, etc., Rushall; Cream, Robert Chevalier, surgeon, Rushall; Hayward, John, surgeon, Rushall.

1070 HAYWARD, John, surgeon.

1858/59 marked "Cream, Robert Chevallier, surgeon now Hayward, John".
1859/60 marked "charged in Market Lavington".
Cross references: Bartlett, John, surgeon, etc., Rushall; Cream, Robert Chevalier, surgeon, Rushall; Febb, Thomas H., surgeon, Rushall; Hayward, John, surgeon, Market Lavington.

1071 LEWIS, James, blacksmith.

1842/43 returned and assessed £57.6.8.
1846/47 assessed in absence of return £100.
1847/48 assessed in absence of return £100; income proved at £80; exempt.
1848/49 returned and assessed £150.
1849/50 assessed in absence of return £150; assessment discharged on appeal but no sum recorded.

1847/48 £2.6.8 left in charge.

1072 LLOYD, Revd. William.

1842/43 name only recorded.

1073 SIMPSON, Edward.

1851/52 marked "of Netteravon".

STANTON ST. BERNARD

1074 ABRAHAMS, Morris, tailor.

1846/47-1850/51 assessed in absence of return £130; exempt.
1851/52-1852/53 assessed in absence of return £100; exempt.
1853/54-1855/56 assessed in absence of return £80; exempt.
1856/57-1859/60 recorded; no assessments made; exempt.

1075 BERRY, Isaac, miller.

1850/51-1852/53 assessed in absence of return £70; exempt.
1853/54 recorded but no assessment made.

1850/51 marked "late John Stadden miller".
1854/55 marked "late now Maslen, James".
Cross references: Maslen, James, miller, Stanton St. Bernard; Stadden, John, miller, Stanton St. Bernard.

1076 CHANDLER, Thomas, innkeeper, grocer.

1851/52 returned and assessed £130; exempt.
1852/53 assessed in absence of return £130; reduced to £120 on appeal.
1853/54-1855/56 assessed in absence of return £130.
1856/57 recorded but no assessment made.
1857/58-1859/60 recorded; no assessments made; exempt.

1851/52 innkeeper, grocer, etc.; 1852/53-1855/56 innkeeper, grocer;
1856/57-1859/60 grocer.
1852/53 marked "Wiltshire, William see Chandler".
1856/57 marked "Query".
Cross reference: Wiltshire, William, brewer, cooper, Stanton St. Bernard.

1077 CLARKE, John, coal & platt merchant, coal & slate merchant. [also CLARKE, William, CLARKE, Executors of William]

1842/43 returned and assessed £200.
1846/47 returned £160; assessed £200.
1847/48 assessed in absence of return £200.
1848/49 returned £160; assessed £200.
1849/50 returned £150; assessed £200.
1850/51 assessed in absence of return £250.
1851/52 returned £160; assessed £250.
1852/53 returned £150; assessed £250.
1853/54 returned £120; assessed £250.
1854/55-1856/57 assessed in absence of return £250.
1857/58 returned £160; assessed £250.
1858/59 assessed in absence of return £150.
1859/60 recorded but no assessment made.

1842/43, 1846/47-1852/53 John Clarke; 1853/54-1858/59 William Clarke; 1859/60 Executors of William Clarke.
1842/43, 1846/47-1847/48 coal & platt merchant; 1848/49-1859/60 coal & slate merchant.
1858/59 marked "see return".
Pigot & Co's Directory, 1842: John Clarke, coal, salt & slate merchant, Wharf, Devizes.
Cross reference: Hilliard, Benjamin, agent to Clark (*sic*), Stanton St. Bernard.

1078 HILLIARD, Benjamin, agent to Clark, accountant.

1858/59-1859/60 assessed in absence of return £75.

1858/59 agent to Clark (*sic*); 1859/60 accountant.
1858/59 William inserted but deleted, Benjamin substituted.
Cross reference: Clarke, John, (for William) coal & slate merchant, Stanton St. Bernard.

1079 MASLEN, James, miller.

1854/55 assessed in absence of return £100.
1855/56 estimated at £100 but no assessment made.
1858/59-1859/60 recorded but no assessments made.

1854/55 marked "Berry, Isaac late, now Maslen, James, miller".
1855/56 marked "late Berry, charged at Allcannings".
1856/57-1857/58 marked "charged at Allcannings".
Cross references: Berry, Isaac, miller, Stanton St. Bernard; Maslen, James, butcher, Allcannings; Stadden, John, miller, Stanton St. Bernard.

1080 MASLEN, John, innkeeper, Barge.

1859/60 assessed in absence of return £120.

1859/60 marked "Sparks, William Henry now Maslen, John, innkeeper (Barge)".
Cross references: Naish, Jacob Hobbs, innkeeper, Stanton St. Bernard; Sparks, William Henry, innkeeper, Stanton St. Bernard.

1081 NAISH, Jacob Hobbs, innkeeper, Barge.

1856/57 assessed in absence of return £120.
1857/58 returned and assessed £120.
1858/59 assessed in absence of return £120.

1858/59 marked "now William Henry Sparks, innkeeper, Barge".
Cross references: Maslen, John, innkeeper, Stanton St. Bernard; Sparks, William Henry, innkeeper, Stanton St. Bernard.

1082 SPARKS, William Henry, innkeeper, Barge.

1859/60 marked "Naish, Jacob Hobbs now Sparks, William Henry, innkeeper, Barge"; entry deleted, marked "now John Maslen, innkeeper".
Cross references: Maslen, John, innkeeper, Stanton St. Bernard; Naish, Charles Hobbs, innkeeper, Stanton St. Bernard.

1083 STADDEN, John, miller.

1842/43 returned and assessed £70; exempt.
1846/47-1849/50 assessed in absence of return £70; exempt.

1850/51 marked "Berry Isaac late John Stadden, miller".
Cross references: Berry, Isaac, miller, Stanton St. Bernard; Maslen, James, miller, Stanton St. Bernard.

1084 TASKER, Michael, blacksmith, etc.

1842/43 returned and assessed £80; exempt.
1846/47 returned and assessed £20.
1847/48 assessed in absence of return £20; exempt.
1848/49 returned and assessed £60; exempt.
1849/50-1852/53 assessed in absence of return £60; exempt.
1853/54 returned £20; assessed £40.
1854/55-1855/56 assessed in absence of return £40; exempt.
1856/57-1859/60 recorded; no assessments made; exempt.

1842/43, 1846/47-1847/48, 1856/57-1859/60 blacksmith; 1848/49-1855/56 blacksmith, etc.

1085 WILTSHIRE, William, brewer, cooper, dealer.

1842/43 returned and assessed £80; exempt.

1846/47 returned and assessed £95; exempt.
1847/48 assessed in absence of return £95; exempt.
1848/49 returned and assessed £100; exempt.
1849/50-1850/51 assessed in absence of return £100; exempt.
1851/52 assessed in absence of return £60; exempt.

1842/43 brewer, cooper & dealer; 1846/47-1851/52 brewer, cooper, etc.
1852/53 marked "see Chandler".
Pigot & Co's Directory, 1842: Wiltshire, William, saddler, East Lavington.
Cross reference: Chandler, Thomas, innkeeper, grocer, Stanton St. Bernard.

STERT

1086 BEAVEN, John, miller.

1853/54 returned and assessed £40; exempt.
1854/55 assessed in absence of return £100; income proved at £50; exempt.
1855/56 returned and assessed £50; exempt.
1856/57-1857/58 recorded; no assessments made; exempt.
1858/59 returned £25; no assessment made; exempt.
1859/60 returned £30; no assessment made; exempt.

1087 COOKE, George, brickmaker.

1859/60 assessed in absence of return £25 (Stert), £65 (Etchilhampton); assessment on
    profits at Stert deleted.

1859/60 marked "at Stert & Etchilhampton"; against Stert entry marked "commenced in May
    1859".
1859/60 marked "Dunford, James, brickmaker now George Cooke".
Cross reference: Dunford, James, brickmaker, Stert.

1088 DUNFORD, James, brickmaker.

1853/54 returned and assessed £20; exempt.
1854/55 assessed in absence of return £100.
1855/56 returned £20; assessed £100.
1856/57-1857/58 assessed in absence of return £100.
1858/59 returned £30; assessed £100.

1853/54-1856/57 Durnford; 1857/58-1858/59 Dunford.
1854/55 [Wedhampton] Dunford, James, brickmaker Stert.
1859/60 marked "now George Cooke".
Cross references: Cooke, George, brickmaker, Stert; Dunford, James, brickmaker,
    Wedhampton.

1089 HISCOCK, Abel, miller. [also HISCOCK, Mary]

1855/56 returned £15 miller, £20 interest; assessed £50; exempt.
1856/57-1857/58 recorded; no assessments made; exempt.
1858/59 returned £16 but no assessment made.
1859/60 returned £25 miller, £25 interest but no assessment made.

1855/56-1858/59 Abel Hiscock; 1859/60 Mary Hiscock.

1090 POPE, James, miller.

1853/54 returned and assessed £10; exempt.
1854/55-1855/56 assessed in absence of return £50; exempt.
1856/57-1859/60 recorded; no assessments made; exempt.

UPAVON

1091 AKERMAN, J.P., Relieving Officer.

1842/43 returned £40 interest on money on loan but deleted.
1846/47-1848/49 marked "Schedule E".
1851/52 returned and assessed £111; income proved at £134.9.8; exempt.
1852/53 assessed in absence of return £134 but deleted; marked "Schedule E".
1853/54 returned and assessed £70; exempt.
1854/55 returned £109.3.8 but deleted; assessed £70.
1855/56 returned and assessed £40.17.4.
1856/57-1859/60 marked "Schedule E"; no assessments made.

1849/50-1850/51 no assessments made.

1092 BONNER, John, beerseller, butcher.

1842/43 returned and assessed £50; exempt.
1846/47-1849/50 assessed in absence of return £50; exempt.
1851/52 returned and assessed £80; income proved at £83.10.0; exempt.
1852/53 returned £70; assessed £80; exempt.
1853/54 returned £60; assessed £80; exempt.
1854/55 returned £75; assessed £100.
1855/56 returned £90; assessed £100.
1856/57 assessed in absence of return £100.
1857/58-1858/59 returned and assessed £100.
1859/60 returned two amounts of £30; assessed £100.

1842/43 butcher & beerseller; 1846/47-1849/50, 1851/52-1857/58 butcher; 1858/59-1859/60 butcher & retailer of beer.

1850/51 no assessment made.

1093 CARTER, Henry, draper & grocer.

1842/43 returned and assessed £150.
1846/47-1847/48 assessed in absence of return £150.
1848/49-1855/56 returned and assessed £150.
1856/57 assessed in absence of return £150.
1857/58-1859/60 returned and assessed £150.

1094 COPELAND, -.

1846/47-1847/48 surname only entered; no assessments made.

1095 CROOK, Revd. Henry S.C., private tutor.

1842/43 returned and assessed £100.
1850/51-1851/52 returned and assessed £70.
1852/53 returned and assessed £80.

1846/47-1847/48 recorded but no assessments made; 1846/47 marked "Return".
1853/54 recorded but no assessment made; marked "call for return".
1854/55 marked "nil".
1855/56 marked "none in year".
1856/57-1859/60 recorded but no assessments made.

1096 CROOK, Miss Sarah.

1848/49 name only entered but deleted.

1097 FORD, Edward, mealman, miller, baker.

1842/43 returned and assessed £80; exempt.
1846/47-1849/50 assessed in absence of return £80; exempt.
1851/52 returned £25; assessed £50; income proved at £80; exempt.
1852/53 assessed in absence of return £80; exempt.
1853/54 returned £40; assessed £70; income proved at £50; exempt.
1854/55 assessed in absence of return £100; income proved at £80; exempt.
1855/56 assessed in absence of return £80; exempt.
1856/57-1859/60 recorded; no assessments made; exempt.

1842/43, 1846/47-1849/50 mealman; 1851/52-1852/53 baker; 1853/54-1859/60 miller.
1850/51 no assessment made.

1098 HEDGES, John, innkeeper.

1842/43 returned £95; assessed £120; exempt.
1846/47-1852/53 assessed in absence of return £120; exempt.

1099 HUTCHENS, John, innkeeper & baker.

1842/43, 1846/47-1849/50 assessed in absence of return £50; exempt.

1842/43, 1846/47 Hutchins; 1847/48-1849/50 Hutchens.

1100 LANCASTER, William, brewer.

1851/52 returned and assessed £50; exempt.
1852/53 returned and assessed £70; exempt.
1853/54 returned £50; assessed £70; exempt.
1854/55-1856/57 assessed in absence of return £100.
1857/58 returned and assessed £100.
1858/59 returned £70; assessed £100.
1859/60 returned £100; assessed £120.

1101 MASTERSON, John, drillman.

1842/43 returned £50; assessed £75; exempt.
1846/47-1848/49 assessed in absence of return £130; exempt.
1849/50 assessed in absence of return £130; assessment discharged on appeal but no
    amount recorded.

1102 ORAM, John, baker.

1842/43 returned and assessed £100; exempt.
1846/47-1849/50 assessed in absence of return £80; exempt.

1103 SMITH, Edward, grocer, shopkeeper.

1842/43, 1846/47-1849/50 assessed in absence of return £100; exempt.
1851/52 returned and assessed £70; exempt.
1852/53 returned £70; income proved at £107.15.0; exempt.
1853/54 assessed in absence of return £100; income proved at £60; exempt.
1854/55-1855/56 assessed in absence of return £70; exempt.
1856/57 recorded; no assessment made; exempt.
1857/58-1858/59 returned and assessed £75 and £18 interest.
1859/60 returned £70 and £18 interest; assessed £93.

1842/43, 1846/47–1849/50 shopkeeper; 1851/52–1859/60 grocer.
1850/51 no assessment made.
1857/58–1859/60 returned "interest of money".

1104 SMITH, James, carrier.

1842/43 returned and assessed £30; exempt.
1846/47–1849/50 assessed in absence of return £30; exempt.

URCHFONT

1105 BURT, John, cordwainer.

1842/43 returned £20; assessed £50; exempt.
1846/47–1849/50 assessed in absence of return £50; exempt.

1106 BUNGLEY, George, tailor.

1842/43 returned £30 but no assessment made.
1846/47–1849/50 assessed in absence of return £30; exempt.

1107 CLELFORD, William, cordwainer.

1842/43, 1846/47–1849/50 assessed in absence of return £50; exempt.

1108 DAVIS, George, tailor.

1846/47–1849/50 assessed in absence of return £50; exempt.

1109 DOWSE, John, innkeeper, farmer, Bell.

1846/47 assessed in absence of return £150; income proved at £136; exempt.
1847/48 assessed in absence of return £150; income proved at £120; exempt.
1848/49–1850/51 assessed in absence of return £120; exempt.
1851/52 returned and assessed £116; exempt.
1852/53 returned £100; assessed £120.
1853/54 returned £40; assessed £120.
1854/55 assessed in absence of return £120.
1855/56 returned £40; assessed £120.
1856/57 returned £80; assessed £120.
1857/58 returned £40; assessed £120.

1846/47-1850/51, 1855/56-1857/58 innkeeper; 1851/52-1854/55 innkeeper & farmer.
1846/47-1847/48 no appeal noted.
1856/57 Bell noted.
1858/59 marked "now Charles Hobbs Naish.
Cross reference: Naish, Charles Hobbs, innkeeper, Urchfont.

1110 EDWARDS, James, innkeeper, Nags Head. [also EDWARDS, Jane; EDWARDS, William]

1842/43 returned £50; assessed £100; exempt.
1846/47-1849/50 assessed in absence of return £100; exempt.
1851/52 returned £35; assessed £70; income proved at £55; exempt.
1852/53 returned £50; assessed £55; exempt.
1853/54 returned and assessed £35; exempt.
1854/55-1855/56 assessed in absence of return £100.
1856/57 returned £100; assessed £150.
1857/58 returned £90; assessed £160.
1858/59-1859/60 returned £100; assessed £160.

1842/43, 1851/52-1854/55 James Edwards; 1846/47-1850/51 Jane Edwards;
1855/56-1859/60 William Edwards.
1850/51 no assessment made.
1856/57 Nags Head noted.

1111 EDWARDS, John, lime burner.

1857/58 assessed in absence of return £20.
1858/59 returned and assessed £20.
1859/60 returned £10; assessed £20.

1112 EDWARDS, William & Thomas, blacksmiths, etc.

1842/43, 1846/47-1849/50 assessed in absence of return £60; exempt.

1842/43, 1846/47 blacksmiths; 1847/48-1849/50 blacksmiths, etc.

1113 GIDDINGS, Robert, baker & mealman.

1842/43 returned £30 and £7.10.0 interest; assessed £120 and £7.10.0 interest.
1846/47-1848/49 returned £30; assessed £130.
1849/50 assessed in absence of return £130.
1850/51 returned £15; assessed £150.
1851/52 returned £20; assessed £150.
1852/53-1854/55 returned £30; assessed £150.
1855/56-1859/60 assessed in absence of return £150.

Pigot & Co's Directory, 1842: Robert Giddings, miller, Urchfont.

1114 GIDDINGS, Sarah, grocer, chandler. [also GIDDINGS, Robert]

1842/43 returned and assessed £10; exempt.
1846/47-1848/49 assessed in absence of return £10; exempt.
1849/50 returned and assessed £25; exempt.

1842/43 Robert Giddings, chandler; 1846/47-1849/50 Sarah Giddings, grocer.

1115 GILLETT, James, bricklayer, grocer & tea dealer.

1842/43 returned and assessed £15g, £50b; exempt.
1846/47-1849/50 assessed in absence of return £65; exempt.
1851/52-1855/56 assessed in absence of return £50; exempt.
1856/57-1859/60 recorded; no assessments made; exempt.

Abbreviations: b, bricklayer, g, grocer & tea dealer.
1842/43, 1846/47-1849/50 bricklayer, grocer & tea dealer; 1851/52-1859/60 bricklayer.
1850/51 no assessment made.

1116 HAMLEN, John, innkeeper.

1842/43 returned £50; assessed £150; income proved at £100; exempt.

1842/43 no appeal noted.

1117 HIBBERD, Robert, carpenter.

1842/43 returned £70; assessed £100; exempt.
1846/47-1849/50 assessed in absence of return £80; exempt.
1851/52 returned and assessed £50; exempt.
1852/53 returned and assessed £50; income proved at £64.3.3; exempt.
1853/54 returned and assessed £65; exempt.
1854/55-1855/56 assessed in absence of return £65; exempt.
1856/57-1859/69 recorded; no assessments made; exempt.

1850/51 no assessment made.
Pigot & Co's Directory, 1842: Robert Hibbard (sic), carpenter & wheelwright, Littleton.

1118 HIBBERD, William, carpenter, beerseller.

1842/43 returned £20; assessed £50; exempt.
1846/47-1849/50 assessed in absence of return £50; exempt.

1852/53 returned £30; assessed £50; exempt.
1853/54-1855/56 assessed in absence of return £50; exempt.
1856/57-1859/60 recorded; no assessments made; exempt.

1842/43, 1846/47-1849/50 carpenter; 1852/53-1859/60 beerseller.
1850/51-1851/52 no assessments made.

1119 LANCASTER, John, castrator.

1842/43 returned and assessed £85; exempt.
1846/47-1848/49 returned and assessed £85 and £12.10.0 interest; exempt.
1849/50 returned and assessed £85 and £2.2.0 interest; exempt.
1851/52 returned and assessed £85.
1852/53 returned £80; assessed £85; income proved at £87.14.0; exempt.

1850/51 no assessment made.

1120 LYNE, John, butcher.

1842/43 returned £30; assessed £75; exempt.
1846/47-1849/50 assessed in absence of return £130; exempt.
1851/52 returned £20; assessed £50; exempt.
1852/53-1855/56 assessed in absence of return £50; exempt.
1856/57-1859/60 recorded; no assessments made; exempt.

1850/51 no assessment made.

1121 MATTHEWS, Roger, chandler, baker.

1842/43 returned and assessed £25; exempt.
1846/47-1849/50 assessed in absence of return £25; exempt.
1851/52 returned and assessed £20; exempt.
1852/53 assessed in absence of return £20; exempt.
1853/54 returned and assessed £20; exempt.
1854/55-1855/56 assessed in absence of return £60; exempt.
1856/57-1859/60 recorded; no assessments made; exempt.

1842/43, 1846/47-1849/50 chandler & baker; 1851/52-1859/60 baker.
1850/51 no assessment made.

1122 NAISH, Charles Hobbs, innkeeper. [by comparison, Bell]

1858/59-1859/60 returned £40; assessed £120.

1858/59 marked "late Jno. Dowse innkeeper".
Cross reference: Dowse, John, innkeeper, Urchfont.

1123 NEW, James, bailiff.

1842/43 returned and assessed £40; exempt.
1846/47-1849/50 assessed in absence of return £40; exempt.

1124 PIERCE, James, tailor.

1842/43 assessed in absence of return £45; exempt.
1846/47-1849/50 assessed in absence of return £40; exempt.

1125 PLANK, Thomas, shoemaker.

1842/43 returned and assessed £20; exempt.
1846/47-1849/50 assessed in absence of return £20; exempt.

1126 RUDMAN, Noah, carpenter.

1842/43, 1846/47-1849/50 assessed in absence of return £30; exempt.

1127 SCOTT, Richard, bailiff.

1842/43 returned and assessed £80; exempt.

1128 SMITH, Richard, cooper, maltster.

1842/43 returned £35; assessed £80; exempt.
1846/47 assessed in absence of return £80; income proved at £99.13.7; exempt.
1847/48-1848/49 assessed in absence of return £80; exempt.
1849/50 assessed in absence of return £85; exempt.
1851/52 returned £20; assessed £60; income proved at £88.5.1; exempt.
1852/53 returned £18; assessed £40; income proved at £107.9.0; exempt.
1853/54 returned £18; assessed £50; exempt.
1854/55 assessed in absence of return £75.
1855/56 assessed in absence of return £60; exempt.
1856/57 recorded; no assessment made; exempt.
1857/58 returned £18; estimated at £40 but no assessment made; exempt.
1858/59 returned £5; assessed £50.
1859/60 returned £10; assessed £50.

1842/43 cooper & maltster; 1846/47-1849/50, 1851/52-1859/60 cooper.
1850/51 no assessment made.

1129 SMITH, Thomas, shopkeeper.

1842/43 returned and assessed £20; exempt.
1846/47-1849/50 assessed in absence of return £40; exempt.

1130 SNOOK, John Swallow, threshing machine owner, maltster, thrasher.

1842/43 returned £18; assessed £25; exempt.
1846/47-1849/50 assessed in absence of return £25; exempt.
1850/51 assessed in absence of return £25; assessment discharged on appeal but no sum recorded.
1851/52 returned nil, no assessment made.
1852/53 recorded but no assessment made.
1853/54 assessed in absence of return £20; exempt.
1854/55 assessed in absence of return £50; exempt.
1855/56-1859/60 recorded; no assessment made; exempt.

1842/43, 1846/47-1850/51 maltster; 1851/52-1857/58 threshing machine (owner); 1858/59-1859/60 thrasher.
1850/51 on appeal marked "business given up. No successor".
1855/56 marked "discontinued".

1131 STAPLES, James, grocer, draper, bacon factor, shopkeeper, innkeeper.

1842/43 returned £60; assessed £100; income proved at £60.
1846/47-1849/50 assessed in absence of return £73; exempt.
1852/53 returned and assessed £42; income proved at £84.5.10; exempt.
1853/54 assessed in absence of return £84; exempt.
1854/55 assessed in absence of return £100; reduced to £75.
1855/56 assessed in absence of return £75; exempt.
1856/57-1859/60 recorded; no assessments made; exempt.

1842/43, 1846/47-1848/49 grocer, draper & bacon factor; 1849/50 draper, grocer, etc.; 1852/53-1857/58 shopkeeper; 1858/59-1859/60 innkeeper.
1850/51-1851/52 no assessments made.

1132 WHATLEY, Evi, beerseller, brewer.

1842/43 returned £40; assessed £60; exempt.
1846/47-1850/51 assessed in absence of return £100; exempt.
1851/52 returned £30; assessed £80; exempt.
1852/53 returned £30; assessed £80; income proved at £86.11.0; exempt.
1853/54 returned £20; assessed £86; exempt.
1854/55 assessed in absence of return £100; income proved at £50; exempt.
1855/56 assessed in absence of return £50; exempt.

1856/57-1859/60 recorded; no assessments made; exempt.

1842/43 beerseller (brewer entered but deleted); 1846/47-1859/60 beerseller & brewer.

1133 WHITE, Frederick George, surgeon.

1857/58 returned and assessed £200; reduced to £137.

1858/59 returned £159.5.7 but deleted and marked "returned at Market Lavington".
1858/59-1859/60 also marked "Schedule E".
Cross reference: White, Frederick George, surgeon [under Hitchcock, Charles], Market
    Lavington.

1134 WISE, Thomas, brickmaker.

1842/43 recorded but no assessment made.
1846/47-1849/50 assessed in absence of return £40; exempt.

WEDHAMPTON

1135 DUNFORD, James, brickmaker. [also DUNFORD, Thomas]

1842/43 returned and assessed £50; exempt.
1846/47 assessed in absence of return £50; exempt.
1847/48-1852/53 assessed in absence of return £100; exempt.
1853/54 assessed in absence of return £100; income proved at £90; exempt.

1842/43, 1846/47-1847/48 Thomas Dunford; 1848/49-1853/54 James Dunford.
1854/55-1857/58 marked "return in Stert". [1853/54 assessed also in Stert].
1853/54-1856/57 [Stert] Durnford.
1858/59-1859/60 recorded but no assessment made.
Cross reference: Dunford, James, brickmaker, Stert.

1136 FAY, Timothy, woolstapler.

1842/43 returned and assessed £50; exempt.
1846/47 assessed in absence of return £100.
1847/48 returned and assessed £100.
1848/49 assessed in absence of return £140.
1849/50 returned £139; assessed £150.
1850/51-1852/53 returned and assessed £150.
1853/54 returned and assessed £400.
1854/55 assessed in absence of return £400.

1855/56 returned £186; assessed £400.
1856/57 returned £150; assessed £300.

1857/58 marked "dead".

1137 MANNINGS, George, woolstapler.

1842/43 returned and assessed £122.
1846/47-1847/48 returned and assessed £150.
1848/49 assessed in absence of return £140; exempt.
1849/50 returned £105.3.8; assessed £150.
1850/51 returned £117; assessed £150.
1851/52-1852/53 returned and assessed £150.
1853/54 returned and assessed £200.
1854/55 assessed in absence of return £200.
1855/56 returned £100; assessed £200.
1856/57 returned £150; assessed £200.
1857/58 returned and assessed £200.
1858/59 returned £150; assessed £200.
1859/60 returned and assessed £300.

1842/43 marked "pays £25 interest"; 8/9 duty left in charge, otherwise exemption claimed.

1138 RICKETTS, James, beerhouse keeper.

1842/43 returned and assessed £50; exempt.
1846/47-1849/50 assessed in absence of return £50; exempt.

1139 WITCHELL, James, blacksmith.

1842/43 returned and assessed £50; exempt.
1846/47-1849/50 assessed in absence of return £50; exempt.

WILCOT, OARE & DRAYCOT [FITZPAYNE]

1140 CHANDLER, Elizabeth, innkeeper.

1842/43 returned and assessed £20; exempt.
1846/47-1849/50 assessed in absence of return £20; exempt.

1141 COLLARD, G.P., shopkeeper.

1846/47-1849/50 assessed in absence of return £20; exempt.

1142 EDMONDS, John, maltster, baker.

1842/43 returned and assessed £70.
1846/47-1847/48 assessed in absence of return £80.
1848/49 returned £60; assessed £80.
1849/50 returned £50; assessed £80.
1850/51 assessed in absence of return £80.

1842/43 maltster & baker; 1846/47-1850/51 maltster.
1851/52 marked "no business done for 12 months".
1852/53 marked "left the parish".

1143 FERRIS, William, valuer.

1857/58 returned and assessed £150.
1858/59 returned and assessed £275.
1859/60 returned and assessed £320.

1144 GRANT, John & James, maltsters.

1857/58-1859/60 recorded but no assessments made.
Cross reference: Grant, John, maltster, Easterton.

1145 GRANT, Jonathan, valuer.

1850/51-1851/52 assessed in absence of return £67.
1852/53 returned and assessed £83.
1853/54 returned and assessed £46.
1854/55 assessed in absence of return £60.
1855/56 returned and assessed £60.
1856/57 assessed in absence of return £80.
1857/58 returned and assessed £80.
1858/59-1859/69 returned £60; assessed £80.

1146 MARKES, Frances B.

1842/43 name only entered; no assessment made.

1147 WILSON, David, shopkeeper.

1842/43 returned and assessed £20; exempt.

1846/47 marked "left the parish".

WILSFORD

1148 BOLTER, John, beerhouse keeper.

1857/58 returned £60; no assessment made.
1858/59-1859/60 recorded; no assessments made; exempt.

1149 DUNFORD, James, baker & shopkeeper.

1857/58 returned £30; no assessment made.
1858/59-1859/60 recorded; no assessments made; exempt.

1150 LEONARD, Jesse, maltster.

1851/52 assessed in absence of return £100.
1852/53 assessed in absence of return £100; exempt.
1853/54 returned £77; assessed £100; exempt.

1851/52 marked "late Exors. of Jacob Stratton".
1853/54 marked "see Marden". (no entry in Marden)
1854/55 marked "gone".
Cross reference: Stratton, Jacob, maltster, Wilsford.

1151 ORAM, Mary, blacksmith.

1857/58-1859/60 recorded; no assessment made; exempt.

1152 SIMONS, Revd. N., clerk.

1842/43 returned and assessed £100; exempt.

1846/47 marked "q.pupils. return".

1153 SPRINGBETT, Thomas, mealman.

1842/43 returned and assessed £50; exempt.
1846/47 assessed in absence of return £50; exempt.
1847/48 assessed in absence of return £150.
1848/49 returned £75; assessed £150; reduced to £110; exempt.
1849/50 assessed in absence of return £110; exempt.
1850/51-1852/53 assessed in absence of return £120; exempt.
1853/54-1856/57 assessed in absence of return £120.

1857/58 returned £100; assessed £120.
1858/59-1859/60 assessed in absence of return £120.

1848/49 no appeal noted.

1154 STRATTON, Jacob, maltster.

1842/43 returned and assessed £90.
1846/47-1847/48 assessed in absence of return £90.
1848/49 returned and assessed £100.
1849/50 returned £100; assessment discharged on appeal but no sum recorded.

1848/49-1849/50 Executors of Jacob Stratton.
1851/52 marked "Leonard, Jesse, maltster late Stratton, Jacob".
Cross reference: Leonard, Jesse, maltster, Wilsford.

WOODBOROUGH

1155 BROWN, Job, innkeeper, smith.

1842/43, 1846/47-1852/53 assessed in absence of return £75; exempt.
1853/54 returned £15; assessed £75; exempt.
1854/55-1856/57 assessed in absence of return £75.
1857/58 returned £70; assessed £75.
1858/59 returned £50; assessed £75.
1859/60 returned and assessed £75.

1842/43, 1846/47-1852/53, 1858/59-1859/60 innkeeper; 1853/54-1857/58 innkeeper & smith.

1156 BROWN, Philip, blacksmith.

1846/47-1849/50 assessed in absence of return £20; exempt.

1157 CALLADINE, Samuel, tailor, draper.

1842/43 assessed in absence of return £80; exempt.
1846/47-1849/50 assessed in absence of return £70; exempt.
1851/52 returned and assessed £100; income proved at £135; exempt.
1852/53 assessed in absence of return £135; exempt.
1853/54 returned £4; estimated at £135 deleted.

1842/43, 1846/47-1849/50 tailor; 1851/52-1852/53 draper; 1853/54 draper & tailor.

1850/51 no assessment made.
1851/52 entered as Mr.Culladine.
1852/53 marked "late draper".

1158 FIDLER, Hezekiah, smith.

1846/47-1849/50 assessed in absence of return £20; exempt.

1159 FIDLER, William, harness maker, grocer. [also FIDLER, Sarah]

1846/47-1849/50 assessed in absence of return £40; exempt.
1857/58 returned £65; assessed £100; reduced to £75.
1858/59-1859/60 returned and assessed £75.

1846/47-1849/50, 1857/58 William Fidler; 1858/59-1859/60 Sarah Fidler.
1846/47-1849/50, 1857/58 harness maker; 1858/59-1859/60 harness maker & grocer.
1850/51-1855/56 no assessments made.
1856/57 recorded as harness maker & grocer but no assessment made.
1857/58 no appeal noted.
1858/59 marked "Q. Fidler journeyman harness maker".

1160 HIBBERD, John, maltster, grocer, shopkeeper.

1842/43, 1846/47-1849/50 assessed in absence of return £60; exempt.

1842/43 maltster & grocer; 1846/47-1849/50 shopkeeper.

1161 NORTH, John B., miller.

1842/43 assessed in absence of return £80; exempt.

Cross reference: North, John Bunce, miller, Potterne [possible].

1162 PAVEY, James, miller.

1846/47-1849/50 assessed in absence of return £80; exempt.

1163 PINNIGER, Thomas, traveller.

1857/58-1859/60 returned and assessed £120.

1164 ROBBINS, Samuel, timber merchant, coal merchant, tonnage agent, slate merchant, Post Master.

1842/43 returned £150tc, £100a; assessed £300.
1846/47 assessed in absence of return £400.
1847/48 returned £350; assessed £400.
1848/49 returned £300; assessed £400.
1849/50-1850/51 returned £380; assessed £500.
1851/52 returned £300; assessed £400.
1852/53 assessed in absence of return £400.
1853/54 returned and assessed £400.
1854/55 assessed in absence of return £500.
1855/56 returned £500; assessed £600.
1856/57 assessed in absence of return £600.
1857/58 returned and assessed £600.
1858/59 returned £600; assessed £800.
1859/60 returned £700; assessed £800.

Abbreviations: t, timber merchant; c, coal merchant; a, tonnage agent.
1842/43, 1846/47 timber & coal merchant, tonnage agent; 1847/48-1849/50 timber merchant
  & tonnage agent; 1850/51-1858/59 timber merchant; 1859/60 timber merchant, coal &
  slate merchant, Post Master.
1849/50 marked "& at Devizes".
Cross reference: Robbins, Samuel, timber merchant, St.Mary.

1165 SHIPMAN, Thomas, baker.

1842/43, 1846/47-1849/50 assessed in absence of return £50; exempt.

1166 TURNER, William, draper & tailor.

1853/54 returned and assessed £110.
1854/55 assessed in absence of return £100.
1855/56 returned and assessed £100.
1856/57 assessed in absence of return £100.
1857/58 returned £72; assessed £100.
1858/59-1859/60 returned and assessed £100.

1167 WILTSHIRE, Mary, collar & harness maker.

1842/43, 1846/47 assessed in absence of return £30; exempt.

1168 WYLD, Revd. W.T.

1848/49 name only entered and deleted.

INDEX OF OCCUPATIONS

NOTE: References are to entry numbers, not to pages.

Wine merchant, 432, 465, 546, 650, 872, 1041
Wine merchant's clerk, 448, 449
Woolstapler, 26, 234, 594, 792, 1136, 1137
Workhouse, Master of, 36

Worsted dealer or warehouse, 618, 760
Writing clerk, 491

Yeoman, 524, 962

INDEX OF BUSINESS NAMES

Note: Businesses outside the parishes of St.John and St.Mary, Devizes, are shown with the parish or township in which they are recorded; otherwise, remaining businesses are recorded in either the parish of St.John or St.Mary. References relate to both text and footnotes

Angel, 714, 786
Angel, Market Lavingtom, 1034
Antelope, 255, 269, 397, 506, 545, 594
Artichoke, Week, 246, 274

Barge, Stanton St.Bernard, 1080, 1081, 1082
Bear, 434
Bell, Bedborough, 6, 35
Bell, Cheverell Magna, 927, 932
Bell, Market Lavington, 1009
Bell, Potterne, 144
Bell, St.Edith's Marsh, Bromham, 79, 97
Bell, Urchfont, 1109, 1122
Bellevue Lunatic Asylum, Week, 276
Belvedere Mill, Bedborough, 30
Black Dog, West Lavington, 320, 344
Black Horse, 570
Black Swan, 616
Bottle, 432
British Lion, Bedborough, 17, 32, 298

Canal Company, 227
Castle, 683, 746
Cheverell Mill, Cheverell Magna, 942
Church Mill, Chirton, 915, 920
Churchill Arms, West Lavington, 313, 328, 338, 341
Cornbury Mill, West Lavington, 315, 343
Cross Keys, 821, 822, 826, 863
Cross Keys, Rowde, 176
Crown, 514, 518, 578, 585
Crown, Bishops Cannings, 47, 50
Crown, Potterne, 125, 150, 155

Dolphin, 379
Duke of Wellington, 399

Elm Tree, 569, 617

Fiddington House Lunatic Asylum, West Lavington, 327, 347
Fox & Hounds, Picadilly, Rowde, 167, 170, 190

Garretts Mill, West Lavington, 319
George, Potterne, 132, 136
George, Rowde, 175
Green Dragon, Market Lavington, 1016, 1029
Greyhound, Bromham, 70, 84

Hare & Hounds, 430, 523, 558
Hughes, Locke & Co., 537
Hughes, Locke & Olivier, 537
Hurst Mill, Worton, 349, 354, 361, 365

Kings Arms, Green, 242, 290, 302
Kings Arms, Allcannings, 901, 905
Kings Arms, Potterne, 134
Kings Arms, Market Lavington, 1003, 1021, 1036

Lamb Inn, 551, 655
Locke, Olivier & Saunders, 537
Locke, Olivier & Tugwell, 537

Nags Head, 844, 882, 886
Nags Head, Urchfont, 1110
New Inn, Bromham, 55

INDEX OF NAMES

WILTSHIRE RECORD SOCIETY
(As at May 2002)

President: PROF. C.R. ELRINGTON, F.S.A.
General Editor: DR JOHN CHANDLER
Honorary Treasurer: IVOR M. SLOCOMBE
Honorary Secretary: JOHN N. D'ARCY

Committee:
D. CHALMERS
DR D.A. CROWLEY
S.D. HOBBS
M.J. MARSHMAN
MRS S. THOMSON
MRS I.L. WILLIAMS
K.H. ROGERS, F.S.A., representing the Wiltshire Archaeological and Natural History Society

Honorary Independent Examiner: J.D. FOY
Correspondent for the U.S.A.: CHARLES P. GOULD

PRIVATE MEMBERS

ADAMS, Ms S, 23 Rockcliffe Avenue, Bathwick, Bath BA2 6QP

ANDERSON, MR D M, 20 Shakespeare Road, Stratford-sub-Castle, Salisbury SP1 3LA

APPLEGATE, MISS J M, 55 Holbrook Lane, Trowbridge BA14 0PS

ASAJI, PROF K, 5-35-14 Senriyama-nishi, Suita, Osaka, Japan 565-0851

AVERY, MRS S, 33 Cardigan Street, Oxford OX2 6GP

BADENI, COUNTESS JUNE, Norton Manor, Norton, Malmesbury SN16 0JN

BAINES, MRS B M, 32 Tybenham Road, Merton Park, London SW19 3LA

BALL, MR S T, 19 The Mall, Swindon SN1 4JA

BARNETT, MR B A, 17 Alexandra Road, Coalpit Heath, Bristol BS36 2PY

BATHE, MR G, Byeley in Densome, Woodgreen, Fordingbridge, Hants SP6 2QU

BAYLIFFE, MR B G, 3 Green Street, Brockworth, Glos GL3 4LT

BENNETT, DR N, Hawthorn House, Main Street, Norton, Lincoln LN4 2BH

BERRETT, MR A M, 10 Primrose Hill Road, London NW3 3AD

BERRY, MR C, 9 Haven Rd, Crackington Haven, Bude, Cornwall EX23 0PD

BISHOP, MRS S M, Innox Bungalow, Market Place, Colerne, Chippenham SN14 8AY

BLAKE, MR P A, 18 Rosevine Road, London SW20 8RB

BLAKE, MR T N, Glebe Farm, Tilshead, Salisbury SP3 4RZ

BOX, MR S D, 73 Silverdale Road, Earley, Reading RG6 2NF

BRAND, DR P A, 155 Kennington Road, London SE11 6SF

BRITTON, MR D J, Overbrook House, The High Road, Ashton Keynes, Swindon SN6 6NL

BROOKE-LITTLE, MR J P, Heyford House, Lower Heyford, Bicester, Oxon OX25 5NZ

BROWN, MR D A, 36 Empire Road, Salisbury SP2 9DF

BROWN, MR G R, 6 Canbury Close, Amesbury, Salisbury SP4 7QF

BRYANT, MRS D, 1 St John's Court, Devizes SN10 1BJ

BURGESS, MR I D, 29 Brackley Avenue, Fair Oak, Eastleigh, Hants SO5 7FL

BURGESS, MR J M, Tolcarne, Wartha Mill, Porkellis, Helston, Cornwall TR13 0HX

BURNETT-BROWN, MISS J M, Lacock Abbey, Lacock, Chippenham SN15 2LG

CAREW HUNT, MISS P H, Cowleaze, Edington, Westbury BA13 4PJ

CARR, PROF D R, Dept. of History, 140 7th Ave South, St Petersburg, Florida 33701 USA

CARRIER, MR S, 9 Highfield Road, Bradford on Avon BA15 1AS

CARTER, DR B J, JP PHD BSc FSG, 15 Walton Grange, Bath Road, Swindon SN1 4AH

CAWTHORNE, MRS N, 45 London Road, Camberley, Surrey GU15 3UG

CHALMERS, MR D, Bay House West, Bay House, Ilminster, Somerset TA19 0AT

CHANDLER, DR J H, Jupe's School, The Street, East Knoyle, Salisbury SP3 6AJ

CHARD, MR I, 35 Thingwall Park, Fishponds, Bristol BS16 2AJ

CHAVE, MR R A, 39 Church Street, Westbury BA13 3BZ

CHURCH, MR T S, Mannering House, Bethersden, Ashford, Kent TN26 3DJ

CLARK, MR A G, Highlands, 51a Brook Drive, Corsham SN13 9AX

CLARK, MRS V, 29 The Green, Marlborough SN8 1AW

CLEGG, MS R, 12 Brookes Road, Broseley, Salop TF12 5SB

COBERN, MISS A M, 4 Manton Close, Manton, Marlborough SN8 4HJ

COLCOMB, MR D M, 38 Roundway Park, Devizes SN10 2EO

COLE, MRS J A, 113 Groundwell Road, Swindon SN1 2NA

COLEMAN, MISS J, Swn-y-Coed, Abergwili, Carmarthenshire SA32 7EP

COLLINS, MR A T, 11 Lemon Grove, Whitehill, Bordon, Hants GU35 9BD

COLMAN, MRS P, 28 Abbey Mill, Church Street, Bradford on Avon BA15 1HB

CONGLETON, LORD, West End Farm, Ebbesbourne Wake, Salisbury SP5 5JW

COOMBES, MR J, 85 Green Pastures, Heaton Mersey, Stockport SK4 3RB

COOMBES-LEWIS, MR R J, 45 Oakwood Park Road, Southgate, London N14 6QP

COOPER, MR S, 12 Victory Row, Wootton Bassett, Swindon SN4 7BE

CORAM, MRS J E, 38 The Parklands, Hullavington, Chippenham SN14 6DL

COULSTOCK, MISS P H, 15 Pennington Crescent, West Moors, Wimborne, Dorset BH22 0JH

COVEY, MR R V, Lower Hunts Mill, Wootton Bassett, Swindon SN4 7QL

COWAN, COL M, 24 Lower Street, Harnham, Salisbury SP3 8EY

CRIGHTON, MR G S, 68 Stanford Avenue, Springfield, Milton Keynes MK6 3NH

CROOK, MR P H, Bradavon, 45 The Dales, Cottingham, E Yorks HU16 5JS

CROUCH, MR J W, Kensington House, Pensford Hill, Pensford, Somerset BS39 4AA

CROWLEY, DR D A, 16 Greater Lane, Edington, Westbury BA13 4QP

D'ARCY, MR J N, The Old Vicarage, Edington, Westbury

DAVIES, MRS A M, 283 Longstone Road, Iver Heath, Bucks SL0 0RN

DIBBEN, MR A A, 18 Clare Road, Lewes, East Sussex BN7 1PN

DRAPER, MISS R, 12 Sheep Street, Devizes SN10 1DL

EDE, DR M E, 12 Springfield Place, Lansdown, Bath BA1 5RA

EDWARDS, MR P C, 33 Longcroft Road, Devizes SN10 3AT

ELRINGTON, PROF C R, 34 Lloyd Baker Street, London WC1X 9AB

FALCINI, Ms L, Old Forge Cottage, North Lane, West Tytherley, Salisbury SP5 1JX

FAY, MRS M, 40 North Way, Porton Down, Salisbury SP4 0JN

FICE, MRS B, Holt View House, 9 Rosemary Lane, Rowledge, Farnham GU10 4DB

FIRMAGER, MRS G M, 72b High Street, Semington, Trowbridge BA14 6JR

FLOWER-ELLIS, DR J G, Swedish Univ of Agric Sciences, PO Box 7072 S-750 07, Uppsala, Sweden 1972

FORBES, MISS K G, Bury House, Codford, Warminster

FOSTER, MR R E, The New House, St Giles Close, Gt Maplestead, Halstead, Essex CO9 2RW

FOY, MR J D, 28 Penn Lea Road, Bath BA1 3RA

FREEMAN, REV DR J, 1 Cranfield Row, Gerridge Street, London SE1 7QN

FROST, MR B C, Red Tiles, Cadley, Collingbourne Ducis, Marlborough SN8 3EA

FULLER, MRS B, 65 New Park Street, Devizes SN10 1DR

GALBRAITH, Ms C, Box 42, 17 Gill Street, Coldwater, Ontario L0K 1EO, Canada

GALE, MRS J, 169 Spit Road, Mosman, NSW 2088, Australia

GHEY, MR J G, 18 Bassett Row, Bassett, Southampton SO1 7FS

GIBBS, MRS E, Home Farm, Barrow Gurney, Bristol BS48 3RW

GINGELL, Ms B M, 32 Cambridge Lodge, Bonehurst Road, Horley, Surrey RH6 8PR

GODDARD, MR R E H, Sinton Meadow, Stokes Lane, Leigh Sinton, Malvern, Worcs WR13 5DY

GOODBODY, MR E A, Stockmans, Rectory Hill, Amersham, Bucks

GOODFELLOW, MR P S, Teffont Selby, 47 High Street, Mow Cop, Cheshire ST7 3NZ

GOSLING, REV DR J, 1 Wiley Terrace, Wilton, Salisbury SP2 0HN

GOUGH, MISS P M, 39 Whitford Road, Bromsgrove, Worcs B61 7ED

GOULD, MR C P, 1200 Old Mill Road, San Marino, California 91108 USA

GOULD, MR L K, 263 Rosemount, Pasadena, California 91103 USA

GRIFFIN, DR C J, School of Geographical Sciences, University of Bristol, University Road, Bristol BS8 1SS

GRIFFITHS, MR T J, 29 Saxon Street, Chippenham SN15

GRUBER VON ARNI, COL E E, 11 Park Lane, Swindon SN1 5HG

HAMILTON, CAPTAIN R, 1 The Square, Cathedral Views, Crane Bridge Road, Salisbury SP2 7TW

HARE, DR J N, 7 Owens Road, Winchester, Hants SO22 6RU

HARTCHER, REV DR G N, 3-5 Vincentia Street, Marsfield, NSW 2122, Australia

HATCHWELL, MR R C, Cleeve House, Rodbourne Bottom, Malmesbury SN16 0EZ

HAYWARD, MISS J E, Pleasant Cottage, Crockerton, Warminster BA12 8AJ

HELMHOLZ, PROF R W, Law School, 1111 East 60th Street, Chicago, Illinois 60637 USA

HENLY, MR H R, 99 Moredon Road, Swindon SN2 2JG

HERRON, MRS Pamela M, 25 Anvil Crescent, Broadstone, Dorset BH18 9DY

HICKMAN, MR M R, 184 Surrenden Road, Brighton BN1 6NN

HICKS, MR I, 74 Newhurst Park, Hilperton, Trowbridge BA14 7QW

HICKS, PROF M A, King Alfred's College, Winchester SO22 4NR

HILLIKER, MR S, Box 184, Sutherland, NSW 2232, Australia

HILLMAN, MR R B, 18 Carnarvon Close, Chippenham SN14 0PN

HINTON, MR A E, Glenside Cottage, Glendene Avenue, East Horsley, Surrey KT24 5AY

HOBBS, MR S, 63 West End, Westbury BA13 3JQ

HOLLEY, MR R J, 120 London Road, Calne SN11 0AH

HORNBY, MISS E, 70 Archers Court, Castle Street, Salisbury SP1 3WE

HORTON, MR P.R.G, OBE, Hedge End, West Grimstead, Salisbury SP5 3RF

HOWELLS, Jane, 7 St Mark's Rd, Salisbury SP1 3AY

HUGHES, PROF C J, Old House, Tisbury, Salisbury SP3 6PS

HUGHES, MR R G, 60 Hurst Park Road, Twyford, Reading RG10 0EY

HULL, MR J L F, Sandown Apartments, 1 Southerwood Drive, Sandy Bay, Tasmania 7005, Australia

HUMPHRIES, MR A G, Rustics, Blacksmith's Lane, Harmston, Lincoln LN5 9SW

INGRAM, DR M J, Brasenose College, Oxford OX1 4AJ

JACKSON, MR D, 2 Byways Close, Salisbury SP1 2QS

JAMES, MR & MRS C, 18 King Henry Drive, Grange Park, Swindon SN5 6BL

JAMES, MR J F, 3 Sylvan Close, Hordle, Lymington, Hants SO41 0HJ

JEACOCK, MR D, 16 Church Street, Wootton Bassett, Swindon

JELLICOE, RT HON EARL, Tidcombe Manor, Tidcombe, Marlborough SN8 3SL

JOHNSTON, MRS J M, Greystone House, 3 Trowbridge Road, Bradford on Avon BA15 1EE

KENT, MR T A, Rose Cottage, Isington, Alton, Hants GU34 4PN

KING, MR S F, Church Mead House, Woolverton, Bath BA3 6QT

KIRBY, MR J L, 209 Covington Way, Streatham, London SW16 3BY

KITE, MR P J, 13 Chestnut Avenue, Farnham GU9 8UL

KNEEBONE, MR W J R, 20 Blind Lane, Southwick, Trowbridge BA14 9PG

KUNIKATA, MR K, Dept of Economics, 1-4-12, Kojirakawa-machi, Yamagata-shi 990, Japan

LANSDOWNE, MARQUIS OF, Bowood House, Calne SN11 0LZ

LAURENCE, MISS A, 1a Morreys Avenue, Oxford OX1 4ST

LAURENCE, MR G F, Apt 312, The Hawthorns, 18-21 Elton Road, Clevedon BS21 7EH

LAWES, MR G, 48 Windsor Avenue, Leighton Buzzard LU7 1AP

LEGGATT, MR A, 48 High Street, Worton, Devizes SN10 5RG

LODGE, MR O R W, Southridge House, Hindon, Salisbury SP3 6ER

LONDON, MISS V C M, 55 Churchill Road, Church Stretton, Salop SY6 6EP

LUSH, DR G J, 5 Braeside Court, West Moors, Ferndown, Dorset BH22 0JS

MARSH, REV R, Maybridge Vicarage, 56 The Boulevard, Worthing, West Sussex BN 13 1LA

MARSHMAN, MR M J, 13 Regents Place, Bradford on Avon BA15 1ED

MARTIN, MR D, 21 Westbourne Close, Salisbury SP1 2RU

MARTIN, MS JEAN, 21 Ashfield Road, Chippenham SN15 1QQ

MASLEN, MR A, 8 Alder Walk, Frome, Som BA11 2SN

MATHEWS, MR R, P O Box R72, Royal Exchange, NSW 2000, Australia

MATTHEWS, CANON W A, Holy Trinity Vicarage, 18a Woolley St, Bradford on Avon BA15 1AF

MATTINGLY, MR N, Freshford Manor, Freshford, Bath BA3 6EF

MERRYWEATHER, MR A, 60 Trafalgar Road, Cirencester, Glos GL7 2EL

MILLINGTON, MRS P, Hawkstone, Church Hill, Lover, Salisbury SP5 2PL

MOLES, MRS M I, 40 Wyke Road, Trowbridge BA14 7NP

MONTAGUE, MR M D, 115 Stuarts Road, Katoomba, NSW 2780, Australia

MOODY, MR R F, Harptree House, East Harptree, Bristol BS18 6AA

MORIOKA, PROF K 3-12, 4-chome, Sanno, Ota-ku, Tokyo, Japan

MORLAND, MRS N, 33 Shaftesbury Road, Wilton, Salisbury SP2 0DU

MORRISON, MRS J, Priory Cottage, Bratton, Westbury BA13

MOULTON, DR A E, The Hall, Bradford on Avon BA15

NAPPER, MR L R, 9 The Railway Terrace, Kemble, Cirencester GL7 6AU

NEWBURY, MR C COLES, 6 Leighton Green, Westbury BA13 3PN

NEWMAN, MRS R, Tanglewood, Laverstock Park, Salisbury SP1 1QJ

NOKES, MR P M A, Wards Farm, Ditcheat, Shepton Mallet, Somerset BA4 6PR

O'DONNELL, MISS S J, 42 Wessington Park, Calne SN11 0AU

OGBOURNE, MR J M V, 14 Earnshaw Way, Beaumont Park, Whitley Bay, Tyne and Wear NE25 9UN

OGBURN, CHIEF JUDGE ROBERT W, 317 First Avenue, Monte Vista, CO 81144, USA

OSBORNE, COL R, Unwins House, 15 Waterbeach Road, Landbeach, Cambridge CB4 4EA

PARKER, DR P F, 45 Chitterne Road, Codford St Mary, Warminster BA12 0PG

PARROTT, MRS M G, 81 Church Road, Christian Malford, Chippenham SN15 4BW

PATIENCE, MR D C, 29 Priory Gardens, Stamford, Lincs PE9 2EG

PATRICK, DR S, The Thatchings, Charlton All Saints, Salisbury SP5 4HQ

PERRY, DR S H, Priory Cottage, Broad Street, Bampton, Oxon

PERRY, MR W A, Noads House, Tilshead, Salisbury SP3 4RY

POWELL, MRS N, 4 Verwood Drive, Bitton, Bristol BS15 6JP

RADNOR, EARL OF, Longford Castle, Salisbury SP5 4EF

RAYBOULD, MISS F, 20 Radnor Road, Salisbury SP1 3PL

REEVES, DR M E, 38 Norham Road, Oxford OX2 6SQ

ROGERS, MR K H, Silverthorne House, East Town, West Ashton, Trowbridge BA14 6BE

ROOKE, MISS S F, The Old Rectory, Little Langford, Salisbury SP3 4NU

SHELDRAKE, MR B, 28 Belgrave Street, Swindon SN1 3HR

SHEWRING, MR P, 73 Woodland Road, Beddau, Pontypridd, Mid-Glamorgan CF38 2SE

SIMS-NEIGHBOUR, MR A K, 2 Hesketh Crescent, Swindon SN3 1RY

SINAR, MISS J C, 1 Alton Road, Wilcot, Pewsey SN9 5NP

SLOCOMBE, MR I, 11 Belcombe Place, Bradford on Avon BA15 1NA

SMITH, DR C, 2 Wesley Villas, Church Street, Coleford, Frome BA3 5ND

SMITH, MR P J, 6 Nuthatch, Longfield, Kent DA3 7NS

SNEYD, MR R H, Court Farm House, 22 Court Lane, Bratton, Westbury BA13 4RR

SOPP, MR G A, 23952 Nomar Street, Woodland Hills, California 91367, USA

SPAETH, DR D A, School of History and Archaeology, 1 University Gardens, University of Glasgow G12 8QQ

STEELE, MRS N D, 46 The Close, Salisbury SP1 2EL

STEVENAGE, MR M R, 49 Centre Drive, Epping, Essex CM16 4JF

STEWARD, DR H J, Graduate School of Geography, 950 Main Street, Worcester, Mass 01610-1477, USA

STEWART, MISS K P, 6 Beatrice Road, Salisbury SP1 3PN

SYKES, MRS M, Conock Manor, Conock, Devizes SN10 3QQ

SYLVESTER, MR D G H, Almondsbury Field, Tockington Lane, Almondsbury, Bristol BS12 4EB

TAYLOR, DR A J, Rose Cottage, Lincolns Hill, Chiddingfold, Surrey GU8 4UN

TAYLOR, MR C C, 11 High Street, Pampisford, Cambridge CB2 4ES

TAYLOR, MRS J B, PO Box 3900, Manuka, ACT 2063, Australia

TELFORD, MRS L, 1 Dauntsey Court, Duck St, West Lavington, Devizes SN10 4LR

THOMPSON, MR & MRS J B, 1 Bedwyn Common, Great Bedwyn, Marlborough SN8 3HZ

THOMSON, MRS SALLY M, Home Close, High St, Codford, Warminster BA12 0NB

TIGHE, MR M F, Strath Colin, Pettridge Lane, Mere, Warminster BA12 6DG

TOMKOWICZ, MRS C, 2 Chirton Place, Trowbridge BA14 0XT

TSUSHIMA, MRS J, Malmaison, Church Street, Great Bedwyn, Marlborough SN8 3PE

TURNER, MR I D, Warrendene, 222 Nottingham Road, Mansfield, Notts NG18 4AB

WAITE, MR R E, 18a Lower Road, Chinnor, Oxford OX9 4DT

WALKER, MR J K, 82 Wainsford Road, Everton, Lymington, Hants SO41 0UD

WARNEFORD, MR F E, New Inn Farm, West End Lane, Henfield, West Sussex BN5 9RF

WARREN, MR P, 6 The Meadows, Milford Hill Road, Salisbury SP1 2RT

WEINSTOCK, BARON, Bowden Park, Lacock, Chippenham

WELLER, MR R B, 9a Bower Gardens, Salisbury SP1 2RL

WENDEN, MRS P, 21 Eastern Parade, Fareham, Hants PO16 0RL

WHORLEY, MR E E, 190 Stockbridge Road, Winchester, Hants SO22 6RW

WILLIAMS, MRS I L, 7 Chandler Close, Devizes SN10 3DS

WILTSHIRE, MRS P E, 23 Little Parks, Holt, Trowbridge BA14 6QR

WOODWARD, A S, 28-840 Cahill Drive West, Ottawa, Ontario K1V 9K5, Canada

WORDSWORTH, MRS G, Quince Cottage, Longbridge Deverill, Warminster BA12 7DS

WRIGHT, MR D P, Haileybury, Hertford SG13 7NU

YOUNGER, MR C, The Old Chapel, Burbage, Marlborough SN8 3AA

UNITED KINGDOM INSTITUTIONS

Aberystwyth
    National Library of Wales
    University College of Wales
Bath. Reference Library
Birmingham
    Central Library
    University Library
Brighton. University of Sussex Library
Bristol. University Library
Cambridge. University Library
Cheltenham. Bristol and Gloucestershire
    Archaeological Society
Chippenham. Wiltshire College
Coventry. University of Warwick Library
Devizes
    Wiltshire Archaeological & N.H. Soc.
    Wiltshire Family History Society
Dorchester. Dorset County Library
Durham. University Library
Edinburgh
    National Library of Scotland
    University Library

Exeter. University Library
Glasgow. University Library
Leeds. University Library
Leicester. University Library
Liverpool. University Library
London
    British Library
    College of Arms
    Guildhall Library
    Inner Temple Library
    Institute of Historical Research
    London Library
    Public Record Office
    Royal Historical Society
    Society of Antiquaries
    Society of Genealogists
    University of London Library
Manchester. John Rylands Library
Marlborough
    Memorial Library, Marlborough College
    Merchant's House Trust
    Savernake Estate Office

Norwich. University of East Anglia Library
Nottingham. University Library
Oxford
    Bodleian Library
    Exeter College Library
Poole. Bournemouth University
Reading
    Central Library
    University Library
St Andrews. University Library
Salisbury
    Bourne Valley Historical Society
    Cathedral Library
    Salisbury and South Wilts Museum

Sheffield. University Library
Southampton. University Library
Swansea. University College Library
Swindon
    English Heritage
    Swindon Borough Council
Taunton. Somerset Archaeological and
    Natural History Society
Trowbridge
    Wiltshire Libraries & Heritage
    Wiltshire and Swindon Record Office
Wetherby. British Library Document Supply
    Centre
York. University Library

INSTITUTIONS OVERSEAS

AUSTRALIA
Adelaide. Barr Smith Library, Adelaide
    University
Crawley. Reid Library, University of Western
    Australia
Melbourne
    Baillieu Library, University of Melbourne
    Victoria State Library
Sydney. Fisher Library, University of Sydney
    Law Library, University of New South
    Wales

CANADA
Halifax, Nova Scotia. Dalhousie University
    Library
London, Ont. D.B. Weldon Library, Univer-
    sity of Western Ontario
Montreal, Que. Sir George Williams
    University
Ottawa, Ont. Carleton University Library
Toronto, Ont
    Pontifical Inst of Medieval Studies
    University of Toronto Library
Victoria, B.C. McPherson Library, Univer-
    sity of Victoria

EIRE
Dublin. Trinity College Library

GERMANY
Gottingen. University Library

JAPAN
Osaka. Institute of Economic History, Kansai
    University
Sendai. Institute of Economic History,
    Tohoku University
Tokyo. Waseda University Library

NEW ZEALAND
Wellington. National Library of New
    Zealand

UNITED STATES OF AMERICA
Ann Arbor, Mich. Hatcher Library, Univer-
    sity of Michigan
Athens, Ga. University of Georgia Libraries
Atlanta, Ga. The Robert W Woodruff
    Library, Emory University
Baltimore, Md. Milton S. Eisenhower
    Library, Johns Hopkins University
Bloomington, Ind. Indiana University
    Library
Boston, Mass.
    Boston Public Library
    New England Historic and Genealogi-
    cal Society

Boulder, Colo. University of Colorado Library
Cambridge, Mass.
  Harvard College Library
  Harvard Law School Library
Charlottesville, Va. Alderman Library,
  University of Virginia
Chicago.
  Newberry Library
  University of Chicago Library
Dallas, Texas. Public Library
Davis, Calif. University Library
East Lansing, Mich. Michigan State University Library
Eugene, Ore. University of Oregon Library
Evanston, Ill. United Libraries, Garrett/
  Evangelical, Seabury
Fort Wayne, Ind. Allen County Public Library
Houston, Texas. M.D. Anderson Library,
  University of Houston
Iowa City, Iowa. University of Iowa Libraries
Ithaca, NY. Cornell University Library
Las Cruces, N.M. New Mexico State
  University Library
Los Angeles.
  Public Library
  Young Research Library, University of
  California

Minneapolis, Minn. Wilson Library, University of Minnesota
New Haven, Conn. Yale University Library
New York.
  Columbia University of the City of
  New York
  Public Library
Notre Dame, Ind. Memorial Library,
  University of Notre Dame
Piscataway, N.J. Rutgers University
  Libraries
Princeton, N.J. Princeton University
  Libraries
Salt Lake City, Utah. Family History Library
San Marino, Calif. Henry E. Huntington
  Library
Santa Barbara, Calif. University of California
  Library
South Hadley, Mass. Williston Memorial
  Library, Mount Holyoke College
Stanford, Calif. Green Library, Stanford
  University
Tucson, Ariz. University of Arizona Library
Urbana, Ill. University of Illinois Library
Washington. The Folger Shakespeare Library
Winston-Salem, N.C. Z.Smith Reynolds
  Library, Wake Forest University

LIST OF PUBLICATIONS

The Wiltshire Record Society was founded in 1937, as the Records Branch of the Wiltshire Archaeological and Natural History Society, to promote the publication of the documentary sources for the history of Wiltshire. The annual subscription is £15 for private and institutional members. In return, a member receives a volume each year. Prospective members should apply to the Hon. Secretary, c/o Wiltshire and Swindon Record Office, County Hall, Trowbridge, Wilts BA14 8BS. Many more members are needed.

The following volumes have been published. Price to members £15, and to non-members £20, postage extra. Available from the Wiltshire and Swindon Record Office, Bythesea Road, Trowbridge BA14 8BS.

1. *Abstracts of feet of fines relating to Wiltshire for the reigns of Edward I and Edward II*, edited by R.B. Pugh, 1939
2. *Accounts of the parliamentary garrisons of Great Chalfield and Malmesbury, 1645-1646*, edited by J.H.P. Pafford, 1940
3. *Calendar of Antrobus deeds before 1625*, edited by R.B. Pugh, 1947
4. *Wiltshire county records: minutes of proceedings in sessions, 1563 and 1574 to 1592*, edited by H.C. Johnson, 1949
5. *List of Wiltshire boroughs records earlier in date than 1836*, edited by M.G. Rathbone, 1951
6. *The Trowbridge woollen industry as illustrated by the stock books of John and Thomas Clark, 1804-1824*, edited by R.P. Beckinsale, 1951
7. *Guild stewards' book of the borough of Calne, 1561-1688*, edited by A.W. Mabbs, 1953
8. *Andrews' and Dury's map of Wiltshire, 1773: a reduced facsimile*, edited by Elizabeth Crittall, 1952
9. *Surveys of the manors of Philip, earl of Pembroke and Montgomery, 1631-2*, edited by E. Kerridge, 1953
10. *Two sixteenth century taxations lists, 1545 and 1576*, edited by G.D. Ramsay, 1954
11. *Wiltshire quarter sessions and assizes, 1736*, edited by J.P.M. Fowle, 1955
12. *Collectanea*, edited by N.J. Williams, 1956
13. *Progress notes of Warden Woodward for the Wiltshire estates of New College, Oxford, 1659-1675*, edited by R.L. Rickard, 1957
14. *Accounts and surveys of the Wiltshire lands of Adam de Stratton*, edited by M.W. Farr, 1959
15. *Tradesmen in early-Stuart Wiltshire: a miscellany*, edited by N.J. Williams, 1960
16. *Crown pleas of the Wiltshire eyre, 1249*, edited by C.A.F. Meekings, 1961
17. *Wiltshire apprentices and their masters, 1710-1760*, edited by Christabel Dale, 1961
18. *Hemingby's register*, edited by Helena M. Chew, 1963
19. *Documents illustrating the Wiltshire textile trades in the eighteenth century*, edited by Julia de L. Mann, 1964
20. *The diary of Thomas Naish*, edited by Doreen Slatter, 1965
21-2. *The rolls of Highworth hundred, 1275-1287*, 2 parts, edited by Brenda Farr, 1966, 1968
23. *The earl of Hertford's lieutenancy papers, 1603-1612*, edited by W.P.D. Murphy, 1969
24. *Court rolls of the Wiltshire manors of Adam de Stratton*, edited by R.B. Pugh, 1970
25. *Abstracts of Wiltshire inclosure awards and agreements*, edited by R.E. Sandell, 1971
26. *Civil pleas of the Wiltshire eyre, 1249*, edited by M.T. Clanchy, 1971
27. *Wiltshire returns to the bishop's visitation queries, 1783*, edited by Mary Ransome, 1972
28. *Wiltshire extents for debts, Edward I - Elizabeth I*, edited by Angela Conyers, 1973
29. *Abstracts of feet of fines relating to Wiltshire for the reign of Edward III*, edited by C.R. Elrington, 1974

30. *Abstracts of Wiltshire tithe apportionments*, edited by R.E. Sandell, 1975
31. *Poverty in early-Stuart Salisbury*, edited by Paul Slack, 1975
32. *The subscription book of Bishops Tounson and Davenant, 1620-40*, edited by B. Williams, 1977
33. *Wiltshire gaol delivery and trailbaston trials, 1275-1306*, edited by R.B. Pugh, 1978
34. *Lacock abbey charters*, edited by K.H. Rogers, 1979
35. *The cartulary of Bradenstoke priory*, edited by Vera C.M. London, 1979
36. *Wiltshire coroners' bills, 1752-1796*, edited by R.F. Hunnisett, 1981
37. *The justicing notebook of William Hunt, 1744-1749*, edited by Elizabeth Crittall, 1982
38. *Two Elizabethan women: correspondence of Joan and Maria Thynne, 1575-1611*, edited by Alison D. Wall, 1983
39. *The register of John Chandler, dean of Salisbury, 1404-17*, edited by T.C.B. Timmins, 1984
40. *Wiltshire dissenters' meeting house certificates and registrations, 1689-1852*, edited by J.H. Chandler, 1985
41. *Abstracts of feet of fines relating to Wiltshire, 1377-1509*, edited by J.L. Kirby, 1986
42. *The Edington cartulary*, edited by Janet H. Stevenson, 1987
43. *The commonplace book of Sir Edward Bayntun of Bromham*, edited by Jane Freeman, 1988
44. *The diaries of Jeffery Whitaker, schoolmaster of Bratton, 1739-1741*, edited by Marjorie Reeves and Jean Morrison, 1989
45. *The Wiltshire tax list of 1332*, edited by D.A. Crowley, 1989
46. *Calendar of Bradford-on-Avon settlement examinations and removal orders, 1725-98*, edited by Phyllis Hembry, 1990
47. *Early trade directories of Wiltshire*, edited by K.H. Rogers and indexed by J.H. Chandler, 1992
48. *Star chamber suits of John and Thomas Warneford*, edited by F.E. Warneford, 1993
49. *The Hungerford cartulary: a calendar of the earl of Radnor's cartulary of the Hungerford family*, edited by J.L. Kirby, 1994
50. *The Letters of John Peniston, Salisbury architect, Catholic, and Yeomanry Officer, 1823-1830*, edited by M. Cowan, 1996
51. *The Apprentice Registers of the Wiltshire Society, 1817- 1922*, edited by H. R. Henly, 1997
52. *Printed Maps of Wiltshire 1787–1844: a selection of topographical, road and canal maps in facsimile*, edited by John Chandler, 1998
53. *Monumental Inscriptions of Wiltshire: an edition, in facsimile, of* Monumental Inscriptions in the County of Wilton, *by Sir Thomas Phillipps*, edited by Peter Sherlock, 2000
54. *The First General Entry Book of the City of Salisbury, 1387-1452*, edited by David R. Carr, 2001

VOLUMES IN PREPARATION

Wiltshire glebe terriers, edited by S.D. Hobbs and Susan Avery; *Marlborough probate inventories*, edited by Lorelei Williams; *Wiltshire papist returns and estate enrolments, 1705-87*, edited by J.A. Williams; *The Diary of William Henry Tucker*, edited by Helen Rogers; *Early vehicle registration in Wiltshire*, edited by Ian Hicks; *Wiltshire probate records index*, edited by Lucy Jefferis; *Crown pleas of the Wiltshire eyre, 1268*, edited by Brenda Farr; *The Hungerford cartulary, vol.2: the Hobhouse cartulary*, edited by J.L. Kirby; *The Parish registers of Thomas Crockford, 1613-29*, edited by C.C. Newbury; *Farming in Wiltshire during the seventeenth century*, edited by J. H. Bettey. The volumes will not necessarily appear in this order.

A leaflet giving full details may be obtained from the Hon. Secretary, c/o Wiltshire and Swindon Record Office, County Hall, Trowbridge, Wilts. BA14 8BS.